MUSLIMS, NATIONALISM AND THE PARTITION, 1946 PROVINCIAL ELECTIONS IN INDIA

Muslims, Nationalism and the Partition: 1946 Provincial Elections in India

SHO KUWAJIMA

MANOHAR
2026

First published 1998
Reprinted 2026

ISBN 978-81-7304-211-9

Published by
Ajay Kumar Jain *for*
Manohar Publishers & Distributors
4753/23 Ansari Road, Daryaganj
New Delhi 110 002

Printed at
Replika Press Pvt. Ltd.

Contents

List of Tables 7

Preface 9

Acknowledgements 15

Abbreviations 17

Introduction 19

I THE SIMLA CONFERENCE AND AFTER 29
Steps for the Elections 29
Enrolment 36
Nomination 48

II THE POST-WAR PEOPLE'S MOVEMENT 72
The *Prati Sarkar* Movement and the Elections 72
The Civil Service in the Critical Period 79
Movement against the Trial of the Officers of the Indian National Army 85
The Royal Indian Navy on Strike 109

III THE 1946 PROVINCIAL ELECTIONS 130
Elections and Political Parties 130
The Election Campaign 141
Polling and Polling Stations 157

IV ELECTION RESULTS 166
General Review 166
Results in the Provinces 170
A Case Study of Bihar 192

CONCLUSION 209

Appendix I	The Indian Franchise Act, 1945	239
Appendix II	Election Bill of the Palamu District Kisan Sabha	242
Glossary		244
Bibliography		245
Index		251

List of Tables

Table I	Labour Electoral Colleges in Bengal	43
Table II	Seats in Provincial Legislative Assemblies, 1946	216
Table III	Provisional dates of Nominations, Polling and Completion of the General Election to the Legislative Assemblies in the Provinces, 1945-6	217
Table IV	Programmes for the Work of Revision of Electoral Rolls and holding Election for the Bihar Legislative Assembly and Bihar Legislative Council	218
Table V	Candidates and Voters in the Elections to the Provincial Assemblies in 1946	220
Table VI	Votes polled by various Political Parties in Elections to the Provincial Assemblies in 1946	221
Table VII	Number of Women Voters in Elections to both Reserved and Unreserved Seats in the Provincial Legislative Assemblies	223
Table VIII	Provincial Assembly Elections, 1946, Results and Analysis by Economic Research Department, All India Congress Committee	224
Table IX	Communist Analysis of the Election Results	233
Table X	Ambedkar's Analysis of the Elections in the Scheduled Caste Constituencies in case of Bombay	235
Table XI	Provincial Assembly Election Results, 1946	238

Preface

On 10 April 1946, the first post-War General Election was held in Japan on the basis of universal adult franchise.

I have some unforgettable recollections of those days. A few months after the end of the Second World War, the American Army marched through the main street of our small town near Tokyo and occupied it for some time. With a few of my primary school classmates, I observed this scene without uttering many words. We were overwhelmed and felt uneasy with the creaking sound of the American tanks which drove over this rural town. We were forced to realize that the War had ended.

Only recently, I found out that Jawaharlal Nehru had said in a Press Conference on 13 November 1945 that no Indian Army should be sent to any territory, not even to Japan, to humiliate anybody. Yet at that time I could not imagine what had happened in Asia where the Japanese Army had been active during the War.

Another scene lingers in my memory. Most probably it is related to the campaign for the General Election of 1946 in Japan. On our way back from school, we were passing through the same street, when an elderly candidate was making his speech, the only listeners were a few of us who had not reached the age of voting. In the elections of 1946 the size of each constituency was much larger than today, and the candidate may well have been a stranger to this rather closed area. Nevertheless, it was a really desolate scene, even if not totally unusual in the post-War days. This candidate himself was uncertain about the future of Japan, and of course, about his own future too.

The General Election of Japan in 1946 was held under the extreme strain of post-War political crisis, unstable rehabilitation, food scarcity and inflation. On the polling day many voters preferred food to vote, and caught suburban trains early morning to get rice or other foodstuffs in rural areas. That year, after the May Day celebration (revived after 11 years), another May Day demanding 'More Food to the People' was called on 19 May. In the confusion, the preparation of electoral roll was defective, and the names of 256,988 voters were not registered. Though this number was less than 1 per cent of the total qualified persons, omissions reached 10.8 per cent in Kagoshima Ken (Prefecture) in southern Japan. In Nagano Ken, one village headman accused of negligence of his duties committed suicide. The most painful fact was that the people of Okinawa Ken were deprived of their franchise on the grounds that administrative rights over Okinawa had not been transferred back to Japan. Parliamentary democracy began in Japan with the denial of voting rights to a substantial part of the country which suffered most in the last war.

There were other aspects of the elections. The Japan Communist Party which was legalized could gain 5 seats for the first time in the National Diet. Also Japanese women for the first time got an opportunity to vote for the destiny of Japan and for their own future. The Ministry of Education appealed to women to vote and issued the following statement:

> The time has come when the votes of women are crucial. We expect women to keep in mind following three points:
>
> 1. You are more sincere than men. Therefore you should not waste a precious chance to use your right to vote.
> 2. Women have their own sense of justice. You should decide independently whose political view is right without being influenced by others.
> 3. You have more sense of perception than men. With the help of this ability of yours you should vote for the right person. [Japanese Diet (ed.), *Gikai Seido Hyakunen-Shi* (Hundred Year History of Parliamentary System), *Supplement*, Tokyo, 1990, p. 149.]

It is unbelievable that the Japanese Ministry of Education had such 'progressive' ideas in 1946, even if they were not free of their usual pedagogy.

In India the Provincial Assembly Elections were held from January to April 1946. These elections were crucial in deciding the political destiny of the subcontinent. Elections were prepared in the background of the people's 'Quit India' upheaval of 1942 and the growth of the Pakistan movement for a Muslim majority state or states. The Congress was eager to claim the success of the 'Quit India' struggle as its own victory through the medium of the election results. On the other hand, the Muslim League which lost the 1937 Provincial Elections, had to prove within the framework of the Government of India Act, 1935, that it was the only organization that represented Indian Muslims. In tandem with the election campaign, there was the post-War upsurge of the freedom movement symbolized in the movement against the trial of members of the Indian National Army and the strike in the Royal Indian Navy, and also the movement of workers, peasants and other people for their daily demands in various parts of India. Very often it was difficult to distinguish these movements from the election campaign. The food situation in the beginning of 1946 was very critical, and the memory of the Bengal Famine of 1943 was still fresh. Popular discontent penetrated even into the naval ratings and policemen, expected to play the role of the guardians of British rule.

In the 1946 election of Japan, advice was extended to the illiterate voters. They could take to their polling booths their slips of paper on which the names of the candidates they had chosen were written, in order to copy down these names on the ballot papers. In the case of the Indian elections of 1946, it was not necessary to write a candidate's name. It was enough to select a coloured box. But, franchise was restricted by property and literacy. Many of those who took part in the freedom movement including the Quit India movement, or in the working class and peasant movements, had no right to vote. There is a view which asserts that there would have been no difference in the election results even if they had been given their right to vote. The situation does not seem to be so simple, because the significance of the elections does not lie only in the results. And, of course, the results may possibly have been different. In this connection, we have to answer the following two basic questions : to what extent two political forces, the Indian National Congress and the Muslim League could represent the views of the disenfranchised majority, and how the provincial elections were related to the people's movement. The 1946 Provincial Elections already hinted at problems which independent India and Pakistan, would face in the future, besides giving the answer to the choice of 'unity' or the 'partition'.

The importance of the Provincial Elections in 1946 can be gauged from the fact that the Convention of the Muslim League members of the new Central and Provincial Assemblies held at Delhi on 8 and 9 April, adopted a resolution which defined Pakistan as 'a sovereign independent state' in the background of the victory of the elections which showed that the League occupied most of the seats in the separate constituencies reserved for the Muslims. The chance of an independent Muslim majority state in Bengal waned but was floated again on the eve of the Independence of India and Pakistan.

It is also to be noted that the new Provincial Assemblies after the elections played a decisive part in the constitution-making process, the partition of Bengal and the Punjab and the abolition of the statutory landlord system in India. Many of the new legislators joined the power structure by occupying important posts in the governments, parliaments or military regimes in South Asia.

Letters of Sardar Vallabhbhai Patel who was actually in charge of the Central Election Board of the Congress show how seriously this architect of the state apparatus in India was concerned with the management of the electoral process from the nomination of candidates to the formation of ministries.

On the part of the British Government, the elections meant the chance to select Indian political parties with whom they could negotiate a peaceful transfer of power without disturbing the continuity of the 'constitutional' framework which they had made before the Second World War. Now the Congress and the Muslim League took it for granted to contest the coming elections provided by the Government of India Act, 1935. At the first stage of its election campaign the Congress took notice of the meaning of the fact that the elections would be held on a restricted franchise for only about one-fourth of adult population. The Communist Party of India, in particular, stated that the workers and peasants who were its mainstay were deprived of their right and that this would be really disadvantageous to the party. However, as the campaign proceeded, this issue receded into the background. This common understanding of the participation in the same constitutional process made easier the transition from the stage of the elections to that of the discussion around the Cabinet Mission Plan of 16 May 1946, though it was partly disturbed by the movements against the trial of the officers of the Indian National Army and also by the Royal Indian Navy strike.

Recently some books and monographs have appeared in connection with the various aspects of the Provincial Assembly Elections in 1946. There are some analyses of the election campaign and election results in the Punjab, North-West Frontier Provinces, Sind and Bengal. In Pakistan and Bangladesh studies have emphasised the importance of the elections which led to the victory of the Muslim League. But a comprehensive picture of the 1946 Provincial Elections is yet to emerge despite their historical significance. Partly this is due to the fact that the length of time between the start of the election campaign and the last stage makes difficult a bird's-eye view of the whole picture. The Muslim League was ready to fight the elections in July 1945 immediately after the failure of the so-called Simla Conference, but the Bengal Ministry headed by H.S. Suhrawardy was sworn in on 24 April 1946 as the results of the elections and the new Ministry of Madras headed by T. Prakasam appeared as late as 30 April. The main reason however is that the serious controversy on the elections was submerged by the discussion between the Indian leaders and the British Cabinet Mission which started in the end of March 1946.

My study explores the historical meaning of the 1946 Provincial Assembly elections in the context of the contemporary history and politics of South Asia. It is not my intention to analyse the details of the elections in each province. My main interest in this work is what the elections meant for those who had already reached voting age, but who had no right to vote, for instance, the rickshaw-walas who had joined the 'Quit India' movement enthusiastically in Patna, the agricultural labourers who were the main victims in the Bengal Famine of 1943, and the people of Isur in Mysore Princely state who had to suffer severe repression at the hands of the army and police.

In 1972, I wrote a monograph in Japanese on the process towards the independence of India and Pakistan (1937-47), in which I spared one part to the analysis of the 1946 elections with limited sources. After a few years, the relevant British official documents were published as *The Transfer of Power, 1942-47*. These documents are very useful in tracing how the British political, administrative and military leaders responded to the various demands of the Indian leaders and people, but they do not appreciate correctly the historical role of the people's movement in this critical period. Actually the elections of 1946 were fought in the arena where the regime under the Government of India Act, 1935, and the upsurge of the post-War people's movement crossed each other.

This is an enlarged work of my earlier paper prepared in Japanese and a revised version of my report to the Indian Council of Social Science Research as a Senior Research Fellow. I worked in India under this scheme for a year from December 1988 to September 1989, and then from July to September 1990.

On 4 January 1946 many Japanese leaders connected with Japanese War-time policy were expelled from their official posts by the General Headquarters of the Allied Forces. In the General Election of 10 April, 95 per cent of the candidates and 81 per cent of the elected were newcomers. Many candidates campaigned for the defence of the basic structure of the Japanese polity under the Meiji Constitution in which the locus of the sovereignty was placed in the Emperor. The elections of 1946 were fought under this Constitution. However, after the elections it was this new Assembly that passed the new Constitution which clearly provided for the popular sovereignty and forever renounced war as a sovereign right of the nation.

The Second World War is not over and done with in Japan. Recently the main principles of the present Constitution (including that of the renunciation of war as the means of solving international conflicts) have been under severe trial, and there are strong voices from various quarters demanding constitutional revision on the grounds that times have changed. It has to be asked whether, we really have learnt the relevance of our war-time and post-war experiences to the present.

So also in South Asia the historical choice of the people and the non-participation of the majority of the people in the constitutional decision-making process during the late 1940s is closely related to the nature of the problems that the people are facing in the 1990s.

In the fiftieth year after the end of the Second World War the people in Asia are in a position to reconsider the meaning of the 1940s in the present context.

SHO KUWAJIMA

Acknowledgements

The present work was made possible by a Senior Fellowship awarded by the Indian Council of Social Science Research. I owe a particular sense of gratitude to Professor Iqbal Narain, ex-Member-Secretary of the ICSSR for his warm arrangement. Dr Reena Burman Chandra and Dr Sita Radhakrishnan, Directors of the ICSSR kindly extended their timely help and encouraged my work. From Mr A.P. Mangla and Dr K.N. Jahangir, Deputy Directors, I could always receive their friendly and prompt service in various stages of my work.

During the period of my fellowship, I was attached to the School of International Studies, Jawaharlal Nehru University. Dr P.A. Narasimha Murthy and Dr Rahmatullah Khan, Deans of the School kindly took much trouble to make my work fruitful and my stay in India comfortable. To the late Dr Urmila Phadnis and Dr I.N. Mukherjee, Chairpersons, Centre for South, Central, Southeast Asian and South West Pacific Studies of the School, I express my grateful thanks for facilities during the whole period of my fellowship.

I read many official records in the National Archives of India and the State Archives located in Calcutta, Patna, Bikaner, Madras and Bombay. I am thankful to the Directors and Commissioners and their staffs who kindly provided facilities for my work. I would like to express my special thanks to Mr Tara Sharan Singh, Director of the Bihar State Archives for providing me very useful records from which I could have a concrete image of the Provincial Assembly Elections in 1946. As for the technical side of the elections, I could get most appropriate information from Mr S. Bhatnagar, ex-Chief Electoral Officer, Government of Bihar.

Besides these, I was able to read in the private paper section of the Nehru Memorial Museum and Library, Hindi section of the National Library, and the Library of the Election Commission of India.

Also, I received useful information about the candidates who stood in the Provincial Elections of 1946. In this aspect, I am very grateful to Dr Amalendu De (in connection with Bengal), Dr Sachchidananda and Dr Arvind N. Das (Bihar), Dr D.N. Dhanagare and Dr Gail Omvedt (Maharashtra), Dr Suryanath U. Kamath (Karnataka), Dr K.C. Alexander (Andhra), and Dr K.P. Karunakaran (Kerala). I am also thankful for the suggestions and help from Professor Bipan Chandra, Professor C.E. Ramachandran, Professor K. Veerthappa, Professor S. Nagarajan, Professor H.S. Chopra, Dr J.A. Naik, Professor H.G. Pant and Professor K.V. Kesavan.

I troubled Dr D.N. Dhanagare, former Member-Secretary of the ICSSR at the last stage of my Fellowship work.

In 1992, after completing my report, I met Mr Mazhar Ali Khan, Editor, *Viewpoint* in Lahore who kindly helped in my work on the Punjab elections in 1946. This was our first and last meeting though there was contact through correspondence and he had called me a 'pen friend'. He passed away on 28 January 1993. Also, I would like to express my thanks for generous assistance from Dr Sarfaraz Hussain Mirza, Deputy Director, Centre for South Asian Studies, University of the Punjab.

As for the elections in Bengal, Professor K.M. Mohsin, Department of History, University of Dhaka, who was attached to our University as a Fellow in 1994-95, was of great help to me.

My work could not have come out in this form but for the suggestion of Dr Arvind N. Das. Since 1975 I have learnt many aspects of the contemporary history of India including peasant studies in general and politics in Bihar in our informal talks in Delhi, Patna and Osaka.

Last, I would like to express my thanks to Mr Ramesh Jain for waiting patiently for the completion of my delayed work.

Abbreviations

NAI	National Archives of India
NMML	Nehru Memorial Museum and Library
TSA	Tamilnadu State Archives
MSA	Maharashtra State Archives
WBSA	West Bengal State Archives
BSA	Bihar State Archives
RSA	Rajasthan State Archives
TOP	Nicholas Mansergh (ed.) *The Transfer of Power 1942-7* Vol. 6 and Vol. 7, London, 1976 and 1977

Introduction

The Second World War was one in which the people of the world were involved. Both the combatants and 'the people behind the war' were affected, and South Asia was no exception. Even the remote mountain land of Nepal sent no less then 200,000 sons to the war front and faced a decline in production, leading to nation-wide shortages and inflation.[1]

In India the Quit India movement spread on an unprecedented scale and protested against the policy of the British War-time Government which was reluctant to concede any substantial part of the civil and military administration to the Indian side during the War. In Bihar, one of the centres of the movement, both rural and urban lower classes of the people joined. On 12 August 1942 in Patna the *rickshaw ikka chalanewale* (rickshaw and horse carriage pullers) and others who knew politics to the extent that they recognized the British as the enemy, played a prominent part in the *hartal* (general strike). Few heroic descriptions of the Quit India movement refer to this incident which was recorded in the autobiography of Rahul Sankrityayan, a man of letters, Buddhist scholar, Marxist historian and peasant leader. He was critical of the movement as a whole from the standpoint of the 'People's War' theory.[2] Participation of the urban lower classes meant that their movement was also an expression of protest against high prices and shortages of food and daily goods caused by the War.

In 1943 famine covered many parts of Bengal (presently Bangladesh and West Bengal of India). This famine was 'man-made', and basically the results of the War and colonial rule. From the later half of 1943 many 'paupers' came to Calcutta from the suburban areas in search of food and died on the streets.

The bombing of Calcutta by Japanese aircraft in December 1942 and in December 1943 not only confused the rice market in the area but also badly affected the lives of the people. The *Statesman* dated 1 December 1943 reported about the first Japanese daylight raid on

Calcutta area and wrote that the coolies' quarters suffered in the raid, the home of several families being destroyed. There were a number of casualties. The same paper of Tuesday 7 December 1943 carried the news that the air raid on Sunday had led to 500 civilian casualties, over one-third of these were fatal.

At that time Calcutta was in the throes of famine. This makes meaningless the Japanese War-time statement that the War aim of Japan was to liberate the Asian people from the clutch of the European and American colonialism, though the Japanese papers told the Indian people repeatedly that the purpose of the bombing was not to disturb the lives of the people. The *Statesman* published in Calcutta carried daily statistics of starvation in Calcutta and suburbs. For instance, the statistics for 1 October 1943 in these areas were as follows:

Died in Hospitals	70
Admitted to Hospitals	173
Discharged	111
Bodies disposed of by relief organisations	104
Total admission of staying to Hospitals, 16 August to 30 Sept.	6,514
Total deaths among these	1,574
Bodies disposed of by Police Corpse Disposal Squad and two non-official relief organisations 1 Aug. to 30 Sept.	3,494

Later, the statistics for 1 December were as follows:

Died in Hospitals	34
Admitted to Hospitals	55
Discharged	29
Bodies disposed of by relief organisations	58
Total admission of staying to Hospitals, 16 Aug. to 30 Nov.	15,746
Total deaths among these	5,812
Bodies disposed of by Police Corpse Disposal Squad and two non-official relief organisations, 1 Aug. to 30 Nov.	8,803
Total deaths among 'paupers' recorded by the City Corporation's Health Officer between 1 Aug. and 27 Nov.	15,293

Moreover, the tragedy in Calcutta was merely a fraction of what was prevalent in the rural parts of Bengal. According to the studies conducted by P.C. Mahalanobis and others, the subdivisions of Arambagh, Chandpur, Chittagong, Contai, Diamond Harbour, Madaripur, Manikganj, Munshiganj, Nilpharmari, Noakhali, Tamluk and 24-Parganas were 'most affected' by the famine. Barisal, Bhola, Coxbazar, Dacca, Feni, Goalanda, Kandi, Midnapur, Narayanganj, Satkhira, Serajganj, Tangail and Tipperah were also 'severely affected'.

The largest numbers of victims came from the agricultural labourers.[3] Amartya Sen writes in his recent studies that the deaths in the Bengal famine of 1943 were approximately three million.[4] What did war mean to these victims? Neither the 'Anti-Fascist War' fought by the British nor the 'Asian War of Liberation' by Japan could save their lives. The slogans of the War meant nothing to them.

At the end of the Second World War the people of South Asia rejoiced at the defeat of the Fascists, but also were jubilant over the defeat of the Conservatives led by Churchill in the British General Election in July 1945. The Indian people decided to stand on their own feet. The people most affected by the War had their reason to expect something in the post-War world.

The Provincial Elections of 1946 were crucial in deciding the destiny of the people in the post-War years. However, it was based on the limited franchise which excluded about the three-fourths of the adult people in British India for the reason that they were not literate or had not enough property. From November 1945 to February 1946 there were three waves of the people's movement, the movement against the trial of the officers of the Indian National Army in November 1945 and February 1946, and the Royal Indian Navy Strike in February 1946. But the Congress and the Muslim League had already decided to contest the elections which were to be held from January to April 1946, and on the occasion of the RIN Strike both Congress and League advised the naval ratings to surrender, and promised to solve *constitutionally* the problems that they were facing. This phase of the post-War history will be discussed in detail later.

The results of the Provincial Elections were very clear. The Indian National Congress won the contests in the General seats, while the Muslim League was victorious in most of the Muslim seats. The British Cabinet Mission which visited India at the end of March 1946 tried to accommodate demands of both the Congress and the League. They proposed the Cabinet Mission Plan of 16 May, which conceded the possibility of the secession of the Pakistan areas after ten years while maintaining a Union of India for the moment. Though it seemed that both organizations accepted the plan *as a whole*, they interpreted even its main parts differently. Thus the Muslim League, in the meeting of its Council held on 29 July, adopted the following resolution:

> Whereas the League has today resolved to reject the proposals embodied in the statement of the Cabinet Delegation and the Viceroy of May 16, 1946, due to the intransigence of the Congress on the one hand and the breach of

faith with the Muslims by the British Government on the other; and whereas Muslim India has exhausted without success all efforts to find a peaceful solution of the Indian problem by compromise and *constitutional* means; whereas the Congress is bent upon setting up a Caste Hindu Raj in India with the connivance of the British; and whereas recent events have shown that power politics and not justice and fair play are the deciding factors in Indian affairs; whereas it has become abundantly clear that the Muslims of India would not rest content with anything less than the immediate establishment of an independent and full sovereign State of Pakistan and would resist any attempt to impose any constitution, long-term or short-term, or setting up of any Interim Government at the Centre without the approval and consent of the Muslim League, the Council of the All-India Muslim League is convinced that the time has now come for the Muslim nation to resort to *direct action* to achieve Pakistan and assert their just rights and to vindicate their honour and to get rid of the present slavery under the British and contemplated future of Caste Hindu domination.[5] (italics mine)

'Resort to direct action' meant that the Muslim League and its leader, Jinnah finally relinquished *constitutional* means, even though Jinnah had stressed on many occasions that he believed in constitutional methods. For this purpose the League took full advantage of its election results which had been already secured by constitutional means.

The period between July and August 1946, when the constitutional process reached a critical stage in India, was also the peak of the post-War Labour movement. *The Times* estimated the figure of persons displaced from War-time employment (including ex-servicemen) at between five and seven million. Also, the war-time cost-of-living bonus, never adequate to compensate for the enormous rise in prices, was reduced after the War even as the cost-of-living indices of the working class in various industrial cities were rising.[6] A quantum increase in the number of labour strikes was caused by the conditions that the workers faced in the post-War days. After the Congress became more involved in the constitutional process with its negotiations with the British Cabinet Mission, all-India strikes were planned by the labour leaders in some important sectors. An All-India Railway Strike which was planned for 27 July, demanding (1) no retrenchment; (2) revision of scales of pay; (3) adequate dearness allowance; (4) three months' bonus, was avoided with an assurance by the Railway Board about the appointment of a committee to examine retrenchment and to ensure it would be held in abeyance pending the report of the adjudication. It also agreed to recommend the Government that the Pay Commission should be ready within six months.[7]

However, on 11 July began a strike of employees of the Posts and Telegraphs Department under the leadership of V.G. Dalvi. The strike was finally withdrawn on 6 August. Sardar Vallabhbhai Patel had to intervene in the meantime. On 29 July there was a sympathy strike in support of the Posts and Telegraphs strikers in Calcutta. Nikhil Chakravarty, a Communist reporter, highly appraised the significance of this strike in Calcutta:

> But it was a day the like of which you and I had read before in books but had never seen with our own eyes.
>
> It is a strike which by the numbers participating in it has broken all records. From Hooghly point to Diamond Harbour, over 16 lakhs of people, workers and babus, took part. And this despite the fact that the Trade Union Congress had exempted railway, water works and also electric workers from it. *If the hartal as a whole is considered, then the number of those responding to the call—including shopkeepers, students, teachers, along with workers—would come to over 40 lakhs.* IT WAS COMPLETE STOPPAGE OF CALCUTTA'S LIFE.[8] (italics original)

In South India, the strike of the South Indian Railway workers began on 25 August and was withdrawn on 22 September 1946 with the assurance of Asaf Ali, railway minister, that all legitimate grievances would be attended to.[9]

Asaf Ali was a member of the Interim Government headed by Jawaharlal Nehru which started on 2 September without the participation of the League. The Congress Working Committee took this labour situation seriously in its meeting from 8 to 13 August and, while expressing 'the sympathy of the Congress with the working class in its struggle to improve its economic position and its status', adopted a resolution warning the workers about lack of discipline and disregard of obligations, and certain individuals and sections for exploiting the ignorance of the workers. The resolution says:

> The Committee feel further that it is necessary in the general interest to point out that avoidable strikes cannot have the backing of public opinion, and in view of the dire need of the country for more goods and services, hasty or ill-conceived stoppages and the refusal to take advantage of the available means of settlement by negotiation, conciliation and arbitration, constitute a distinct dis-service to the community and the working class itself.
>
> The Committee in this connection emphasise that in particular industries and services, which are essential for the existence of the community and on

which the continuity of public administration depends, should be immune from dislocation by strikes and lockouts and all disputes between the employee and employers (including governments) should be finally settled by arbitration and adjudication.[10]

This meeting was held in Wardha where Gandhi's ashram was located. Earlier (3 August) Gandhi had without qualification criticized the strikes:

The statement in the daily press that I had approved of the postal strike is not true . . . .

Obviously there should be no strike which is not justifiable on merits. No unjust strike should succeed. All public sympathy must be withheld from such strikes . . . .

Strikes for economic betterment should never have a political end as an ulterior motive. Such a mixture never advances the political end and generally brings trouble upon strikers, even when they do not dislocate public life, as in the case of public utility services such as the postal strikes . . . .

In the present case we have National Provincial Governments. Postmen should consult these Governments before resorting to the extreme step . . . .

Sympathetic strikes must be taboo until it is conclusively proved that the affected men have exhausted all the legitimate means at their disposal and until the Congress has been proved to have betrayed or neglected their interests or until the Congress has called for sympathetic strikes in order to secure justice from obdurate and unsympathetic authorities.

One hears of strikes all over the country to paralyse the Government. This paralysis is an extreme political step, open only to a body like the Congress, not even to unions, however powerful they may be . . . .

At the present moment, the Congress is engaged in making a success of the proposed Constituent Assembly. There are interminable difficulties in the way. Paralysing strikes must seriously hamper Congress action. . . . Therefore, my humble suggestion to all strikers is to make a frank declaration of submission to arbitration or adjudication, to seek the guidance of the Congress and abide by its advice and for all sympathetic strikes to stop whilst the Congress is engaged in making the contemplated Constituent Assembly a success and while Provincial National Governments are functioning.[11]

Gandhi's idea was realized in the form of the resolution of the Congress Working Committee. Gandhi thought that the functions of the Provincial Congress Governments and the Constituent Assembly should not be hampered. That meant that he set great store by the results of the Provincial Elections too. There was no longer room for political strikes on the initiative of the people. Economic strikes should have been avoided and referred to arbitration or adjudication. The members of the Congress Working Committee endorsed this view of

Gandhi fully. This was the last meeting of the Working Committee in Wardha. After this Gandhi was busy dealing with communal riots with his strong will in the last stage of his life, and the Congress Working Committee often differed from him concerning the communal situation.

The Muslim League also worried about the development of the postal strikes. However, it seemed there was no difference in the approach to the situation between the Congress and the League although there was now confrontation between the two in their approach to the Cabinet Mission Plan.

On 11 July 1946, the editorial of *Dawn*, the Muslim League paper, said:

> No one will grudge an increase in the salaries and emoluments of the overworked and underpaid postal employees, but no one will allow them to extort concessions, by periodic threats of laying down tools, at the expense of their equally miserable counterparts in other walks of life. . . . If the union leaders are not determined to alienate public sympathy, they must advise their men to abandon the strike as their demands have already been referred to the Pay Commission and the Adjudicator who cannot possibly belittle their legitimate grievances.

This paper only reported without comment news of the general strike called by the Bengal Committee of the All-India Trade Union Congress, in sympathy with the Post and Telegraph strike for 29 July.[12]

On 3 August the same paper welcomed the decision of the All-India Posts and Telegraphs Lower Grade Union to call off the postal strike. As we have noted, in this decision the intervention of Sardar Vallabhbhai Patel had also played an important part:

> The public will heave a sigh of relief that the postal strike which has been going for the last 23 days is at last to end. Already much inconvenience and heavy losses have been suffered by the people. This could have been avoided if the authorities had from the beginning shown a slightly better appreciation of the difficulties of the low-paid staff in these days of high cost of living . . . .
>
> The concessions given to the postal employees were reviewed by Sir Eric Conran-Smith, Member for Postal and Air, in his broadcast talk on Thursday (1st). The relief granted is considerable and there should be no reason why the men should not accept it in the spirit in which it has been offered . . . . Sir Eric's handsome tribute to the service is well merited and it is hoped that normal working will be restored of a 'great public utility service with a record of which its members have every reason to be proud'.

Though the League's organ showed sympathy for the postal labourers, the Congress and the League shared the same view in connection with the constitutional developments and the labour situation. In this respect there was no basic change in the views on the people's movement on either side between February 1946 and July-August 1946.

Writing on Gandhi's article which has been quoted earlier, the *Dawn* tried to prove that the League was more sympathetic to the right of the postal labourers than the Congress:

> The postal men have their own recognised Unions through which they speak and put forward their demands. One cannot find any reason why they should get the 'approval' of Mr. Gandhi or any other Congress leader before they decide on a strike. Besides, what earthly connection is there between the convening of a Constituent Assembly or the coming into power of 'national provincial Governments' and the postal employees demanding better wages and living conditions? Throughout the article there is not a word of sympathy for the low-paid men in their present hard lot but there is ill-conceived warning that if the men reject the advice of the Congress leaders they do so at their peril. This is a threat as well as blackmail.[13]

The League also tried to separate the constitutional process from the labour movement. There was no perception that, though the postal labourers were demanding better wages and better living conditions in their strike, their destiny was closely related with the negotiations about the Cabinet Mission Plan although many of them were deprived of their voting right in the Provincial Elections. From the end of July to the first half of August, the League was busy preparing for Direct Action Day (16 August). On 5 August, Jinnah asked the people to observe the day of 'direct action' for Pakistan peacefully and in a disciplined manner. But, from the standpoint of the Pakistan movement, the postal strike seemed the matter of another world though the League was very much concerned with the development of the labour situation.

On 16 August, 'Direct Action' day, against the appeal of Jinnah, Calcutta experienced ghastly killings in which Hindus, Muslims and Sikhs were involved, and from which women and children were not spared. Four to five thousand people died. The first and last sentences which I quoted from Chakravarty's article that praised the General Strike in Calcutta 18 days before can be read in their original form in a completely different context. It was a day the like of which you and I had read before in books but had never seen with our own eyes. It was complete stoppage of Calcutta's life.

Why could not the General Strike in Calcutta, said to have involved more than 4 million people and even carried the slogan of 'Hindu-Muslim Unity', prevent this tragedy? Was it a result of the separation of the labour movement from the constitutional process? The 'direct action' was a result of the negotiations inside the constitutional framework. Many of the victims in the killing had no voting right, but lost their lives as a result of the constitutional process from which they were excluded.

In this respect, the transitional period during which the people's movement and the constitutional process overlapped rather than remained completely separate is very meaningful and is worth examining.

After the 'great Calcutta killing' the communal riots spread first to East Bengal (presently Bangladesh) in October 1946 and then to Bihar. In 1947, the year of independence of India and Pakistan, the Punjab faced the agony of communal killing and the gruesome experience of the painful movement of refugees. This part of the history of the subcontinent is well-known and is described in literature and non-fiction, though it appears that historical studies have not yet grappled with this theme squarely.

From the late 1940s to the beginning of the 1950s, the independence of India and Pakistan (August 1947), of Sri Lanka (February 1948) and the end of the Rana Regime (February 1951) in Nepal were epoch-making in the history of South Asia.

In this process towards independence and the end of autocratic rule, to what extent did the people of these areas played a decisive part? In India there was only limited franchise. In Nepal there was no parliamentary system. The end of the Rana Regime cannot be attributed only to the intervention of a Government of India that worried about the instability of Nepal in the context of new developments in Tibet. A long tradition of anti-Rana movements in Nepal certainly contributed to this epoch-making event. If so, what was the role of the movement against the INA trial, the naval strike and the Post and Telegraph strike?

Also, it was a wonder that the Provincial Elections were held in India during this critical period just after the Second World War. This may partly explain the stability of the parliamentary system in India after her Independence. It is ironical that the parliamentary system took roots in Pakistan only towards the end of the 1980s: Jinnah had been a constitutionalist since the years of the non-cooperation movement, 1919-22. In Nepal, Padma Shamsher, who announced a new constitution on 26 January 1948 with a bicameral parliament and the hereditary Rana as Prime Minister, was forced to retire in February.[14] After the end of the Rana Regime, the parliamentary system that had just appeared was abolished by a coup by King Mahendra in 1960, and was revived only in 1991 after the 'Revolution of 1990' which all classes of people joined. In Sri Lanka, the elections of 1956 brought politics nearer to the people and also carried Sinhala nationalism deeply into the political consciousness of the political workers and the people. Though the parliamentary system has been working in this country since Independence, the character of the elections of 1956 and the Constitution of 1972 are closely related to subsequent political crisis in Sri Lanka.

The Provincial Elections of 1946 in India, their positive and negative aspects included, are not a page of history that we can afford to forget.

NOTES

1. Prem R. Uprety, *Nepal: A Small Nation in the Vortex of International Conflicts 1900-1950*, Kathmandu, 1984, pp. 239-40.
2. Rahul Sankrityayan, *Meri Jivan-Yatra*, Ilahabad, 1950, Vol. 2, pp. 594-5.
3. P.C. Mahalanobis *et al.*, 'A Sample Survey of After-Effects of the Bengal Famine of 1943', *Sankhya*, Vol. 7, Part 4, 1946.
4. Amartya Sen, *Poverty and Famines—An Essay on Entitlement and Deprivation*, Oxford, 1982, p. 202.
5. Anil Chandra Banerjee and Dakshina Ranjan Bose, *The Cabinet Mission in India*, Calcutta, 1946, pp. 358-9.
6. Chamanlal Revri, *The Indian Trade Union Movement—An Outline History 1880-1947*, New Delhi, 1972, pp. 276-7.
7. *People's Age*, 30 June 1946.
8. Ibid., 11 August 1946.
9. Ibid., 29 September 1946.
10. A.M. Zaidi, *INC—The Glorious Tradition Volume Four 1939-1950—Texts of the resolutions passed by the INC, the AICC and the CWC*, New Delhi, 1988, p. 254.
11. *The Collected Works of Mahatma Gandhi, LXXXV (June 16, 1946—October 20, 1946)*, Ahmedabad, 1982, pp. 116-17.
12. *Dawn*, 30 June 1946.
13. Ibid., 6 August 1946.
14. Association of Asian Studies, Osaka University of Foreign Studies, *Chronology of Asia in the 1940s*, Osaka, 1995.

I

The Simla Conference and After

Steps for the Elections

On 21 August 1945, the Viceroy Lord Wavell announced in a press note that the elections to the Central and Provincial Legislatures would be held in the coming cold weather. After discussion with the newly formed Labour Government in London, he returned to New Delhi with its proposal on 16 September and stated again in his broadcast three days later:

It is the intention of His Majesty's Government to convene as soon as possible a constitution-making body, and as a preliminary step they have authorised me to undertake, immediately after the elections, discussions with representatives of the Legislative Assemblies in the Provinces, to ascertain whether the proposals contained in the 1942 declaration are acceptable or whether some alternative or modified scheme is preferable. Discussion will also be undertaken with the representatives of the Indian States with a view to ascertaining in what way they can best take their part in the constitution-making body. . . .

During these preparatory stages, the Government of India must be carried on, and urgent economic and social problems must be dealt with. Furthermore, India has to play her full part in working out the new World Order. His Majesty's Government have therefore further authorised me, as soon as the results of the Provincial Elections are published, to take steps to bring into being an Executive Council which will have the support of the main Indian Parties. . . .

The task of making and implementing a new Constitution for India is a complex and difficult one which will require goodwill, cooperation and patience on the part of all concerned. We must first hold elections so that the will of the Indian electorate may be known. It is not possible to undertake any major alteration of the franchise system. This would delay matters for at least two years. But we are doing our best to revise the existing electoral rolls efficiently. After the elections I propose to hold discussions with the representatives of those elected, and of the Indian States to determine the form which the Constitution-making body should take, its powers and procedure. . . .

> The Constituent Assembly that is to find the constitution for the new India will be elected by the Provincial Assemblies except for the four members to represent small political units and the 93 to represent the Indian States.[1]

In this statement we find the basic framework of the Provincial Elections in 1946 and the role the Labour Government expected the Provincial Assemblies to play in the drafting of the Constitution.

The main factor which made the Provincial Elections an imminent issue was the breakdown of the Simla Conference. From 25 June 1945, the leaders' conference was held in Simla at the invitation of Lord Wavell for the purpose of forming a new Executive Council that would be more representative of Indian political opinions. Dates for fresh elections to the central and provincial legislatures was one of the subjects to be discussed. In the new Council all members except the Viceroy and Commander-in-Chief would be Indians, and the Council would have the same number of caste Hindu and Muslim members. The Muslim League insisted that it would nominate all Muslim members in the Council as it was the only body that could represent all the Muslims of India. However, the Congress could not agree to this view and claimed to be the national organization that included Muslims.

Meanwhile, L.S. Amery, Secretary of State for India, wrote to Wavell before the end of the Simla Conference, 'So all our plans have for the moment broke down in face of Jinnah's intransigence.' He found two positive results however, in the breakdown of the conference. First, the breakdown was 'further confirmation of the fact that the difficulty does not lie as between India and His Majesty's Government, but within India itself. For the time being, at any rate, there should be a considerable diminution of bitterness against this country . . . .'[2] This was the view to which the British Government adhered until the last stage of the transfer of power. Second, Amery judged that the attitude of the Congress could hardly be as bitter against them as it had been before their proposal were put to the Congress. The British Government could take advantage of this *dĕtente.* (This view also did not change.)

In this letter, Amery suggested that Wavell would carry on with his existing Executive Council with minor changes. But Wavell did not agree to this, because seven of his Indian colleagues were, according to him, disloyal. Amery's other proposal was meaningful. It was he who had suggested the holding of elections in 'the coming cold weather'.

Wavell was not at all sure what the Governors would think about the Provincial Elections; he himself thought that the holding of the elections as soon as possible would be 'a political diversion'. The conclusion which the Governors' Conference reached in the meetings on 1 and 2 August 1945 was in favour of early elections. All except the Governor of the Punjab wanted Central Elections before the end of 1945 so as to produce the new Assembly for the next budget session. Provincial Elections would be held in all Section 93 Provinces under Governor's rule by the end of March 1946. As for the provinces not under Section 93, again all favoured early elections except Sir Bertland Grancy, Governor of the Punjab.[3] He thought that 'until the absurdity of the crude form of Pakistan was exposed, Punjab Muslims would vote simply on what appeared to them to be a religious issue'. Grancy did not want Central Election before September or October 1946, and favoured Provincial Elections in the autumn of 1946.[4] Wavell reported that there was general agreement that Provincial Elections should be synchronized as far as possible though complete uniformity would be difficult.

The conclusion of the Governors' Conference set the pace for the later constitutional development.

Earlier, when the Labour Party won the elections on 26 July 1945, Wavell wrote in his diary, 'I am afraid there will be a lot of foolish, inexperienced and rather wild legislators amongst the 400 odd of Labour. However there were very many stupid and tiresome Tories in the late Conservative majority. I think Labour is likely to take more interest in and be more sympathetic towards India, but they will have some weird ideas about it.'[5] He also feared that Pethick-Lawrence, the new Secretary of State for India, might have fixed and old-fashioned ideas derived mainly from Congress contacts.[6]

On 17 August, Pethick-Lawrence in a telegram to Wavell stated that Government was in favour of early elections, and advised Wavell to hasten preparatory measures for elections in the coming cold weather.[7] On the same day, Attlee clarified at the India and Burma Committee of the Cabinet that they should regard the forthcoming elections as designed primarily to provide an electoral college for the framing of a new constitution.[8]

Afterwards, the Secretary of State for India again sent a message to Wavell, that Government authorized the Viceroy to announce forthwith that elections would be held both for the Central Assembly and for Provincial Assemblies during the coming cold weather. Wavell was asked to confine his announcement to the bare decision that elections overdue were to be held. Details of the constitution-making were left to discussions between the Cabinet and Wavell who was invited to London for consultation.[9]

After arriving in London on 26 August, George Abell, Wavell's Private Secretary, told him that Cripps was the only man in the Government who was really in a hurry, and wanted to get back to the 'Cripps Offer'. The remainder of the Government was not in a hurry, and the rank and file of the Labour Party and the country at large took little interest in India.[10] This indicates the priorities in Labour polity immediately after the War.

Wavell attended the meeting of the India and Burma Committee of the Cabinet on 29 August and reviewed the Indian political situation.

He thought that Jinnah would not enter into a discussion without any previous guarantee of acceptance of Pakistan in principle, and that the League leader spoke for 99 per cent of the Muslim population of India in their apprehension of Hindu domination. Wavell predicted from the reports of the Governors that in the forthcoming elections the Muslim League would strengthen their position considerably. Also, he stated that the Cripps Offer of 1942 still held the field, but that there had been a very hardening in the feeling of the Indian parties since 1942.[11]

According to Wavell's view, 'before further progress could be made, we should face up to the root problem which was the problem of Pakistan'. He felt that the Pakistan idea had never been properly brought into the light of day, and that it would not stand up to objective analysis. If one could arrange for such an objective analysis, the effect on the Muslim electorate might be considerable, and greatly reduce the vigour with which the Muslims would support the idea. At that stage a declaration of the British Government calling for examination of the Pakistan issue may be necessary.

But the discussion in London could not reach a final conclusion. Wavell got an impression that the Cabinet were interested and in earnest about Indian problems, and were determined to solve them, and that there was 'much genuine goodwill'. But he was not sure the difficulties were fully realised.[12] He was consistently firm on the dangers of forcing the pact and imposing a constitution making body.[13]

Thus, in London the gap between Wavell's concept of 'objective analysis' before further progress and Attlee's 'genuine goodwill' without definite policy was not narrowed. This forced Wavell to broadcast his half-hearted statement of 19 September, and it did not much depart from the press note of 21 August. For the moment, there was no alternative but for the British to make preparations for the Central and Provincial Elections. In the meantime jubilation over the Labour victory had finally disappeared in India: Labour's attitudes could not meet the 'overwhelming urge to change the present government'.[14]

Among the Indian political forces, it was the Muslim League that took the first decision to participate in the elections. The last elections to the Central Assembly had been in 1934, and to the Provincial Assemblies, in 1937. The League had not proved its representative character for the Indian Muslims in the strength of legislators in the Provincial Assemblies, as it had been defeated in the 1937 elections. The Simla Conference contributed to the consolidation of the position of Jinnah, League leader, and weakened non-League Muslim parties, particularly the Unionist Party in the Punjab. Now the League needed its strength in the legislatures to prove that it was 'the sole and authoritative organization of the Muslims of India by a verdict from the electorate'.[15]

The Muslim League took its decision immediately after the failure of the Simla Conference. On 15 July 1945, the Working Committee of the All-India Muslim League demanded that 'fresh elections to the Central and Provincial Legislatures should no longer be delayed and immediate steps should be taken to hold them as soon as possible because important questions await solutions which can only be properly dealt with by representatives in touch with public opinion and sentiment of the people'.

The next day, Jinnah appealed for election funds in Simla: 'You know that elections cannot be fought without money. Therefore, everywhere from now onwards collect funds in each province and systematically organise our people'.[16]

On 30 August 1945, Jinnah confirmed that the paramount issue before the Muslim League in the coming elections were (1) Pakistan and (2) the Muslim League as the only authoritative and representative organisation of the Musulmans of India.[17] In this appeal, he stressed that he would welcome any earnest change-over on the part of any Muslim, and disclosed that Sir Feroz Khan Noon, a member of the Executive Council of the Governor-General (later Prime Minister of Pakistan, 1957-8) would resign from his post and join the League. For the Muslim League, its purpose for fighting the elections was clear, though it had to surmount its own organizational difficulties.

As for the Indian National Congress, it was in the meeting of the

All-India Congress Committee held in Bombay, 21-3 September 1945, that it decided to participate in the elections. The Congress noted that the Central Assembly was still governed by the Act of 1919 and was constituted on a franchise of less than one per cent of the population. Further, it referred to the ban on several organizations and thousands of people in detention without trial or undergoing sentences of imprisonment. Yet the Congress resolved that the forthcoming elections should be contested in order to demonstrate the will of the people, especially on the issue of the immediate transfer of power.

While moving the resolution on the movement of 1942, Jawaharlal Nehru said:

> It is the duty of the leaders to direct the enthusiasm of the people into proper channels. Elections are not the things that ultimately matter. It is the strength and determination of the people to win freedom that matters and it is the duty of the leaders of the people to direct the enthusiasm and spirit of the people in the right channels.[18]

On 4 October 1945 in Lucknow, Nehru said, 'I am not unduly enthusiastic about the elections'.[19] It is also the same Nehru who said in Lahore on 25 August that he was not very such interested in elections as such, but that at certain moments they assumed particular importance.[20]

The Congress fought the demand of the League for Pakistan with its slogan of 'Quit India'. But, at the same time the Congress had to advise the people who joined the Quit India movement to direct their enthusiasm into the 'right channel'. On the other hand, Nehru feared that the energy of the people might be frittered away in petty conflicts in the process of the election campaign. Though Nehru's speeches in public meetings were full of fiery assaults on the bureaucracy, the League leadership and the Communist Party of India, they also reflected his ambivalent feelings towards the people and the Congress organization.

Before we proceed to the election policy of the Communist Party of India, it is necessary to trace a brief history of Congress-Communist relations immediately after the War. In September 1945, the Congress Working Committee decided to go into the 'charge of indiscipline brought against the Congress members of the Communist Party' who objected to the Quit India movement. After the beginning of the Russo-German War on 22 June 1941 Indian Communists came to grasp the character of the Second World War as an Anti-Fascist People's War, and opposed the Quit India movement. Instead of joining the movement, they proposed the establishment of the national united front against Fascists on the basis of the Congress-League unity. The CPI found the urge to the 'national self-determination' of the Muslim-majority areas in the growth of Pakistan movement. This basic view did not change for some time even after the War. The report of the three-men's committee of the Congress was submitted quickly to the AICC in Bombay. They were of opinion that there was ample evidence on the record before them to establish a strong *prima facie* case against the Communists within the Congress, and asked them to justify their position and policy and to show cause why action should not be taken against them. The Congress was already considering whether the Communists should be allowed to remain on the Congress executive bodies.[21] In responding to this demand, the CPI issued a directive instructing all Communists to resign forthwith from the Congress except the members of the AICC.[22]

Finally, the Congress Working Committee which met in Calcutta from 7 to 11 December took its disciplinary decision to remove the Communist members of the AICC, and asked the Provincial Congress Committees to take similar action. The rift between the Congress and the Communists was complete.[23]

Despite this adverse background Indian Communists were still confident of their theoretical stance which they had taken since 1941. Already, in an editorial in their weekly, *People's War* dated 29 July 1945, Communists supported the demands of the Muslim League for fresh elections:

> Our Party fully supports the League demand for elections as an elementary democratic right and the best way to put our internal differences to the test of the people's verdict. Our appeal to the Congress is that when you deny the League's representative claim, it is your own bounded duty to join hands with it to demand new elections from the British Government and see for yourself if the League can prove its claim by people's votes, the only alternative to a civil war.
>
> Let all parties enter the electoral contest in the spirit of brother parties, who may differ but are pledged to accept the verdict of our common parent, the people.[24]

Here, the Communists appealed to all Parties to contest the elections, but it was not clear how they would keep their independent policy on constitution-making in the future. Also, it was not clarified how a people's verdict was possible under restricted franchise. At this moment it seemed that they thought the 'people's verdict' would be in favour of Pakistan.

Enrolment

The Sixth Schedule of the Government of India Act, 1935 provided that a person shall be included in the electoral rolls after having attained the age of 21 years.

No person would be included in the electoral roll for a Sikh constituency, a Muhammadan constituency, an Anglo-Indian constituency, or an Indian Christian constituency, unless he is a Sikh, a Muhammadan, an Anglo-Indian, or an Indian Christian, as the case may be. Further no one entitled to be included in the electoral roll for any Sikh constituency, Muhammadan constituency, Anglo-Indian constituency, or Indian Christian constituency in any Province would be included in the electoral roll for a general constituency in that province.

The barrier dividing General voters and Muslim voters, and General seats and Muslim seats is very clear. General electors could not vote for Muslim seats or Muslim electors for General seats. The Muslim League that claimed to represent all the Muslims of India need not bother about the General seats, or exert influence in the General constituencies. The Indian National Congress that claimed to represent all the Indian people must prove that it had the support not only of the General electorates but also of the Muslim voters.

At this stage, whether the separate electorate system was desirable or not was no longer a central issue. The Congress had to win the substantial part of Muslim seats in areas where the League was concentrating its activities. In the Provincial Elections of 1937 the League had won only 108 seats in 484 Muslim constituencies, but now the situation had changed. While the Congress organizations were paralysed during the movement of 1942, the Pakistan movement prevailed among various sections of Indian Muslims. There is no doubt that, at this moment of the history of the subcontinent, the separate electoral system worked most favorably for the Muslim League.

Another noteworthy character of the electoral rolls in the Provincial Elections of 1946 was that franchise was restricted by property and literacy.

Before leaving London, Lord Wavell said that the Congress now talked of boycotting the Elections unless they could be conducted on the basis of adult suffrage and a completely new electoral register.[25]

Even though some of the Congress members talked of adult suffrage, this was not its main issue. In fact, Nehru said at the All-India States People's Conference in Udaipur on 1 January 1946:

Adult franchise is a worthy ideal. The goal of the Congress is also adult franchise. But it is not practical politics at the present juncture to demand representation to the constituent assembly based on adult franchise . . . . At present adult franchise is not practicable even in British provinces. It will be inadvisable to demand adult franchise just now from the rulers.[26]

On 9 January, Nehru confirmed this point:

The Congress will not insist on the adopting of adult franchise of the constituent assembly. Enlargement of the franchise will cause delay in establishing a constituent assembly. It is a bitter pill to swallow. I do not know how much wider the franchise can be made. The people will be represented by elected representatives.[27]

Nehru's preference was for 'wider franchise' and not adult franchise. What he criticized in his election campaign was that electoral registers were full of errors, omissions and bogus entries. In his letter to Krishna Menon dated 3 September 1945, he took up this problem:

. . . the voters' registers are just a mass of errors and omissions. Many are full of bogus entries. Congress people, spending their time in prison, seldom think of these registers till the eve of the elections. Muslim Leaguers and others of their kind have full leisure for this business and are more interested in it than in anything else. We are told that no changes can be made in the registers now.[28]

M. Hashim Kidwai, biographer of Rafi Ahmad Kidwai, Congress leader of U.P., writes that the latter succeeded in getting the electoral roll of U.P. revised and that those who had been excluded were now included in it.[29]

Nehru also asked the *kisans* to make sure that their names were entered in the voting registers. The Congress workers were told to undertake this job.[30] But when Nehru asked the Punjab Congress workers to penetrate the villages where the real India lived and educate the masses on their right to vote, what did he mean by the 'masses'?

The contradiction between the admiration for the people's heroism during the Quit India movement and the restricted franchise system in the elections was not fully examined in Congress circles. Or else it can be said that one of the main objects of Nehru's 'violent' speeches was to solve this contradiction in his own style.

It was the Communist Party of India that pointed out the problems of restricted franchise as one of 'all round handicaps' which it was facing. The editorial of the *People's War* was of the same view that the electoral rolls were not correct and that the ritual of revision of rolls was a bad farce. In addition to this, it said that the handicap of the party was due to restricted franchise:

> The restricted property franchise disenfranchises the vast majority of the toiling masses out of whom our Party is born, and to whom its main appeal is directed.
>
> Everyone knows that we are the only working-class party in our country, but the majority of the working-class is disenfranchised.
>
> In the rural areas besides the vested interests, the vote extends to the rich peasants and a section of the middle peasants, and the vast mass of agricultural labourers and the poor peasants representing 70 to 80 per cent of the rural population are disenfranchised.
>
> This implies that our Party candidates have no chances of success even where the Kisan Sabha has won a great hold and the party can command the vote of the majority of the toiling peasantry. Our Party can thus contest only those rural seats where through its long and hard work in the interest not only of the peasantry, but of the entire rural population it has won the majority even of the upper rural strata and can get their vote even against the old traditional parties like the Congress and the League, whose main base lies in this very upper strata and through which they influence the rest of the village.
>
> In other words, it will be a case of our contesting among the rural bases of other parties and not they contesting us among our bases, nor would it be a contest for the majority of the ACTUAL rural population.
>
> Except the few labour seats, our Party will thus be demanding a hearing and seeking the confidence of those sections of the population that follow other parties, and will be deprived of the vote of its own supporters, the working classes, the peasantry and the agricultural labourers who spontaneously follow our banner wherever we work.[31]

There is room for discussion concerning the strength of the Communist Party of India immediately after the War, but this view shows clearly how the franchise system, restricted by property, deprived the lower strata of the people of their basic right. It is very interesting that the CPI made a class analysis of the social basis of the Congress and the League through its criticism of the existing franchise system. For during and immediately after the War, the Communists emphasized the *national* character of these two organizations. In a sense, this editorial unconsciously made a critical review of their own policy.

I will now examine how the restricted franchise system worked against the lower social strata. I will use mainly the materials provided by the *People's War.* Though not totally correct and only a rough estimate that needs re-examination, it is one of the few papers available which tries to throw light on this aspect of the elections in detail. In many General constituencies the Congress candidates were elected unopposed, even the Communists supported the Congress candidates in the constituencies where their own candidates did not stand.

(i) General Constituencies: Rural

The United Provinces restricted the qualification of voting right which depends on property as follows in the Sixth Schedule, Part V of the 1935 Act:

3. Subject as aforesaid, a person shall also be qualified to be included in the electoral roll for any territorial constituency if he is the owner or tenant of a house or building in the constituency the rental value whereof is not less than twenty-four rupees per annum, or, in the case of a member of the scheduled castes if he is the owner or tenant of a house or building in the constituency the rental value whereof is not less than twelve rupees per annum.
4. Subject as aforesaid, a person shall also be qualified to be included in the electoral roll for any territorial constituency if he
   (a) owns land in the constituency on which land revenue of not less than five rupees per annum is payable; or
   (b) owns land in the constituency free of land revenue, if the land revenue nominally assessed on the land for determining the amount of rates payable in respect of the land, either alone or together with any land revenue payable by him as owner of other land in the constituency, amounts to not less than five rupees per annum;
   (c) is a tenant of land in the constituency in respect of which rent of not less than ten rupees per annum, or rent in kind equivalent to not less than ten rupees per annum, is payable; or
   (d) is an under-proprietor in Oudh of land in the constituency in respect of which under-proprietary rent of not less than five rupees per annum is payable; or
   (e) in the case of a constituency comprising any part of the Hill Pattis of Kumaun, is resident in those Hill Pattis and, in the

> constituency, either is owner of a fee simple estate in those Hill Pattis, or is assessed to the payment of land revenue or cesses of any amount in those Hill Pattis, or is a Khaikar.

In its analysis of 'Election Handicaps', the Communists concluded that the basic property qualification in the rural areas restricted the franchise to those who paid land revenue as landowners, or rents as tenants. All others, such as landless agricultural workers, petty artisans etc., were totally disenfranchised. The *People's War* adds:

> The total number of persons recognised as land owners and tenants by the revenue department of the United Provinces is *about seventy-five lakhs out of a total agricultural population of four and a half crores.* (italics original)
>
> But even among those who pay land revenue or rent, not all are entitled to vote. The franchise is restricted to those who pay Rs. 5 annually as revenue or Rs. 10 as rent. This means the total exclusion from the electoral rolls of all peasants cultivating less than about three bighas or about one and a quarter acre.
>
> *In a poor province like the U.P. where small uneconomic holdings predominate, this amounts to disenfranchising no less than 33 to 40 per cent of the cultivators of the soil.*

A re-examination may be necessary for a correct picture of the rural social structure in U.P., but we may point out that many of those lower strata of the peasantry who enthusiastically participated in the Quit India movement were deprived of their right to vote.

The rural poor in Bihar had to face the same position. The Sixth Schedule—Provisions as to Franchise, Part VII of the 1935 Act—provides the following franchise qualification dependent on taxation and property in case of Bihar:

2. Subject to the provisions of Part I of this Schedule and to any overriding provisions of this Part of this Schedule, a person shall be qualified to be included in the electoral roll for a territorial constituency if he was assessed during the previous financial year to income tax or was, in the previous financial year, assessed to an aggregate amount of not less than one rupee eight annas in respect of municipal tax or is assessed, otherwise than in the Santal Parganas, to chaukidari tax of an annual amount of not less than nine annas or, in the case of a member of the scheduled castes, of an annual amount of not less than six annas;

   Provided that, in relations to the original preparation of electoral rolls and revisions thereof within three years from the commencement of Part VIII of this Act, this paragraph shall have effect as if there were substituted for the reference to nine annas to a reference to twelve annas.

Bihar was the province that had a strong peasant movement under the leadership of Swami Sahajanand Saraswati in the 1930s and where the peasantry including both rich peasants and the rural poor participated in the Quit India movement. However, the franchise divided the peasants of Bihar into two classes, enfranchised and disenfranchised peasants. The *People's War* wrote:

> Here only those who either pay income tax or pay nine annas *choukidari* tax, or who are matriculated or have passed any other equivalent examination can be voters. That is, *choukidari* tax of nine annas is the minimum property qualification of voters in the rural areas. Only those kisans who have at least five bighas of land are supposed to be thus taxed.
>
> Out of the total population in the rural areas nearly 35 per cent are agricultural labourers—practically without any land and another 25 per cent are poor kisans possessing less than five bighas of land. Thus nearly 60 per cent of the total rural population is disenfranchised.
>
> It is exactly this section of the kisans that is most oppressed in the rural areas and amongst whom our party has the biggest following. This means that our main following cannot vote in the coming elections.[32]

Here again, it needs a separate study to assess the strength of the Communists in the rural areas of Bihar in the later half of 1945. But many recent studies point out that small peasants and landless labourers joined the Quit India movement in Bihar.

Further, after the formation of the Congress Ministry in Bihar on 2 April 1946, *bakasht* struggle broke out in various parts of Bihar, demanding the return of the land forcibly ejected by zamindars. Abdul Rasul writes that the first wave of the *bakasht* movement raged in Gaya, Shahabad and Monghyr districts during April-July 1946, when *kisans* asserted their occupancy right in nearly 5,000 acres of *bakasht* land.[33] In her recent study, Vinita Damodaran writes that, in June 1946, a long drawn-out struggle over *bakasht* land broke out once again in several districts in Bihar. She concludes that the struggles affected all sections of the peasantry, from the middle peasant cultivator to the small low-caste sharecropper. Landless labour also played an unprecedented part in the agitation.[34]

For those tenants and landless labour who had no right to vote but joined the *bakasht* struggle, what was the meaning of the elections of 1946? Did the elections only provide an armistice? How could the political forces which claimed to represent the peasantry connect the demands of peasants with their election campaign? Did the *bakasht* struggle mean a radical criticism of the whole constitutional process including the elections? Clearly restricted franchise was not just a technical matter, but closely related to the basic nature of the 'constitutional development'.

(ii) Labour Constituencies

Under the Government of India Act, 1935, apart from the General seats including the seats reserved for the scheduled castes, there were special constituencies reserved for (1) Backward areas and Tribes, (2) Sikhs, (3) Muhammadans, (4) Anglo-Indians, (5) Indian Christians, (6) Commerce, industry, mining and planting, (6) Landholders, (7) Universities, (8) Labour.

The *People's War* which we cited earlier, writes that the opinions of the labourers were only partially represented in the Provincial Assemblies. We will pick up the case of Bengal where the labour movement was very strong during this period:

> Out of the eight labour seats, four are allotted to Railways, Tea Gardens, Collieries and Seamen.
>
> The remaining four represents factory workers of Calcutta, Howrah, Hooghly and 24 Parganas.
>
> 30,000 workers from textile, jute, press, jetty and hosiery in Dacca, as also over 20,000 rickshaw pullers, tram workers, and motor-drivers in Calcutta, though recognised voter in the Corporation Elections, have no franchise for the Assembly. The vast majority of these would vote Communists.[35]

Furthermore, many eligible workers were still left out. According to rules, a worker of six month's standing had the vote, but the present list was prepared three of four years ago and omitted all workers recruited since. In Table I the *People's War* gives details of how a huge per centage of workers were denied the franchise.

In connection with the labour constituencies in Bihar, the same issue reports the position in detail:

> Bihar is a province where big industries like coal, mica, iron and steel, sugar, railways, cement are run employing in all nearly five lakhs of workers.
>
> But the labour constituencies in Bihar have been delimited in such a manner as to deprive lakhs of industrial workers of the right to participate in the election of labour representatives. This particularly affects our Party, which is the strongest force among industrial labour.
>
> There are three labour seats and four labour constituencies. One

constituency is eliminated by rotation in every election.

One seat is reserved for the organised workers in the mining area of Jharia. Only those workers are entitled to vote who are members of Trade Unions which are duly registered and of one year's standing.

There are nearly 90,000 coal workers in Jharia and not more than 35,000 are organised in duly registered Unions, *which means no voting right for more than 60 per cent of the workers.*

Hazaribagh mining area covering 70,000 coal and mica workers is another constituency. This area is our strongest working-class base and a large number of workers are organised in Trade Unions both in coal and mica. The Union and our Party wields tremendous influence over the unorganised workers also.

But, in the coming elections, this is the one Labour constituency out of the four which has been eliminated, according to the rule mentioned before.

The two other labour seats are allotted to the unorganised factory labour of Monghyr-cum-Jamalpur and Jamshedpur.

So the vast mass of workers in sugar, cement and jute industries, and railways do not get any representation and are totally disenfranchised for the labour constituencies.[36]

However, the Election Officer, Bihar showed a different picture of the enrollment and placed stress on his fair administration.[37] According to him ordinarily the draft electoral rolls for the Labour and University constituencies were complete in themselves and did not need supplement by means of notices of claim for registration, because the rolls are prepared from lists of persons possessing the prescribed franchise qualifications, obtained from the secretaries of the

TABLE I: LABOUR ELECTORAL COLLEGES IN BENGAL

Name of Company	*Approximate Number of Workers*	*Number of Voter's List*
I.G.N. Co.	3,000	207
Jessoi & Co.	7,000	566
Cossipore Gun & Shell	12,000	5,799
G.R.W.	9,000	3,244
Kanchrapara Railway Shop	13,000	6,175
Kesoram Cotton	7,000	5,586
Bata Shoes	7,000	3,465
Jaya Iron	1,800	631
Maya Iron	900	412
Braithwaite Iron	2,400	172
Steel Products	900	163
Assansole Collieries	80,000	39,492

constituent trade unions, the owners or managers of the factories concerned and the University authorities. But in the case of the Trade Union (Mining) constituency, the original lists supplied by the Mazdoor Union, Jharia, contained a very large number of names of qualified persons without the names of their fathers. Subsequently the executives of the Union collected the requisite information which enabled the names of these persons to be included in the final notices of claim for registration. On the other hand, in the case of the Monghyr *cum* Jamalpur Factory Labour constituency as many as 339 claims were preferred and all were disallowed for default at the hearing. The claims were fraudulent.

Despite this indication it may be concluded here that the Labour constituencies represented the interests of limited proportion of the working class.

(iii) Literacy

As we have seen universal suffrage was out of the question in Government circles. Wavell's diary dated 4 September 1945 records that Sir Reginald Maxwell, Home Member of the Governor-General's Executive Council, 1938-44 came to see him to suggest an enlarged franchise which was 'surprising'. (Because he thought that Maxwell ought to have known better then anyone 'the ignorance of the present electorate'.[38])

However, illiteracy does not mean ignorance. Wavell was not in a position to understand the meaning of the political awakening of the 'ignorant' people.

In the elections of 1946 even the 'literate' people faced difficulties to prove their literacy. On 2 September 1945, Cripps, President of the Board of Trade spoke in the India and Burma Committee that all Governors should take the greatest possible care to see that the registers were fairly and fully compiled.[39] This was the maximum which the Labour Government could propose. But this was hardly realized at the grass roots level.

Though the following cases in Bengal which the *People's War* mentioned may be a partisan interpretation, it may also be difficult to reject it as untrue:

> The new education qualification denies franchise to lakhs of kisans, who have been roused to active political consciousness by the Red Flag.
>
> But the worst thing is that even this educational qualification is often

ignored by petty bureaucrats. At Nilphamari, the Government clerk had not even heard of it! In most of the districts, the forms have not reached at all.

The rule that it has to be certified by a Gazetted Officer makes it almost impossible for thousands to get enrolled even when they are eligible, because a Gazetted Officer is either unapproachable by local Kisan Sabha workers or he flatly refuses to testify, in many cases afraid of being associated with Communists.

Women voters in the districts have particularly faced this difficulty: at Susang in Mymensingh, for instance the local Sub-Registrar refused to certify the educational qualification of a number of eligible women candidates on the ground that as the Enrolling Officer, he should not certify. When the Rural Magistrate was approached, he also flatly refused to do so.

In Chittagong and Dacca, many women voters were deprived of the franchise because a number of Gazetted Officers approached refused to certify their educational qualification without having the women brought into their presence. This, in the prevailing social set-up, often becomes an impossibility.[40]

The Communists write that in most cases these were not cases of negligence, but discrimination against the Kisan Sabhas or Trade Unions or those people under their influence. It can also be said that there were no careful arrangements to promote women's enrolment.

Even Communists who examined 'election handicaps' in detail in October 1945 could not pursue this theme continuously.

The fortnightly report from the Punjab had already in the first half of September 1945 noted that election fever was rising in all districts and that practically the only reference to the war concerned the fate of the Indian National Army prisoners.[41] Then in the second half of the same month, the report from the Punjab indicated that the party workers were feverishly checking electoral rolls, to see that the names of possible supporters of their parties had not been omitted or overlooked, and that the candidates were being chosen for various constituencies.[42] From these reports we know that election fever emerged before the Viceroy's statement on 19 September.

The report from Bombay in the first half of September sent the information that many quarters were criticizing the lack of uniformity in the decisions of various Provincial Governments in respect of elections and particularly the unwillingness of certain Provincial Governments to undertake the revision of electoral rolls.[43]

On the other hand, the Government report from Bengal had doubts about the method of claiming inclusion in the electoral rolls. The Report from the Dacca Division for the first half of October stated that every party was preparing for the elections. According to this report, in many constituencies, parties were busy seeing that their supporters got on the voter's list. In the General constituencies in Dacca and Bakarganj, this had been very marked, and some officers suspected that there were many attempts to get unqualified persons on the lists, through false certificates of educational qualifications, and by misrepresenting the real age of voters—especially women.[44]

In Bihar, the Election Officer opened on 13 August 1945 at Hazaribagh under the charge of the Election Officer, Rai Bahadur Nandalal Sinha, and was moved to Patna when the Government moved there from Ranchi. The electoral rolls for the territorial and special constituencies of the Bihar Legislative Assembly prepared in 1941-2 were to continue in force till 1 April 1947. But, as the electoral rolls would be nearly four years old by the time the elections have taken place, it was decided that the electoral rolls for the Labour and University constituencies should be completely revised and that, in view of the shortness of the time available, only lists of amendments should be prepared in respect of all other electoral rolls.[45]

Government policy in respect of amendment of the electoral rolls was explained in a communique on 12 September 1945. The procedure for amendment of the rolls on application was briefly stated, the date by which rolls should be amended, and the last date for application were announced. On 18 September the provisional time-table for all important stages of the electoral operations was given to the press in a second communique. On 29 September, a press note was issued which described the requirement of the new rule for amendments of electoral rolls. Simultaneously 'wide publicity' was given through the press and local officers to notices of amendment of electoral rolls and to the franchise qualifications for different classes of constituencies both of the Bihar Legislative Assembly and the Bihar Legislative Council.[46] As for the constituencies of the Legislative Assembly other than Indian Christians, Labour and University constituencies, 1 October 1945 was prescribed as the date by reference to which the lists of amendments should be prepared (i.e. persons qualified on that date were made eligible for enrolment), and 15 October was prescribed as the latest date for applications for enrolment. The fee payable on each such application was reduced from Rs. 10 to 12 annas.[47]

The Subdivisional Officers were made responsible for the preparation of lists of amendments not only in respect of the electoral rolls for the constituencies of which they were the Registration Officers, but for all other constituencies (except Commerce and Industry, Mining and Planting constituencies). In the case of the latter lists were prepared by the Registration Officer himself. namely, the Legislative Secretary.

This was the main process of enrolment in Bihar. But the Election Officer had to admit that there was a gap between the 'election fever' and the actual number enrolled. He wrote:

> The coming elections created an all-round enthusiasm and excitement in the public mind; and the stagnation of the past six years (after the Congress Ministry resigned in protest against the British war policy in 1939) gave place to much agitation and activities on all sides. It looked as if every qualified person was eager to enrol himself as an elector. Arrangements were, therefore, made to record a possible increase of twenty per cent over the existing electorate. The actual number enrolled, however, fell far short of expectation. One reason for this was, as reported by a Returning Officer, that the fee of 12 annas kept away many applicants. Another reason, probably, was that the Congress was confident of its victory at the polls and therefore did not care to bring new electors on to the rolls.[48]

The cost of elections was recovered partly by the sale of the electoral rolls and the lists of amendment (Rs. 8,508) and partly by the forfeiture of deposits by unsuccessful candidates for the Assembly and Council (Rs. 16,000). The largest income for the recovery was derived from the fees on applications for enrolment.[49] It is ironical that this sum of Rs. 34,132 contributed simultaneously to both the success and failure of the elections.

The total electorate in the 1946 Provincial Elections in India were 41,075,839.[50] According to the study of Kingsley Davis, the estimated population of British India in 1945 was 299,621,000. The Census of India, 1931 showed that the proportion of the population over 20 years to the total population as 50.9 per cent and the proportion of the distribution for the 20-39 year group and for the 10-19 year group as 32.0 per cent and 20.7 per cent respectively.[51] If we take these into consideration, the proportion of the total electorate to all the population of the same age group may be roughly less than 28 per cent.

The number of women voters was 6,620,589 only 16 per cent of the total electorate. Most of women and lower classes were deprived of their voting right. Gail Pearson who followed the women franchise movement in India and analysed the 1937 elections in Bombay Presidency concluded:

> Political participation for women, or rather, the participation of the female leadership, was now ensured. Reserved seats ensured that the female elite would remain in parliaments and deal with legislation for social reform. This participation linked with the hollow shell that the universalisation of women's participation in civil disobedience movement had become, plus the ideology of the home, obscured divisions among women and their real condition.[52]

However, the movement for enrolment among women at the grass roots level, though it led to 'bogus' registration in some cases, made many women notice the social gulf between the enfranchised classes and the disenfranchised people.

We have referred to Nehru's comment on the demand for universal adult franchise. As for the League, within its circles there was demand for adult franchise. For instance, six Muslim League members of the Punjab Assembly, headed by the Nawab of Mamdot, President, Punjab Provincial Muslim League stated in a cable to the Secretary of State for India in September 1945: 'The coming elections are going to decide the fate of 400 million Indians for decades to come. Pray, do not rush elections on present restricted franchise. Grant of universal adult franchise is the need of the hour to enable India's teeming millions to shape their destiny themselves.'[53]

The Muslim League, and at least some leaders of the League in the Punjab, were confident of their victory even in universal adult franchise.

The Nawab of Mamdot thought that the Muslim League would sweep the polls in the rural areas of the Punjab, once the citadel of the Unionist Party.[54] This conviction seems to have led him to this demand for adult franchise. In this case the demand of the candidates and the will of the disenfranchised majority were closely related.

However, despite the seriousness of the election issue which would affect the destiny of the people in the subcontinent, internal competition for nominations was far from encouraging. It is also true however that this strife indicated one of the main trends of post-independent politics in South Asia.

Nomination

The nomination of candidates was a problem both the Congress and the League had to solve for the success of the elections.

In his appeal to the Muslims on 30 August 1945, Jinnah emphasized that their best men should be returned, and that the selection of the candidates should be made on the basis of merit, justice and fairplay. He said, 'We should do our best to send up a first class team that will work in the various legislatures with earnestness for the welfare of our people, and to maintain prestige and the honour of the All-India Muslim League.'[55] Actually he knew well what he and the League were facing. In Karachi, on 6 September, he made it clear that the Provincial Muslim League Parliamentary Board would finally select candidates from amongst all the applicants, and that the persons so selected would be the official Muslim League candidates. But any candidate who had not been given a Muslim League ticket by the Provincial Parliamentary Board and was dissatisfied with their decision had a right to appeal to the Central Parliamentary Board, whose decision as the appellate tribunal would be final.[56]

The Central Parliamentary Board was composed of Chowdhry Khaliq-uz-Zaman (Governor, East Pakistan 1953-4), Liaquat Ali Khan (Prime Minister of Pakistan 1947-51) and Nawab Ismail Khan selected by Jinnah. All of them came from U.P.[57] It tried to have a final word in the nomination, but faced resistance from the provincial branches like the Sind Muslim League and could not prepare a consolidated list for the elections.

In July 1945, G.M. Syed set up the Provincial Parliamentary Board with the backing of the Provincial League to select the League candidates. Sir Ghulam Husain Hidayatullah (Sind Premier) and the men of the Mir (Chief of Baluchi tribes) group opposed Syed. In the Sind Legislative Assembly, most of the Muslim seats were captured by the big jagirdar and zamindar factions. Hidayatullah leaned heavily on the support of the Mirs and big zamindars. G.M. Syed was the leader of the 'Syed group', also powerful zamindars, but traditionally opposed to the jagirdar groups of Mirs. It is also well-known that G.M. Syed tried to protect the rights of the *Hari* tenants who were the most oppressed in Sind. In September 1945, Jinnah visited Karachi and asked Syed to reconstitute the Parliamentary Board. The reconstituted Board consisted of the three members belonging to the Syed Group including Syed himself, and the four of the other group. But this Board meeting failed to select candidates and Syed and his two supporters walked out, and appealed all irregularities to the League Central Parliamentary Board. Finally it was decided that the Central Board should select all the candidates. Though the Provincial League under Syed asked the Centre to consult a Committee chosen by it, the Centre ignored this resolution, and finally selected 27 members in which the group opposing Syed had a large majority.[58]

Jinnah removed G.M. Syed from the Muslim League in January 1946. Sajjad Zaheer, a Communist writer, wrote that responsibility for this deplorable state of affairs must be placed on the League high command who tried to appease the reactionaries. Also, he was critical of Syed's act, saying that without any mass peasant movement to support him, and deprived of the backing of the All-India Muslim League, Syed was bound to lose the support of the Sind Muslims. Sajjad Zaheer's conclusion was pessimistic: 'Syed's revolt is a dangerous portent for all patriots: for the League because it will strengthen anti-democratic reactionary elements in it; for the Congress because it will weaken the pro-unity, freedom trend inside the League.'[59]

Though Sajjad Zaheer's view was biased by the Communist policy of the 'Congress-League unity', it reflected the increasing trend in the character of the Pakistan movement and indicated the nature of the post-independent Sind politics.

On the occasion of the Provincial Elections in 1937, the Sind Muslim League was dominated by the rural elite of large landholders, clan leaders (Mirs) and religious leaders (Pirs).[60] Since 1942 there were some endeavours to enrol its members among the rural areas. But in the stage when the Sind League scrambled for seats under the limited franchise system, it could not cast off its earlier character.

The position of the Muslim League was not much different in the North-West Frontier Province. There was serious strife for tickets between the Aurangzeb Khan (Premier 1943-5) group and the Bakht Jamal Khan group.[61] Sajjad Zaheer writes that, out of 38 candidates selected by the Muslim League Parliamentary Board for election to the Provincial Assembly, there were seven *Khan Bahadurs*, one knight, five *Nawabs*, one *Khan Saheb* and two army recruiting officers.[62] Many leading *Khans* were among the candidates and a number of important Pir families supported the League.[63] In those days the social base of the League in the Frontier was still limited to the towns and the non-Pathan Hazara district.[64]

As for the social background of the League in the Punjab, Sajjad Zaheer wrote in the end of 1945 that the entire Muslim educated class of the towns and villages were with the League, and the largest sections of Muslim peasants, zamindars and town poor supported it. But, he confessed that, of the total of six League nominees for the Central Assembly, three were a member of the big Pir family, an old paralytic gentleman of a powerful landlord clan, and a feudal lord whose loyalty even to the League was doubtful.[65] He said that the other three could be satisfactory candidates 'from any democratic point of view'. He had to concede that, in the choice of candidates for the Central and Provincial Assemblies, the Punjab League leaders were following the line that anyone who had the greatest chance of wangling through to success should be given a ticket. It cannot be denied that the Punjab League organization was also in the grip of the Pirs and the clan leaders who were big landlords and shifted their political loyalty from the Unionist Party to the League. Sajjad Zaheer could not diagnose the main cause of the contradiction between the 'undemocratic' candidates and the Muslim 'mass upsurge' for Pakistan.

Both Mian Iftikhar-ud-din, a left Congress leader and Feroz Khan Noor, a member of the Viceroy's Executive Council joined the Punjab League in September 1945.

In a meeting of the All-India Congress Committee in Bombay in September 1945, Mian Iftikhar-ud-din, a left leader, who had some time earlier resigned as President of the Punjab Provincial Congress Committee, proposed an amendment to the resolution moved by Sardar Vallabhbhai Patel. He asked the following parts to be added:

> . . . the AICC resolves that the forthcoming elections be contested, and directs the Working Committee to take all necessary steps in this behalf.
>
> In these elections the Congress will raise the basic demand of the convening of a Constituent Assembly, elected by adult franchise, as the immediate programme of action. . . .
>
> The Congress realizes that any plan of calling a Constituent Assembly, if it is to be the victorious assertion of the people's united will against foreign rule and is to lead to the creation of an independent and democratic India, must be such as will win the backing of all the main parties and of all major sections of our people, especially the Muslims.
>
> The Congress, therefore, assures that the elected representatives of the Constituent Assembly of areas in which the Muslims are in a majority, as in the North-Western and Eastern zones of India, that they would be free to mould their own destiny and to make their own decision whether they join the Indian Union or not.[66]

During the later part of the War the view of Iftikhar-ud-din had come closer to that of the Communist Party of India both in the theory of an anti-Fascist People's War and in the idea of Congress-League or National Unity. But the amendment was rejected, and on return from Bombay, Mian Iftikhar-ud-din resigned the primary membership of the Congress and joined the Muslim League in the end of September

1945. In his statement and an explanatory note, he expressed that he had always believed that Hindu-Muslim unity was the foundations of Indian freedom, but that the new tendencies of the Congress leadership made it impossible to work for the cause of unity in the Congress. In fact, Nehru declared that the Congress would not make any approach to the League, but, on the contrary, would fight it. Patel clearly stated that any one who believed in the right of self-determination for the Muslim zones and was an advocate of Congress-League settlement had no place in the Congress.[67]

Concerning this issue Nehru actually said:

> As far as I can see, it is better to be miles and miles away from the Muslim League. Again and again we went to it with folded hands only to receive kicks. . . .
>
> . . . those who have put obstacles in the way of country's freedom, those who have made us gulp many a bitter cup, with them we can have no truck. The time has therefore come to declare that there would be no more approaches to the League. We shall take the Muslim masses into our confidence. The Congress will be prepared to go to peasants, the workers, the poor and the oppressed of the land—be they Hindus or Muslims.[68]

Here it is to be examined whether the Congress could indeed reach the masses in the Punjab: judging from the words of the Congress leaders (see chapter III), the answer is negative.

When Mian Iftikhar-ud-din joined the Muslim League, Nehru wrote, 'Iftikhar, middle-hearted man that he is, thinks he can reform the Muslim League from within—a foolish idea, but he is foolish enough to do anything.'[69]

It is true that in his election campaign and in the post-independent history of Pakistan, Iftikhar-ud-din fought his isolated struggle for reform of the political system. He was one of a few League leaders who warned against military-cum-bureaucratic rule in Pakistan. *The Viewpoint* made its comment, 'if the art of politics lies in the ability to predict the course of events, then Mian Iftikhar-ud-din was a politician without peer in the land'.[70]

On the other hand, Sir Feroz Khan Noon who also joined the Muslim League in September 1945 recollects his uncomfortable feelings and consciousness of his status:

> I knew the feelings of the prominent Muslim Leaguers of the Punjab. These young men, full of ambition and confidence, having full backing of Mr. Jinnah, looked my return to politics with suspicion, worrying lest I should either take away the credit for their work or try to capture power. In spite of their

hesitation to trust or to cooperate with me, I never felt any resentment, I came back only to help to win the elections for the Muslim League and I knew that this would not be easy without my pitting myself against the Unionists and the old well trenched leaders. My position and my prestige as a former Minister and Defence member of the Viceroy's Executive Council was a counterpoise the Muslim League had against the Unionist Party in the rural areas and officialdom. A sovereign Muslim State of our own was the main force of the forthcoming elections.[71]

Feroz Khan Noon stood as a League candidate in Rawalpindi Division constituency and Mian Iftikhar-ud-din stood in Kasur constituency. The 'establishment' and 'anti-establishment' leaders could keep their uneasy relations in control so long as they fought for Pakistan.

It was in Bengal that relations between the League central leadership and the Provincial League took the most serious turn in the selection of the candidates.

After Abul Hashim was elected as the new Secretary of the Bengal League in November 1943, its organization and activities were vitalized. Now the League came to be free from the clutches of the Nawabs of Dhaka. Abul Hashim toured the rural parts of Bengal where the famine was still casting a serious shadow on the life of the people, and tried to organize the League on the district level on the ideological basis of the Lahore Resolution (March 1940) of the All-India Muslim League which, he interpreted, had no trait of communalism, but contemplated two independent sovereign states as homelands for the Muslims of India. In this process a nucleus of young enthusiastic activists was formed, and they succeeded in enrolling more than half a million two-anna members of the Bengal League in 1944.[72] On 24 March 1945, the draft manifesto of the Bengal Muslim League was published, which declared that the Muslims had a right to mould their life according to the fundamentals of Islam without interference. It also proposed the constitution of a Constituent Assembly through universal adult franchise, nationalization of key industries, and peasant proprietorship.[73] Hashim recollects that the draft manifesto was accepted by the progressive elements of the Muslim League of Bengal and Assam as a guide to their thought and action. (Nikhil Chakravarthy helped prepare the draft.)

On 6 September 1945, Abul Hashim published his press statement entitled *Let us go to War*, and asked the League members to prepare for the elections, because, he said, the ballot box was the only medium through which public opinion could be ascertained with the greatest possible accuracy. He claimed that the Pakistan scheme of the All-India Muslim League represented the views of the entire body of Muslims. In this statement, he appealed to League members to 'bundle up all their differences and to preserve them if necessary in cold storage during the pendency of our common struggle.[74]

But, the squabblings between the 'left' and 'right' inside the Bengal leadership continued abated even as they now boasted a membership of one million.

Actually, in the council meeting of 29 September to start the Provincial Parliamentary Board, the proceedings were obstructed by the shouting down or by the removal of the microphone followed by hand-to-hand scuffles.[75] Finally the Parliamentary Board was formed, in which the group of Nazimuddin (Bengal Premier 1943-5) of the Nawab family got 4 seats, while Hashim's group and Suhrawardy's men held 3 and 2 seats respectively. The results showed the change of trends in the Bengal League. The 'rightists' had already occupied 4 seats of the board before the council meeting according to the rule. The President of the Bengal Muslim League, Maulana Aklam Khan and the leader of the Parliamentary Party, Khwaja Nazimuddin, were ex-officio members of the board. The old Muslin League Assembly members of the Provincial Council elected one member, and the members of the Provincial Assembly elected another. The candidates set up by the leader of the Parliamentary Party were to be official League candidates and were elected without contest. Though Suhrawardy, deputy leader under Nazimuddin, had applied for nomination, he was rejected. Hence started the Suhrawardy-Hashim combine. The remaining 5 members had to be selected by the Provincial Muslim League Council, which elected all seats from the 'leftists'.[76] Not only was Nazimuddin's group defeated in the selection of the board members, but the council adopted a resolution dissolving the Election Fund and Propaganda Committees on which his supporters had had a considerable influence, and the Parliamentary Board was empowered to exercise all these functions. The Parliamentary Board was further expected to consult primary members and public opinion before nominating candidates.[77]

Harun-or-Rashid, a Bangladeshi political scientist, evaluates this as highly significant:

> The election to the Provincial Parliamentary Board was not simply a leadership race between Nazimuddin and Suhrawardy. It was far more significant. The success of the Hashim-Suhrawardy group marked a victory for the Organization against the Parliamentary coterie. The verdict of the League

Council heralded the prominence of the middle class whose representatives comprised the majority. Furthermore, it was tantamount of a vote of non-confidence in Jinnah's confidants in Bengal.[78]

It can be concluded that the decision of the League Council meant the victory of 'Bengal Muslim Nationalism' over the central leadership of the League and simultaneously the victory of the 'middle class upsurge' over the small Nawabi coterie and a few others loyal to Jinnah.

But this showed a remarkable aspect of the new stage of the Bengal Muslim League. Election politics did not end there. After the council meeting, there was some gesture of reconciliation from the side of Suhrawardy. A new Election Fund Committee was set up with Nazimuddin as its President and Hasan Ispahani as the Treasurer. Ispahani represented non-Bengali Muslim merchants and was the right hand man of Jinnah in Bengal, and had been the Treasurer of the former Election Fund Committee.[79] This was not enough to lessen the friction. Though there was a limit to the influence which Jinnah could exert, he acted against the idea of Suhrawardy and Hashim. When Abul Hashim started the Bengali weekly, *Millat*, as the official organ of the Bengal Provincial Muslim League on 16 November 1945 (against the existing daily *Azad* which represented the opinions of the Nazimuddin group) Jinnah did not conceal his displeasure. Furthermore, when Jinnah made a contribution of Rs. 200,000 from the Central Fund, it was not handed over directly to the Provincial Parliamentary Board, but he appointed a special committee to administer the sums on behalf of the All-India Muslim League.[80] Finally, the intervention of the centre came in the form of the revision of the original list of nominations. After his defeat in September, Nazimuddin decided not to contest the election himself, but asked Suhrawardy not to victimize his followers.[81] The official fortnightly report has explained:

> The nominations of Muslim League candidates by the Provincial Parliamentary Board have given rise to considerable dissatisfaction. The Provincial League office in Calcutta was raided by students and a demonstration was made before the house of Mr. Suhrawardy who is supposed to have influenced these nominations in his favour. Similar demonstrations are also reported from Dacca and some other areas.[82]

When the list of 119 Muslim League nominees was announced in early February 1946, a large number of appeals were filed to the Central Parliamentary Board, protesting the elimination of the Khwaja

Nazimuddin group. The Central Board accepted 22 appeals, almost all belonging to his group, so that now he could send about 50 supporters as candidates to the Provincial Assembly.[83] The Government report also confirms that the Central Parliamentary Board had set aside on appeal a number of nominations made by the Provincial League and that this had reduced the volume of discontent which was being felt by large sections against the provincial selections.[84]

In his *Let us go to War*, Abul Hashim, a 'progressive' leader of the Bengal League, wanted to avert the internal strife in the organization for the purpose of winning the elections. Citing the words of Jinnah, Hashim appealed:

> Quaid-i-Azam Mr Mohammad Ali Jinnah wants us to send a first class team to the Legislature. During the last eight years of Provincial Autonomy we have had enough experience of a bad and unreliable team. We can only select the right type of men if we can constitute a Parliamentary Board which would, while nominating the candidates for the legislatures have no other consideration than honesty, integrity and efficiency. The personnel of the Parliamentary Board be such as may inspire confidence among the people.[85]

The slogan of Pakistan united the various Muslim social strata which expected the solution of their own problems in the new state(s). Simultaneously within this framework of thought it allowed a free play of factionalism on the personal or ideological level. 'Sindhi Nationalism' under the leadership of G.M. Syed was excluded from the League movement because it threatened to challenge this framework, and 'Bengal Nationalism' under the leadership of Abul Hashim was accommodated because he wanted to avert internal rivalry at least during the period of election campaign. To that extent the scope of the 'progressive' activities of the Hashim group was curbed.

However, the politics of nominations hinted at the existence of the strong ruling class in rural areas of Sind, the destiny of the struggle which Mian Iftikhar-ud-din initiated in the Punjab and, above all, the strength of the movement of Bengal Muslims for their self-government in post-independent Pakistan.

Meanwhile, the All-India Congress Committee which met in Bombay in September 1945, decided to set up the Assembly Elections Sub-Committee consisting of seven members to take steps for the selection of candidates and for organizing the elections to the legislatures. They are Maulana Abūl Kalam Azad, Sardar Vallabhbhai

Patel, Rajendra Prasad (President of India 1950-62), Govind Vallabh Pant (Chief Minister of U.P. 1947-54), Asaf Ali, Pattabhi Sitaramayya and Shankar Rao Deo. Patel opened the office of the Central Election Board of the Congress in Bombay on 1 October. He was the man who played the most important role in deciding the names of the Congress candidates.

In his letter to Nehru dated 4 November 1945, Patel wrote that the selection of candidates for the elections was a bad business and said, 'It is a sad thing to see this mad competition for going into the Councils. Most of these complaints are absolutely false. No selection is possible which would satisfy all.'[86]

Nehru who was outside the Board, said in Jorhat on 15 December 1945, 'If I had the power I would have adopted a new policy and given nomination in other ways. I would have prohibited the submission of applications for nominations by individual Congressmen. The entire selection should be done by committees selecting candidates on the basis of their past work and on their ability to carry on the Congress work in the legislatures.'[87] Nehru also spoke in Sodapur on 7 December 1945, 'Elections are always a tough work, but they pale into insignificance in the presence of the fundamental issue, namely, the freedom of India.'[88]

However, the reverse was also true. In the presence of entangled bickerings and complaints regarding nominations, even the slogan of 'Quit India' or 'Pakistan' seemed to pale into insignificance. These conflicts mostly occurred outside the sphere of the life of the disenfranchised people.

Patel who actually managed the Central Election Board of the Congress, undertook first the work for the elections to the Central Assembly, because the nominations were required by the end of October 1945. In uncontested constituencies where there was only one candidate, there was no problem. In other cases, he was required to circulate the applications with his recommendation among the seven members of the Election Board, but as this work proceeded, Patel found himself in a position to have the last word.[89] In November 1945, he began to prepare for the nominations for the Provincial Elections.

As for the nominations, it was arranged that Azad, chairman of the Central Election Board, would deal with candidates in Bengal, Assam and the eastern areas, and Patel would handle the cases of Bombay, Gujarat, Maharashtra and the western areas. The south was in charge of C. Rajagopalachari. There were also provincial leaders like Rafi Ahmad Kidwai for U.P., Rajendra Prasad for Bihar, Maulana Baksh for Sind, Gopal Reddy for Andhra and Kamaraj (Chief Minister of Tamilnadu 1954-63) for Tamilnadu.[90]

As the franchise to the Central Assembly was very limited, in the case of Deccan Sardars' and Inamdars' constituencies, Patel even obtained the list of voters, and came to the conclusion that all voters were reactionary and conservative and there was no chance of seats even if the Congress put up its candidates.[91]

Though there was serious rupture between Patel and Azad and it reached breaking point in February 1946, the prominent role of Patel in the election management of the Congress cannot be denied.

As noted earlier, Mian Iftikhar-ud-din left the Congress in September 1945. It came as a big blow to the Punjab Congress, and particularly to the pro-Nehru faction to which Iftikhar-ud-din had belonged.[92] Even before Iftikhar-ud-din left the Congress, it was ridden with factionalism, and Nehru and Patel were of the same view that it was in a deplorable condition.

Already in the beginning of September 1945, Nehru wrote to Partap Singh Kairon (Chief Minister of the Punjab 1956-64), Secretary of the Punjab Congress, saying that if the public thought the Congressmen were split up into different parties, quarreling among themselves, their enthusiasm for the Congress would wane. Nehru admitted that the Punjab Congress had been in the past a somewhat narrow organization without sufficient representation of important elements, especially rural.[93]

Amidst the election campaign in the Punjab, Patel regretted that the Punjab Congress had been divided into groups and factions of a very bitter type and hardly two men trusted each other. Patel was distressed to find that even *good Congressmen* were not united in the Punjab. He asked 'Can nothing be done to make Congress workers realize their sense of responsibility at this critical period?'[94]

In such a situation there was a serious rift between Azad and Patel. They had different approaches to the election campaign and nominations of candidates. Azad took a soft attitude towards the Ahrars and other Nationalist Muslims, while Patel thought that the Congress should send its candidates on the Congress tickets, not as Nationalist Muslims, and did not lay his hope on the Ahrars who had some influence in the Punjab. Relations between the two leaders were not smooth in their approach to the Akalis either. Azad sent a telegram to Patel on 14 November 1945, saying that 'if Akalis approach you please refer them to me. Punjab situation much complicated. We should form opinion very carefully.' Patel wrote back immediately, 'you will see that I was not going to do anything without consulting you'.[95]

It can be said that this rift was basically caused by the absence of a mass Congress base in the Punjab, particularly in its rural areas. The Congress had to find its allies among the Nationalist Muslims or the Akalis, to contain the Muslim League and the Communists.

The Congress organization in Sind too was weak. Nehru wrote to Patel in October 1945,

> I have been receiving many telegrams of protest against the nominations of candidates for election from various provinces. No doubt you have received far more and are in a better position to judge. I cannot, however, help feeling disturbed at some of the choices made or proposed in the Punjab, in Bengal and in Sind.[96]

Though the *National Herald* wrote that Syed's place was in the Congress to which he once belonged,[97] the party on its own initiative was not in a position to respond to the changing scenario.

The position of the Congress in Bengal, a key province in its objection to the Pakistan scheme, was not hopeful. Sarat Chandra Bose wrote to Patel that there was no contact between us (the Congress) and them (the Muslim masses).[98] Like the Punjab Congress, the Bengal Congress was far from united, and there was discord between Sarat Bose and Prafulla Ghosh over the nomination of Congress candidates. Patel expressed his irritation at the delay of nominations to the Central Assembly and his uneasiness with preparations for the Provincial Assembly:

> I hope that all efforts will be made to present a united front in these elections against all opposition to the Congress, either from the Hindu Mahasabha or the Muslim League or any other anti-Congress group. This is a question of now or never. Bengal has suffered tremendously in the past five years and it is for us to make or mar the future of Bengal. The Congress must present a united front and sink all its personal differences.[99]

Yet the disunity did not lessen even in January 1946 when the Congress had to concentrate its activities on the Provincial Elections. Patel again had to emphasize the same appeal in his letter to a Bengal leader:

> You know we were in Calcutta for more than a fortnight only recently. Mahatma Gandhi is still there and he is trying his level best to induce

Congressmen in Bengal to give up quarrels and party differences so that Bengal can be raised once again to its former premier place of pride. We also did our best during our stay. . . . I am hoping, however, that the past five years' sufferings of Bengal will not go in vain and Congressmen in the province will realise their responsibility.[100]

The lack of a mass base for the Bengal Congress, and its leadership crisis, led to a serious rift between Patel and Azad as in the Punjab. When Azad expressed his dissatisfaction about the establishment of a finance committee without his knowledge (which, he thought, came into being with the advice of Patel while he was in Calcutta), the latter vented his anger:

I have done nothing there without your consultation and approval. . . . I know nothing of any finance committee being constituted there by anybody. . . .

I do not know what method you devised for smooth working in Calcutta and you have never told me anything about it.

A Muslim board (Nationalist Muslim Parliamentary Board) was formed after I left, of which I was not informed. Shamsuddin, the Secretary of this board, joined the League immediately after that. . . .

My information, according to reports from Bengal, is that we can expect no more than about 8 to 10 Muslim seats. The rest will all go to the League. In my opinion, the proper course all over India would have been to contest the elections on Congress tickets. The independent machinery will give us no more seats in Bengal, but I have subordinated my opinion in these matters both in the Punjab and in Bengal and elsewhere to yours without question.[101]

During 1939-45, Bengal faced the sacrifice of the people in Midnapur during the Quit India movement and the famine of 1943 in addition to the dislocations of their life accompanying the War. However, Patel's appeal for the unity of the Congressmen did not produce any remarkable results.

In the provinces demanded for Pakistan by the Muslim League, the Congress could not make contact with the Muslim urban and rural middle class who were voters in the restricted franchise system, and despite Nehru's strong desire to reach the Muslim masses who were not voters, it also could not find stable supporters among the Muslim masses except in the North-West Frontier Province. The case of Bengal was typical. Internal strife within Congress leadership was caused by the organizational stagnancy due in its turn to the lack of daily contact between the leadership and the masses though outside the arena of the election campaign there was the strong current of the movement against the trial of the men and officers of the Indian National Army.

There was a different style of political approach between Azad and Patel, but this rift was mainly caused by their opinions as to how the Congress could find allies against the Muslim League in the Punjab and Bengal.

In other provinces the situation was different for the Congress. It did not bother much about the Muslim constituencies and, generally speaking, these were centres of the Quit India movement fought under the leadership of the Indian National Congress.

In Bihar the movement penetrated deep into the rural areas, and it was believed that the Congress would sweep the polls except for the Muslim seats.

However, some symptoms of the post-Independence politics had already appeared in the process of nominations. For instance, the following letter written by a Congressman from Shahabad was sent to the General Secretary, AICC on 21 November 1945:

> The upper classes are not the only people fighting for the freedom of India. Very few of Kayasthas, Brahmins, Bhumihars and Rajputs came forward for the real fight. It is merely the lower community which form the bulk of the population and fought and are fighting more vigorously in great numerical strength than the upper communities for the liberation of their motherland. The upper classes being educationally and economically more advanced come up to the helm of affairs in the Congress and exploit and tread over the interests and rights of other communities instead of giving them lift. This is because in spite of their education they are very reactionary and selfish. Here is an example in the district of Shahabad. Out of five seats in this district for the Provincial Legislature, three have been allotted to the Rajputs and two to the Brahmins, as if there is no other community living in this district.
>
> Therefore, I appeal especially to our Revered Mahatma Gandhi, Pt Jawaharlal Nehru, Maulana Azad, Sardar Patel and Dr Rajendra Prasad to kindly look into the matter and I humbly solicit their assurance that such practices will be checked in future and fair and adequate representation of communities other than four upper classes will be made in all the Provinces of India.[102]

Patel thought this in a different way. When S.S. More wrote to Patel and complained that in Maharashtra and Karnataka the non-Brahmins had done their bit for the country's cause, but they were not getting an effective share in the Congress organization and in the other spheres of the Congress activities, Patel was critical of their 'inferiority complex':

> The non-Brahmins must knock off their fear complex and their inferiority complex. I cannot understand why 97% of non-Brahmins should have any

fear of domination from the 3% Brahmins. Whatever might have happened during the period of foreign rule, such things cannot continue any longer. When foreign rule is about to disappear the Congress can and must be managed and controlled by the non-Brahmins who form the bulk of the population.[103]

Thus Patel who was himself non-Brahmin rejected the logic of non-Brahminism. But it is to be noted that this kind of complaint had already appeared in more than one province within Congress circles that did not accept the theory of non-Brahmin movement officially.

Patel was of course well aware how casteism was affecting Congress activities. North Karnataka, a part of the then Bombay province, was also one of the centres of the Quit India movement, where its unique style of movement, supported by peasants and rural artisans like smiths and weavers, endured over a long period of time.[104] It may be recollected here that, in the historic meeting of the All-India Congress Committee which adopted the Quit India resolution in August 1942, just before Gandhi started his speech, R.R. Diwakar, a Karnataka Congress leader, managed to get a message from Gandhi who wrote in Hindi, '*Meri ummid hai ki is yojna men Karnataka apna hissa dega*' (I hope that Karnataka will play its own role in this plan).[105]

However, Patel commented that the growth of factionalism in Karnataka had been disturbing the process of nominations:

Karnataka is a difficult province and people there are easily moved by passion. There is very little tolerance among public workers. In the disposal of the election of candidates, the little province of Karnataka has given us more trouble than the biggest one in India.[106]

The Fortnightly Report from the Government of Bombay describes the infighting in the Karnataka Congress as follows:

. . . there has been considerable controversy over the selection of candidates on both Congress and League tickets. Feelings have run particularly high over the selection of candidates by the Congress Parliamentary Board in the Karnataka which omitted. A.B. Latthe, ex-Finance Minister, on the ground that he dissociated himself from the 1942 movement. The Lingayat-Brahmin controversy has also been revived in an acute form in this area and the quarrel culminated in an open assault being made on the President and Secretary of the Parliamentary Board while the latter was in session. The Central Parliamentary Board has given a ticket to A.B. Latthe and this may mean that he is being considered again for the Finance portfolio. Mr Gandhi has severely condemned the indiscipline shown by Karnataka Congressmen and deplored their 'indecent longing' to enter the legislature. Similar controversies have been in evidence in Maharashtra where it is freely alleged that attempts are being made to revive the Brahmin-non-Brahmin fight. . . .[107]

A.B. Latthe confessed in his letter to Patel that he was critical of the 1942 movement and therefore had no wish to stand as a candidate on a Congress ticket. He said that he did so only at the request of the District Selection Committee:

There is a degree of opposition to me from those who think that, if elected, I would stand in their way to ministership. A section of Brahmin friends also oppose because they think that I am not as good a Kannadaman as they want. Their two groups headed by some Lingayat leaders and Mr Diwakar, are trying to have my application rejected.[108]

On 1 February 1946, a hectic scene developed in the meeting of the Provincial Parliamentary Board, and Hardikar, a veteran Karnataka Congress leader, sent his telegram to Patel:

Diwakar and Mallya assaulted and manhandled in Parliamentary Board meeting today by some Congress communal-minded fanatics alleging Diwakar responsible for changing Congress candidates by Central Parliamentary Board. Public feel deeply distressed.

His last words communicate the distress in the Karnataka Congress. Finally the situation was saved by the Centre for the moment, and confrontation prevented. Latthe and Patel disclosed the same feelings of displeasure with this ugly drama.[109]

Latthe wrote to Patel:

I am very grateful to you for selecting me and putting me in the Northern Division of this district. . . .

I hope by now you have come to know how far malice has gone in Karnataka and you will not disbelieve me when I tell you that in the predominantly Lingayat South Belgaum, there would be much malicious opposition to me, and possibly some treachery as well.

Patel replied, 'Let us hope that you will be more helpful to strengthen affairs in Karnataka or at least keep the Karnataka Assembly Party in order. It is a crowd of irreconcilables and people of incompatible temperament. It is difficult to work with such people.'

Latthe had been Finance Minister in the Government of Bombay headed by B.G. Kher, but resigned in 1940-1 because he could not accept the principle of non-violence absolutely in meeting the war crisis. He also differed on the issue of the Quit India movement. There was enough reason for the Congress to reject his candidacy in consideration of the probable response of the voters.

Therefore, Patel took the pragmatic decision to permit him to stand as an independent candidate with the understanding that he would sign the Congress pledge and join the party after the elections.[110] Simultaneously, the nomination of A.B. Latthe, a Jain leader and Diwan of Kolhapur State, 1926-30, who was a lieutenant of the non-Brahmin movement led by the Maharaja of Kolhapur, may have been closely connected with Patel's strategy of maintaining continuity in Congress politics.[111]

It is symbolic that, in Bihar and Karnataka where the people fought intensely for the 'Quit India' and the 'caste politics' was a dominant phenomenon in the post-independent period, a discrepancy between the people's movement and the 'caste politics' was already manifest.

Patel encountered the most stiff defiance from the Provincial Congress in Madras. Here Patel and Gandhi wanted the return of C. Rajagopalachari (Governor-General of India 1948-50) who was the Premier in 1937-9 and resigned the Congress membership due to his bold plan to unite the Congress and the League during the Second World War. In December 1945, Patel wrote to D.R. Arunachalam that all sacrifices would be in vain if they would not absorb talents at their disposal and decide to close doors against those who had rendered service in the past and made sacrifices, simply because on one occasion they differed.[112]

Patel's wish to realize the return of Rajagopalachari to a leading post of the Tamilnadu Congress was firm as his letter to K. Kamraj, President, Tamilnadu Provincial Congress showed:

> It is but natural that we should like to see the formation of a Parliamentary Board for your province so constituted as to include all groups and interests as fast as possible leaving no ground for any reasonable complaint. Mr Asaf Ali was sent to your province to bring about an amicable settlement. . . .
>
> You are aware that the decision in the matter of selection of candidates rests with the Central Parliamentary Board.[113]

At the end of December, the Working Committee of the Tamilnadu Congress formed the Provincial Parliamentary Board, and Kamaraj agreed that he would consult Rajaji (C. Rajagopalachari) in the selection of candidates at all stages.[114] For the moment the open controversy seemed to have ceased, but it did not last long.

Patel had to write again to Kamaraj in February 1946:

> I have asked you to carry out your undertaking with me that Rajaji is to be treated as a member in all respects except his being a formal member of the Board. Consultation before and after has no meaning. He has to hear the

arguments and the discussions in the committee and must have an opportunity to influence the members of the committee by his own presence as well as by his persuasive ability.[115]

Afterwards, Kamaraj sent his telegram communicating his wish to resign from the Parliamentary Board as the expression of his protest against Gandhi's critical article which said, 'His (Rajaji's) political wisdom and integrity are beyond question. I was, therefore, pained to find a clique against him.'[116] But the situation took an unexpected turn, because Rajagopalachari also wrote to Gandhi on 21 February, expressing his desire to retire from politics altogether, and take a long needed rest. The Government report writes that this was due to the reason that members close to Rajaji were omitted from the list of candidates framed by the Centre.[117] This report thought that the official Congress block would proceed with their plan without Rajagopalachari, and went on to say that the opposition against Rajagopalachari, especially in the mofussil, appeared to be mounting.

In March the Government concluded that the controversy over Rajagopalachari had momentarily receded into the background, and that everyone was busy with the elections.[118] Patel's will of iron with the potent help of Gandhi did not work smoothly in the south. The self-confidence of Patel who could work the provincial self-government under the Government of India Act, 1935 during the period 1937-9 moved him to try to send his colleagues and lieutenants back to their old posts. Inversely, it prevented him from observing changes in the political and social climate during the Second World War. In this sense, Patel's objection to Rajaji's move for the Congress-League unity and his stubborn will for the return of Rajagopalachari to a leading post of the Congress came from the same source. Patel's strong personality was given full play in his strategy of utilizing the regime of the Government of India Act, 1935, just as Jinnah, basically a constitutionalist, tried to prove the strength of the Muslim League within the constitutional framework of the same Act.[119]

Sometimes Patel advised would-be legislators to desist from their desire as his letter to Loknath Mishra showed, and in this connection he got forceful support from the way Gandhi lived, though he carried out his election management without Gandhi in most aspects.

I may, however, inform you that the Assembly is not the only place of service nor is it comparatively better place for service. You must be aware that many of us in the Congress Working Committee have never put our foot in any legislatures. Mahatma Gandhi has also never seen any Assembly hall. You must not attach any undue importance to these legislative bodies.[120]

In the meantime, the Congress did not hesitate to put up the man of the Army who had just been discharged on 1 February 1946. Patel wrote:

> I have received several letters from the province against your selection, particularly because the Congress policy during the period of war was to refuse to help the British Government in the war and you were actively engaged in the Defence Forces of H.M. Government. Besides you also happened to be a zamindar of the province. In spite of this, we have selected you because our policy is to adopt suitable persons available in the Defence Forces for nominations in the Assemblies wherever possible. . . .
>
> I would advise you to keep your eyes and ears open but at the same time to keep your mouth shut. Hear all, see everything but don't talk much. . . .
>
> We have fought the country's battles without arms and you have done so with arms (but the battles of other countries) and you are now not to think of your arms or weapons. The conditions of our country and the ways and the habits of our people must not make you impatient or angry. The country's lot is very hard. Our people deserve all the sympathy that we can give and all the services that we can render. No sacrifice is big enough for that purpose. Forget that you are a landlord; and also try to forget that you are a superior person. Try to be one of the people of Orissa and learn to talk with them and live with them on their own level, if you want to serve them. Above all, first learn to talk to them in their own language, so that you can read their thoughts from their eyes and convey to them your ideas in their own language. Let not the people feel that you are arrogant or that you are a foreigner. Please give no grounds for complaint that the Congress made a wrong selection in choosing you.[121]

This may be read as advice to a new candidate by a mature Congress leader. Since the Nehru Report of 1928, a draft constitution of India, the Army was expected to be an indispensable part of the State apparatus in the independent India. Now, as independence was expected soon, how to accommodate the Army which had fought on the other side became an urgent problem. This nomination and his careful advice came in the perspective of Patel who planned the 'peaceful' transfer of power and nation building in the turbulent days. In the same context, the 'intimidation' of Government officers who behaved high-handedly during the Quit India movement which appeared frequently in the election speeches of the Congress leaders should be examined carefully. The Congress also needed the cooperation of those officers who had been working on the other side.

In the case of the Communist Party of India, it published its own way of putting up candidates. The Election Policy of the Communists titled *For a Free and Happy India* writes:

> From the very character of our Party comes our non-sectarian approach to other parties. The Congress and the League make exclusive claims against each other. We will support them both where we are not putting up candidates of our own. We have our very serious differences with them, but we recognise them as our major patriotic political organisations that must be generally supported against their reactionary rivals.
>
> Our Party will put up its own candidates in almost all labour seats to demonstrate that it is the accepted leader of the working-class. We will also contest such rural seats, both General and Muslim, where we are the existing majority of the people to demonstrate the strength and vitality of the organised Kisan movement.
>
> In those General seats except those reserved for Scheduled Castes, where the Party is not putting up its own candidate, we will support the Congress candidate.
>
> In those Muslim seats where the Party is not putting up a candidate we will support the League against all rivals.
>
> If in any constituency a notorious hoarder and hated enemy of the people stands as a Congress or a League candidate the Party will of course not campaign for him.[122]

Official documents of the Communists do not mention anything about internal rivalry for nominations. But here it must be examined whether the 'non-sectarian' approach of the Communists which supported both the Congress and the Muslim League was understood among the voters. While in areas where the labour or peasant movement was intense under the Communist leadership, there was a strong tie between the Communist candidates and the people. And, many well-known Communist leaders stood as candidates for the Provincial Elections. We can mention only a few: S.A. Dange (leader of the labour movement in Bombay) and Godavari Parulekar (leader of the peasant movement among the Warlis) in Bombay, P. Sundarayya (leader of the peasant movement in Andhra), E.M.S. Namboodiripad (Chief Minister of Kerala 1957-9, 1967-9) and A.K. Gopalan (later President of the All-India Kisan Sabha) in Madras, Karyanand Sharma (leader of the the peasant movement in Barahiya Tal in the later half of the 1930s) in Bihar, Jyoti Basu (Chief Minister of West Bengal 1977-) and Moni Singh (peasant leader in Mymensingh) in Bengal, and Sohan Singh Josh (leader of the Naujawan Bharat Sabha and Kirti Kisan Party in the 1920s) in the Punjab. From official documents it is difficult for us to examine how the Communists tried to connect the mass movement under their leadership with participation in the Provincial Elections under the limited franchise system. As for the Communist support for the Pakistan movement during the 'People's War' period, many self-critical reviews appeared including that of D. Adhikari, the then editor of the *People's War*. But no comprehensive study has so far appeared on the relations between the Communist leadership in the mass movement and their participation in the electoral process.

NOTES

1. *TOP*, Vol. 6, pp. 282-3.
2. Amery to Wavell, 12 July 1945, *TOP*, Vol. 5, p. 1237.
3. Wavell to Pethick-Lawrence, Telegram, *TOP*, Vol. 6, pp. 35-36.
4. Ibid., pp. 7, 9.
5. Penderel Moon (ed.) *Wavell—The Viceroy's Journal*, Delhi, 1977, p. 159.
6. Ibid., p.161.
7. Pethick-Lawrence to Wavell, Telegram, *TOP*, Vol. 6, p. 83.
8. Ibid., p. 80.
9. Pethick-Lawrence to Wavell, Telegram, ibid., pp. 98-9.
10. Wavell wrote on 16 September, 'hope that I have introduced some sense of realities into the people to whom I have talked on the Indian situation', Moon, op. cit., p. 172.
11. *TOP*, Vol. 6, pp. 173-5.
12. Wavell to all Governors, 21 September 1945, ibid., p. 288.
13. Moon, op. cit., p. 169.
14. Nehru to Stafford Cripps, 27 January 1946, *Selected Works of Jawaharlal Nehru*. Vol. 14, New Delhi, 1982, p. 141.
15. *Dawn*, 16 July 1945.
16. Jamil-ud-Din Ahmad (ed.), *Speeches and Writings of Mr. Jinnah*, Vol. 2, Lahore 1964, p. 191.
17. Ibid., pp. 201-2.
18. Nehru, op. cit., p. 85.
19. Ibid., p. 211.
20. Ibid., p. 163.
21. Ibid., pp. 528-38.
22. Gene D. Overstreet and Marshall Windmiller, *Communism in India*, Berkeley, 1959, pp. 221-2.
23. A.M. Zaidi and Shaheda Zaidi (eds.), *The Encyclopaedia of Indian National Congress, Vol. 12: 1939-1946 A Fight to the Finish*, New Delhi, 1981, p. 492.
24. *People's War*, 29 July 1945.
25. Moon, op. cit., p. 259.

26. Nehru, op. cit., p. 417.
27. Ibid., p. 327.
28. Ibid., p. 83.
29. M. Hashim Kidwai, *Rafi Ahmad Kidwai,* New Delhi, 1986, p. 109.
30. Nehru, op. cit., pp. 161, 216.
31. *People's War*, 21 October 1945.
32. Ibid.
33. Abdulla Rasool, 'Story of Indian Kisans' Post-War Awakening—Peasant Struggles of Last Year Reviewed', *People's Age,* 25 May 1947.
34. Vinita Damodaran, *Broken Promises—Popular Protest, Indian Nationalism and the Congress Party in Bihar, 1935-1946,* Delhi, 1992, pp. 322, 333.
35. *People's War*, 21 October 1945.
36. Ibid.
37. Rai Bahadur Nandalal Sinha, *Report on the Elections in Bihar, March, 1946,* Patna, 1946, p. 8.
38. Moon, op. cit., p. 169.
39. *TOP*, Vol. 6, p. 203.
40. *People's War*, 21 October 1945.
41. *Report on the situation in the Punjab for the first half of September 1945,* NAI.
42. *Report on the sitution in the Punjab for the second half of September 1945,* NAI.
43. *Report for the first half of September 1945,* Bombay, NAI.
44. *Fortnightly Confidential Report of the Dacca Division for the first half of October 1945,* WBSA.
45. Nandalal Sinha, op. cit., p. 1
46. Ibid., p. 3.
47. Ibid., p. 4.
48. Ibid., p. 5.
49. Ibid., p. 2.
50. *Return showing the Results of Elections to the Central Legislative Assembly and the Provincial Legislatures in 1945-1946,* New Delhi, 1948, p. 54.
51. Kingsley Davis, *The Population of India and Pakistan,* Princeton, 1951, p. 68 and p. 86.
52. Gail Pearson, 'Reserved seats—women and the vote in Bombay', in J. Krishnamurthy (ed.), *Women in Colonial India—Essays on Survival, Work and the State,* Delhi, 1989, p. 217.
53. *Dawn,* 6 September 1945.
54. Ibid., 4 September 1945.
55. Jamil-ud-Din Ahmad, op. cit., p. 202.
56. Ibid., p. 204.
57. Ayesha Jalal, *The Sole Spokesman—Jinnah, the Muslim League and*

the Demand for Pakistan, Cambridge, 1985, p. 137.

58. Sajjad Zaheer, 'Behind G.M. Syed's Revolt—Full Story; Its Meaning for All', *People's Age*, 6 January 1946.
59. Ibid.
60. Ian Talbot, *Provincial Politics and the Pakistan Movement—The Growth of the Muslim League in North-West and North-East India 1937-47*, Karachi, 1988, p. 40.
61. Amit Kumar Gupta, *North West Frontier Province Legislature and Freedom Struggle 1932-47*, New Delhi, 1976, pp. 173-4.
62. Sajjad Zaheer, 'Jagirdars amd Title-holders, not Men of the People—Against Current and Popular Awakening,' *People's Age*, 23 December 1945.
63. Talbot, op. cit., p. 17.
64. Ibid., p. 18.
65. Sajjad Zaheer, 'Mass Upsurge of Muslim People—But Leadership still goes in for Opportunist Toadies', *People's Age*, 2 December 1945.
66. Andullah Malik (ed.), *Selected Speeches and Statements of Mian Iftikhar-ud-Din*, Lahore, 1971, pp. 31-2.
67. Ibid., pp. 34-7.
68. Nehru, op. cit., p. 91.
69. Ibid., p. 98.
70. 'Politician without Peer', *Viewpoint*, 3 June 1982.
71. Firoz Khan Noon, *From Memory*, Lahore, 1969, p. 189.
72. Abul Hasim, *In retrospection*, Dhaka, 1974, pp. 34-42.
73. Ibid., pp. 80-1.
74. Ibid., pp. 171-2.
75. *People's War*, 28 October 1945.
76. Kamruddin Ahmad, *A Socio Political History of Bengal and the Birth of Bangladesh*, Dhaka, 1975, p. 65.
77. Harun-or-Rashid, *The Foreshadowing of Bangladesh—Bengal Muslim League and Muslim Politics 1936-1947*, Dhaka, 1987, p. 198.
78. Ibid., pp. 198-9.
79. Ibid., p. 201.
80. Ibid., p. 202.
81. Kamruddin Ahmad, op. cit., p. 65.
82. *Secret Report on the Political Situation in Bengal for the First half of February 1946*, NAI.
83. Harun-or-Rashid, op. cit., p. 206.
84. *Secret Report on the Political Situation in Bengal for the Second half of February 1946*, NAI.
85. Hasim, op. cit., p. 174.
86. Patel to Nehru, 4 November 1945, Durga Das (ed.), *Sardar Patel's Correspondence, 1945-50*, Vol. 2, Ahmedabad, 1971, p. 68.
87. Nehru, op. cit., pp. 264-5.
88. Ibid., p. 251.

89. Rani Dhavan Shankardass, *Vallabhbhai Patel—Power and Organization in Indian Politics*, Hyderabad, 1988, p. 257.
90. Ibid.
91. Das, op. cit., p. 21.
92. Satya M. Rai, *Legislative Politics and Freedom Struggle in the Panjab 1897-1947*, New Delhi, 1984, p. 311.
93. Nehru to Kairon, 11 September 1945, Nehru, op. cit., p. 77.
94. Patel to Sachar, 25 December 1945, Das, op. cit., pp. 280-1.
95. Patel to Azad, 14 November 1945, ibid., p. 146.
96. Nehru to Patel, 31 October 1945, Nehru, op. cit., p. 114.
97. *Peopls's Age*, 6 January 1946.
98. Sarat Chandra Bose to Patel, 3 January 1946, Das, op. cit., pp. 385-6.
99. Patel to P.C. Ghosh, 26 October 1945, ibid., p. 122.
100. Patel to S.C. Ray, 8 January 1946, ibid., pp. 387-8.
101. Patel to Azad, 2 January 1946, ibid., p. 52.
102. *AICC Papers G2(II)/1946*, NMML.
103. Patel to S.S. More, 5 October 1945, Das, op. cit., pp. 254-5.
104. Suryanath U. Kamath, *Quit India Movement in Karnataka*, Bangalore, 1988, pp. 209-10.
105. Ibid., p. 219.
106. Latthe to Patel, 10 February 1946, and Patel to Latthe, 13 February 1946, Das, op. cit., p. 274.
107. *Fortnightly Report for the first half of February 1946*, Government of Bombay, NAI.
108. Latthe to Patel, 14 January 1946, Das, op. cit., p. 265.
109. Latthe to Patel, 10 February 1946, and Patel to Latthe, 13 February 1946, ibid., pp. 273-4.
110. Shankardass, op. cit., p. 265.
111. Kashinath K. Kavlekar, *Non Brahmin Movement in Southern India 1873 1949*, Kolhapur, 1979, p. 90.
112. Patel to D.R. Arunachalam, 20 December 1945, Das, op. cit., p. 176.
113. Patel to Kamaraj, 26 December 1945, ibid., pp. 184-5.
114. Kamaraj to Patel, telegram, 29 December 1945, ibid., p. 188.
115. Patel to Kamaraj, 6 February 1946, ibid., p. 203.
116. Kamaraj to Patel, telegram, 12 February 1946, ibid., p. 207.
117. *Fortnightly Report for the second half of February 1946*, Madras, TSA.
118. *Fortnightly Report for the first half of March 1946*, Madras, TSA.
119. H.M. Seervai, *Partition of India—Legend and Reality*, Bombay, 1989, p. 53. This book is thought provoking, but is a typical example of the case, how the conclusion digresses from the main theme if we open our eyes only to the 'constitutional' side of the 'Transfer of Power'.
120. Patel to Loknath Mishra, 13 February 1946, Das, op. cit., p. 330.
121. Patel to Kumar Lal Ranjit Singh, 22 February 1946, ibid., pp. 325-6.
122. *People's War*, 14 October 1945.

II

The Post-War People's Movement

The *Prati Sarkar* Movement and the Elections

The All-India Congress Committee which met in Bombay in September 1945, framed the main policy which it should take towards the British Government after the Simla Conference. Many leaders including Jaya Prakash Narayan still remained behind prison bars. In the Resolution on 'The Struggle of 1942 and After', while congratulating the nation on the courage and endurance with which it withstood the fierce and violent onslaught of the British power, it clarified that the appraisal of the struggle was conditional:

> The Committee regrets that in some places the people forgot and fell away from the Congress method of peaceful and non-violent action, but realises the provocative action of the Government in effecting sudden and widespread arrests of all well-known leaders, and brutal and ruthless repression of peaceful demonstrations, goaded them to rise spontaneously to resist the army might of an alien Imperialist power which was trying to crush the spirit of freedom and the passionate desire of the Indian people to gain independence.[1]

The Resolution on the 'Congress Policy' moved by J.B. Kripalani added:

> Bans of some organizations and restrictions and disabilities on individuals have not yet been removed and civil liberties are restricted. The continuance of section 93 rule in the provinces and the recent dissolution of the legislatures in a number of provinces are significant and outstanding instances of the policy of the Government, which is determined to hold on to its authoritarian power and to exercise it arbitrarily and autocratically. It is not possible to derive any hope for the future in the shape of frank cooperation on the part of Government with the people, in bringing them their long overdue freedom and independence.
>
> The method of negotiation and conciliation which is the keynote of peaceful policy can never be abandoned by the Congress, no matter how grave may be the provocation, any more than can that of non-cooperation,

complete or modified. Hence the guiding maxim of the Congress must remain: negotiation and settlement when possible and non-cooperation and direct action when necessary.[2]

In this Congress resolution, references to the Quit India movement were already in the past tense. In fact, the movement was still going on in Satara at this moment despite the embarrassment of the Congress leaders. The limitations of the official sources in revealing the underground activities is confirmed by Omvedt's study on the *Prati Sarkar* movement.[3] In spite of this, it may not be meaningless to check the official sources to see to what extent the Government had recognized the serious character of the movement.

According to Gail Omvedt's analysis based on Marathi materials and interviews with the leaders of the movement, it was in February-June 1942 that the Satara *Prati Sarkar* was consciously established,[4] with *nyayadan mandals*, the core of an alternative government, which dealt with a wide range of cases like the punishment of dacoits, prohibition, and checks on atrocities against women, while retaining the military character of the movement. This study concludes that the *nyayadan mandals* basically sided with the poor, or at least the peasantry as a whole, against moneylenders and landlords.[5]

The Quit India movement was a response to the call of Gandhi, 'do or die'. He was released on 6 May 1944 due to illness after spending about twenty-one months in jail. He got a report of the happenings in Maharashtra from the Secretary of the Maharashtra Provincial Congress Committee, and met about 50 Congress leaders of Maharashtra in Poona on 29 June. Under the condition of medical restriction on his work, the first words that came from his mouth was that 'as a man wedded to truth and non-violence, not merely as a matter of discipline or expedience, but as a rule of conduct in all walks of life, I can endorse nothing untruthful or violent'.[6]

On 3 August, Gandhi reached Sevagram. On his way to Sevagram he visited the place where a humble villager had died as a result of firing during the Quit India movement. From Sevagram Gandhi issued a statement concerning what should be done on the memorable 9 August when the struggle started. One of his messages was addressed to the underground workers:

The second thing that I should like done on August 9th is for those who have gone underground to discover themselves. They can do so by informing the authorities of their movements and whereabouts, or by simply and naturally doing their work in the open without any attempt to evade or elude

> the police. To go underground is to elude the police. Therefore, real discovery is to discover oneself to the party eluded. Nothing should be done unless conviction has gone home that a particular action is essential for the cause. In the absence of such a conviction, those who see this note may ignore it and follow what they consider best for the country.[7]

As a matter of fact, this was the instruction of Gandhi to stop 'do or die' activities. Now spinning could take their place. In a sense, the *prati sarkar* movement had developed its 'constructive programme' introduced by Gandhi and extended its roots in the life of the people in Satara. Even these productive results of the movement were however to be discarded in the name of non-violence. So far Gandhi had often repeated that it was only the Congress Working Committee, not he that could represent the Congress legitimately and truly. But the Congress leaders could no longer freely interpret what 'do or die' entailed.

In Satara, only a part of the activists who had the organizational tie with the Congress Party prior to 1942 surrendered while Gandhi's message was decisive in suspending the activities of the parallel governments in various parts of India.[8]

The Government source also reports that the situation in Satara in the middle of 1945 saw no remarkable change:

> The state of lawlessness in Satara district continues as before. It is understood that the local leaders responsible for it are unwilling to desist, though advised to do so by leading Congressmen from outside the district. It seems that some Congress leaders are perturbed at their loss of influence in the district and the increasing part that local goondas are taking in the disturbances. They find it difficult, however, to denounce the goondaism openly because of their past associations with the movements in the districts.[9]

But in the later half of 1945, the tone of the Government reports began to change, using the word, 'improvement' repeatedly while still keeping cautious attitudes. The weekly letter dated 28 July still writes about the well-organized condition of the *prati sarkar* movement in the south of Satara district:

> Lawlessness continues in the Satara District. From a visit to Satara I find, however, some signs of improvement in the situation. Police activity has been stepped up and made more effective and public confidence is beginning to return in certain areas. The gangs in the northern area are now more on the defensive. In the south, the gangs are still very influential and active. Statements recorded from person recently arrested are beginning to show how well organised the gangsters are in their subversive plans to substitute

a parallel Governments for the authorised law of the land. In my opinion the time seems to have come when this subversive organisation should be banned as an unlawful association under the Criminal Law Amendment Act.[10]

The Quit India movement continued in Satara even as the Congress, Muslim League, and Communist Party began preparations for the elections in the 'coming cold weather'. The official report also had to admit (through reading of the cyclostyled English bulletin 'Destroy Dacoits') that the leaders of the *prati sarkar* were appealing to the public to offer their united resistance to all dacoits, arrest them and hand them over to the underground Congress workers. A warning asking the public to beware of those who extort money in the name of the Congress was also given in the bulletin.[11] Despite the repressive measures of the Government and the cold behaviour of both the Provincial and Central Congress, the movement had not lost sight of its aim.

Gail Omvedt places importance on the first visit of Achutrao Patwardhan to Satara, who had been keeping contact with the movement as one of the Bombay-based Socialist leadership. What conclusion came of his meeting with the *prati sarkar* leaders is not clear, but at this moment the Congress was trying to divert their energy to the elections to the Central and Provincial Assemblies. Actually, underground activists came out openly in support for the Congress candidates. Omvedt concludes that the elections effectively ended the *prati sarkar*.[12]

What is to be examined is to what extent the Congress which decided to contest the elections was ready to learn the 'constructive' aspect of the *prati sarkar* movement. The ironic truth is that the Congress which praised the heroic spirit of the people in Satara hesitated to utilize the new tradition of the freedom movement and to learn from its 'constructive' programme.

The tone of the weekly intelligence reports obviously took an optimistic turn from the later half of August. The names of the Provincial and District Congress leaders began to appear frequently. The weekly report on Satara District dated 22 August noted a remarkable drop in the offences committed, and it thought that this was partly due to intense police activities and the growing conviction amongst the public and underground workers that 'we mean business'. It also reported the movement of the Congress leaders. V.P. Pawar, President, District Congress Committee, published his statement in the *Sakar*, disapproving of the methods employed by the underground workers and appealing to the public to adhere to the principles of truth and non-violence. Shankarrao Deo, a leader of the Maharashtra Provincial Congress Committee, was also supposed to have advised the workers privately to stop their activities. Furthermore, the District Magistrate Satara, A.L. Dias and the District Superintendent of Police met S.S. Batliwalla who asked them to remove the ban on N.V. Gadgil's entry into the district. Batliwalla informed them that leaders like Gadgil were anxious to come into the district and denounce the present movement to reaffirm the official Congress policy.[13]

In the confidential report for the week ending 30 August 1945, the District Magistrate again confirmed that there had been a marked improvement in the situation. He stressed that the public as a whole except the Congressmen had welcomed the publicity campaign and the strong measures adopted recently, and that many of the absconders were leaving the district but had decided not to surrender until further instructions were received from the Working Committee.[14]

The Government report in the beginning of September 1945 gives the information that the Rashtriya Seva Dal, the Dahashatwadi Dal, the Satara Congress Sarkar, the Satara Jilha Congress Sarkar, the Congress Sanstha, the Prati Sarkar, the Patri Sarkar, Village Courts, Village Panchayats, Village Tribunals, Nyayadan Mandals, Congress Nyayadan Committee, Nyadata Congress Committee, Samaj Seva Dals, Congress Mandalis and any others 'which had as their object interference with the administration of the law in Satara district and which were connected with the subversive activities' were banned by the Government under the Criminal Law Amendment Act.[15]

In October and November 1945, several reports that stated 'no gangster activities were reported during the week' reached the Government successively.

But, even in the middle of March 1946, the confidential report from Satara had to admit that:

> In view of the recrudescence of the activities of criminals and underground workers, police pressure is being intensified. Many Congress leaders of this district, who previously supported the activities of the underground workers, are now getting a bit nervous about their ability to control them.[16]

It is to be examined whether the 'recrudescence' of the *patri sarkar* movement meant the radicalization of the movement or the revival of dacoities. At least the movement survived after the Provincial Elections in Satara. The District Superintendent of Police, Satara was pessimistic in his letter to the District Magistrate in May 1946:

The situation in the villages in the district is far from satisfactory. Indeed it may be said to have deteriorated greatly. The terror of the Patri Sarkar still hangs heavily on the villagers. If anything, it has increased due to the fact that all the agents of the Patri Sarkar are now moving freely in the villages. The position of the subordinate police has become very difficult due to the continued non-cooperation of the public which is still living in a state of terror. Irresponsible speeches of the type made by Mr P.K. Atre asking to be prepared for bloodshed and criticizing in a most objectionable way, Government officers in general and the police officers in particular are not likely to help the restoration of peace and order. The fact that the arms possessed illegally by political workers have not been surrendered, has also had a covering effect on the public mind. It is learnt that some of these workers are moving in the villages with arms.[17]

Needless to say, we have to read official documents carefully. But what is to be answered is whether this revolt at this stage of the movement represents the acts of the disenfranchised rural poor.

Already in 1946, D.D. Kosambi, a Marxist historian, wrote that the OM (Indian Official Marxists) had dismissed the Satara peasant uprising of 1942-3 as pure banditry.[18] As we have seen the movement survived even in 1945-6. It is to be noted that this observation was made in his review of *The Discovery of India* by Jawaharlal Nehru, because the official Congress leadership also failed to grasp the correct character of this movement or tried to curb it.

In the AICC meeting in Bombay, while moving the resolution on the Quit India movement, Nehru said that it was a mighty and gigantic revolution, and that the first and foremost lesson from this period was that the people of India were awake. But he did not forget to add that it was the duty of the leaders to direct the enthusiasm and spirit of the people into the right channels, though the elections were not the things that ultimately mattered.[19]

Nehru wrote to Patel that everywhere he went, he found tremendous enthusiasm for the Congress.[20] But in his letter to Krishna Menon, Nehru disclosed his own feelings:

My popularity with all kinds of people, which seems to have grown, has become a burden which I find difficult to carry. It is pleasant and exhilarating of course and deeply moving, but it means a continuous strain and prevents work. Travelling by train or by car means sleepless nights and very tiring days. Demands for me come from every direction and the sense of nervous strain increases. I am glad I went to Kashmir. That has done me good. But the moment I returned from the mountains enormous crowds besieged me—such crowds as I had seldom in the past.[21]

This was evidently a result of the Quit India movement and reflected the undeniable fact that people were awake and wanted to change the present system of bondage. Patel wrote back in the beginning of November 1945:

There is no doubt considerable mass awakening and tremendous enthusiasm all round, but I am afraid much of it is superficial. Demonstrative enthusiasm will not help us much unless we take proper care to divert it into the right channel.[22]

Patel negated the effect of this enthusiasm on the election results. In his view, Nehru's tours created a lot of enthusiasm and huge crowds gathered together, but these demonstrations had no value for the purpose of elections, as they influenced no voters in the Muslim constituencies. The Hindu voters needed no encouragement.[23]

Such cool-hearted calculation on the part of Patel only shows one side of the truth. Nehru spoke to the masses in the public meetings and Patel elaborated his strategy and gave full play to his ability as an election organizer. There was one common understanding between the two, and that was the diversion or direction of the people's 'enthusiasm' into the *right channel.* Nehru and Patel were different in their approach in attaining their aim, but they complemented each other.

The election speeches of Nehru produced remarkable results for the Congress. In October 1945, Nehru spoke in Varanasi:

I warn you that the coming few months are the most crucial in the history of the nation. It is essential that you remain cautious and vigilant. The first task before you is to strengthen the Congress by making it a disciplined and organised body and also by enrolling four-anna members. You should check whether the names of those who are entitled to vote are found in the electoral rolls.[24]

The election campaign provided the best chance to reorganize the Congress which had been paralysed since the repression of the Quit India movement. Nehru noticed that there was a serious hiatus between the enthusiasm of the people and the feelings of the old Congress leaders who had lost touch with the people. The main purpose of Nehru's speeches was how to reorganize the Congress while accommodating the people who participated in the Quit India movement into the 'constitutional' channel. This could not be done in the Congress Election Office in Bombay. Among the Congress High Command only Nehru could play this role fully and did so. In fact, Nehru admitted that the elections had somewhat held people in check though he imagined that, as soon as the elections were over, events would march swiftly.[25]

Most of the rural poor may have been able to enrol their names as four-anna Congress members, but they were not entitled to vote. How this fact affected the movement in Satara is to be seen. In Satara, many grass-root level organizations grew in the name of the Congress and even included the poor peasants and agricultural labourers. But the reorganization of the Congress under the framework of its election campaign must have separated the disenfranchised people from these spontaneous organizations.

The Civil Service in the Critical Period

A recent study on the Quit India movement mentions some of the stringent measures used by the Government to suppress it: the arrest, imprisonment, killing, firing by the Army and the police, insult and even assault meted out in complete disregard of the position and status of the people concerned, whipping and collective fines in many areas.[26] P.N. Chopra specially refers to suppression in Satara:

> The worst atrocities were perpetrated over people of Satara. A group of independent journalists who visited Satara in April, 1945 testified to the terroristic activities of the police which included 2,000 arrests, 6 deaths in jail and 13 killed in police firings. Four old men of village Katewadi were seated in a line with stone slabs on their heads and a boy was mounted on each one of them. Some cases of molestation of women were also reported. Inhuman treatment was meted out to prisoners in the jails and there were instances when they were beaten with leather straps soaked in salt water.[27]

As we have seen, the attitudes of the Congress leaders towards the Satara uprisings turned rather cold in August 1945. According to the official records, on 3 September the Satara District Congress Committee decided to give an ultimatum to the 'absconders' in the district to surrender within fifteen days; if they failed to do so, the Congress would see that they were arrested. Furthermore, the Executive Committee of the Maharashtra Provincial Congress Committee which met at Poona on 8 September adopted a resolution demanding lifting of the ban on meetings and release of persons detained without trial in Satara District and the withdrawal of the entire police and military posted in the district.[28]

Now, even in Satara, the demand for the removal of the restriction on civil liberties was connected with the Congress decision to contest the elections. It is true that the Government report recorded that the Congress leaders continued to defend the activities of the Satara underground workers, but now the concern of these leaders was more towards the future than the present form of the movement. At a meeting of some 3,000 persons under the auspices of the Students' Association of Sholapur on 14 September, M.P. Patel and others said that the people's rule established by the underground Congress leaders in Satara District was in furtherance of the Congress resolution of 1942 and expressed their view that it should be copied by the people in other districts *in the next struggle.*[29] Afterwards, S.K. Deo visited certain parts of Satara District between 27 and 29 September, and condemned the activities of the *patri sarkar*, expressing his sympathy for those who were victimized by the 'gangsters' and advising the people not to make any baseless allegations against the police.[30] Finally, the Fortnightly Report for the second half of October 1945 reports that Achut Patwardhan held meetings in Bombay city inviting the Satara *gangsters*, Congress Socialists and left Congressmen from many districts of Maharashtra, and they decided to launch a struggle of the *patri sarkar* type which would paralyse the Government by intensive propaganda and intimidation *after the elections were over.*[31]

Though we have to use official records carefully, it cannot be denied that, despite the fact that the *prati sarkar* or *patri sarkar* movement was still active in Satara, the Congress leaders referred to it in the past or the future tense.

Inversely, the glorification of the Quit India movement was one of the main themes in the speeches of the Congress leaders in the election meetings. Simultaneously, the Government was concerned with the control of the 'violent' speeches by the Indian leaders. It was a very serious problem in Bihar, another centre of the Quit India movement.

Already in the first half of July 1945, the Fortnightly Report noted the uneasiness on the part of Government servants in the event of a Congress Ministry coming into office. Anugraha Narayan Sinha (Finance Minister of Bihar, 1937-9, 1946-57) is said to have made enquiries from local gentlemen regarding the part played by local officials during the Quit India movement.[32] The report for the second half of July again mentioned that the Government was still receiving reports of threats of reprisals by local Congress workers against those who took part in the suppression.[33]

Patel who was in charge of the election management in later days also responded sharply to this situation and in a public speech on 9 August expressed his anger at the hanging of a young man of Bihar:

> We were told 'Forget and Forgive' when we were released. It was gently said that mistakes have occurred on both sides. We believed them and felt that there was some change in their attitude, for they never owned their mistakes in the past. We thought that there is nothing wrong in starting with a clean slate. But when I got up this morning, and read that a brave young man of Bihar had been hanged, when I thought that though a new slogan 'Forget and Forgive' has been coined, British strategy remains the same, grave doubts have arisen in my mind. . . .[34]

On 29 September, Shri Krishna Sinha (Premier of Bihar, 1937-9, 1946-61) mentioned individual police officers by name, accused them of atrocities, and warned them that before long they would have to answer for them.[35]

This political climate led to a reconsideration of Government policy towards the elections. On 26 September 1945, the Government of Bihar sent a letter to R.F. Mudie, Home Member of the Government of India:

> I have referred in my letters to the Viceroy about the possible danger of the situation in a province such as Bihar if the Congress leaders and their followers, such as Sri Krishna Sinha, late Chief Minister and probably my future Premier, continue in their campaign of vilification of Government servants and glorification of the 1942 troubles and the people who were punished for taking part in them. . . . We are engaged in a policy of appeasement, it seems to me, with no reciprocity on the other side, and there are parts of this province which are, I think, still a powder magazine. In view of the coming elections it will be necessary to very considerably reduce the existing controls on public meetings; and so long as the Congress leaders make the speeches and public statements which they have been doing during recent weeks, it will be practically impossible and unfair to gag the smaller fry of local leaders in their election speeches.
>
> . . . I think the time has come for the Central Government to give a definite lead to provinces as to the attitude to be adopted.[36]

This letter shows how the Government officers felt perplexed in the elections which had to take a democratic guise, about the 'intimidating' speeches of the Congress leaders. Later, on 12 October

1945, R. Tottenham, Secretary to the Government of India, sent a letter to the Provincial Governments clarifying their policy towards the elections and stated that peace must be maintained at all costs while allowing the greatest possible latitude to hold public meetings to avoid criticism both inside and outside India. Two measures were suggested in this letter:

(a) The Provincial Government should announce that no existing Provincial or District ban under 56 of the Defence of India Rule shall apply to meetings or processions held in connection with the Central or Provincial elections, but that the peace must be maintained and District Magistrates have instructions to use the ordinary law to maintain the peace should it be threatened by direct or indirect encouragement of violence or by the danger of communal rioting.

(b) District Magistrates should be instructed not to impose restrictions or bans on meetings and processions held in connection with the elections unless they find it necessary to do so in accordance with the instructions given under (a) above. If District Magistrates have to take action to maintain peace they should do so under section 144 Criminal Procedure Code or section 30 of the Police Act and they should be assured that they will have the full support of Government.[37]

Under these post-War circumstances Congress leaders fully utilized the chances provided by the 'free' elections. Their fervent speeches were needed to fill a gap between the Congress leaders who were in jail in the past two or three years and the people who participated in the Quit India movement but were 'demoralized' by the repression. Only on the basis of the revitalization of the people's feelings and their agreement, could the Congress participate in the elections and make negotiations with the British Government.

In October 1945, Nehru made an election tour of U.P. and said at Ballia, a storm centre of the Quit India movement:

> The days of August 1942 cannot be forgotten. We have no feeling of revenge, but those who acted inhumanly towards the people cannot be excused. Be they big officers or small, British or Indian, they are to be brought to book and tried to demonstrate to the world how bureaucracy behaved during those memorable days. If they were tried today, they would be in places worse than jails.[38]

Nehru's criticism was not limited to particular officers but to the role of the Civil Service during the War days:

> The members of the Civil Service are incapable of grasping the problem of the country. After the resignation of Congress Ministries, these men fully

exploited the mischievous provisions of the D.I.R. (Defence of India Rules). All caution was thrown off and the Government of the country was handed over to the police almost on a plate. For all practical purposes, it was a police raj in the country.[39]

Sucheta Mahajan gives particular importance to the election meetings where huge crowds gathered and to the speeches made there.[40] The admiration for the August Struggle and the unabated narration of what the officers had done in those days was certainly a prelude to the movement against the trial of the officers of the Indian National Army.

Wavell wrote in his diary on 24 October 1945:

Depressing reports continue to come in from Provinces of the intemperate attitude of Congress, their attempts to intimidate the Services by threats of revenge when they come into power, and so on. Nehru, in particular, seems quite unable to restrain himself, and perhaps imprisonment has quite upset his balance which was never his strong point.[41]

Needless to say it was not the personal character of Nehru which was affected by a long jail life, but this was the only available means of diverting the enthusiasm of the people into 'right channel'.

On 6 November 1945, when the trial of the Indian National Army had just started, Wavell sent a Memorandum to the British Government, which reflected his serious perception of the Indian situation (it is a different matter whether Attlee and his colleagues agreed to his view). According to Wavell's judgement, the programme of the Congress was to contest the elections, to serve an ultimatum on the British Government, and, in default of its acceptance, to organize a mass movement on 1942 lines and on an even larger scale. But he thought that it was unlikely that the Congress would attempt their *coup* until all the Provincial elections were completed, unless events forced their hand. Accordingly, he warned the British Government to be prepared for a serious attempt by the Congress, probably in the spring of 1946, but possibly earlier, to subvert by force the present administration in India. The following parts of his Memorandum reveal frankly the disturbed conditions of the Services:

11. We should be justified in moving against the Congress now, on the information already available. The Party is not yet fully re-organized and its immediate suppression would be relatively easy. Moreover, immediate action would rally those Indians who have supported us, and would put heart into the Services. The British members of the I.C.S. and I.P. (Indian Police) are dispirited and discontented: the Indian

members of those services are uneasy about the future and under strong political and social pressure; while the Indian subordinates on whom the administration so largely depends are naturally reluctant to make enemies of the future masters of India.

12. But I do not recommend immediate action, unless it is forced on us before the elections by actual disorder. To abandon our programme now would be to invite criticism all over the world, and to stimulate the general doubts about our good faith. I am afraid that we must wait for the present, and prepare to act quickly as soon as we are compelled to do so. The dangers of inaction are grave, since the capacity of the administration in rural districts to stand up to serious disturbances is largely a matter of morale, and service morale is now bad in many districts and is being steadily undermined.[42]

This Memorandum reflects some features of the post-War Indian situation. Wavell was a person who could rush to Bengal to take prompt steps to mitigate the food situation in 1943 unlike his predecessor, Linlithgow, and at the same time talk bluntly about the 'ignorance of the present electorate'. To what extent the view of the military officer turned Viceroy coincided with that of the British Government (which had to frame its policy towards India in the global context and under the internal political and economic strain) should be traced carefully. The Labour Party had still a personal channel of communication with the Congress as the relations of Nehru and Cripps showed. Wavell writes:

I doubt if they (Congress) are much interested in the elections as such; what is more important to them is the opportunity afforded by the elections to revive and re-organize the Party, and they are already taking full advantage of this opportunity.[43]

However, Nehru's speech in Lahore came close to the point when he said, 'I am not very much interested in elections as such, but at certain moments they assume particular importance.' This pronouncement attracts our attention, because it appeared before the AICC decided to contest the elections officially.[44] In his letter to Krishna Menon probably written not so late after the AICC session in Bombay, he even attempted 'rough estimate' of the results of the Provincial elections. And, as we saw in the last chapter, most of the Congress leaders were obsessed with the electoral politics, and the energy of Patel was devoted to the tiresome adjustment of 'national interests' with the personal interests of provincial leaders and candidates.

It is this situation that led Wavell to conclude that it was unlikely that the Congress would attempt a *coup* until all the Provincial Elections were completed. The Viceroy perceived the gravity of the 'demoralization' of the Administrative Service due to the fierce speeches of the Congress leaders, but it was the movement of 1942 itself that really contributed to this 'demoralization'. The speeches only accelerated this process.

Whether the Congress as an organization was actually prepared to punish those officers who had behaved high-handedly in the repression of the movement seems another matter. In a recent study on the 1942 movement, Gyanendra Pandey cited the following part from Patel's letter (January 1947) to Govind Ballabh Pant, U.P. Premier:

> The punishment of persons who were concerned with the 1942 atrocities is quite a different matter, and it is open to provincial Governments, if they so desire, to deal with official misdemeanor in that connection. But the caricaturing of official activities in the manner reported in the Press at a time when we are in office is open to serious objection. This is likely to affect the morale of the police force which in the present emergency can hardly be considered proper.[45]

This was written about a year after the Congress came back to office. However, how Patel tried to accommodate the Army officer who fought the War on the other side as a Congress candidate to the Provincial Assembly in February 1946 should be recollected here. It was at that very time that he advised the naval ratings who revolted in Bombay to surrender unconditionally.

Movement against the Trial of the Officers of the Indian National Army

The Indian Army also faced a crisis of demoralization. Lieutenant General Sir Francis Tuker, G.O.C.-in-C., Eastern Command, India, was critical of the 'lenient' policy of the Government towards the Indian National Army which 'waged war against the King'. He writes in his memoir:

> The Indian Civil Service has been spoken of as the steel structure of India's fabric. I do not think that is any exaggerated tribute to a great service in its heyday. The Indian Army was the foundation on which that structure rested. With a sound army, India was safe; with a rotten army, she was ruined forever.[46]

The 'rotting' process had already started during the Second World

War when the Indian officers and men joined the Indian National Army in large numbers. The British Government decided to put on trial no less than 600 of the 20,000 I.N.A. prisoners, while another 7,000 would be dismissed from service and detained without trial.[47]

In the words of Tuker, 'the sheep who followed might to an extent be excused and simply externed from their provinces, but those who led and those who actively maltreated our prisoners, whether officer or sepoy, should suffer the severest penalities'.[48] Thus, in the camps near Calcutta, Jingaragacha and Nilganj, these prisoners were grouped into different colours denoting the degree of their 'guilt':

> The White were those who joined the I.N.A. but whose conduct thereafter was such as to clear them of any act of disloyalty beyond the simple act of joining that army; the Grey were lukewarm members of the I.N.A. who had done enough to display disloyalty; the Black were those who had taken an active and evil part on the side of the Japanese. The Whites were sent off to their regimental depots, there to be paid, clothed and sent on leave. The Greys were discharged from the service and their pay and allowances during captivity were forfeited, but they retained certain rights to pension, earned outside the period of captivity. The Blacks suffered the same forfeits and lost all right to pension or gratuity, while a few of them were court-martialled.[49]

The first noticeable reaction came from Nehru who had been critical of the role of the I.N.A. during the War.[50] He spoke at a meeting of the Kashmir National Conference in Srinagar on 19 August 1945, and made it clear that the soldiers were misguided, but that whatever they did was done by them out of a patriotic motive. Nehru feared that, if they were treated harshly, it would create bad blood between England and India. At this stage, the Congress leader confirmed that the I.N.A. committed the 'mistake', and understood positively only the 'motive' which drove the Indian soldiers to participate in the joint military operation with the Japanese Army. This perception was still present in the resolution of the AICC in September 1945 which asserted that the officers, men and women of the I.N.A. had laboured for the freedom of India, however mistaken they were. *They had already suffered heavily and any additional punishment would not only be unjustified but would widen the gulf between India and England.*[51] This was the official view of the Congress on the I.N.A. when it decided to form a Defence Committee that included Nehru. At the end of October, Nehru confessed that much of his time was being taken up by the I.N.A. work and the National Planning Commission.[52]

However, as the movement against the trial of the I.N.A. officers became intense, Nehru was forced to revise his view.

As is well-known, three Indian officers consisting of a Hindu, a Muslim, and a Sikh were put on the first trial. This provided the best lesson of 'communal amity'. In his speech in Allahabad on 2 October 1945, Nehru spoke that all ate together and lived together in the I.N.A. They had thereby no communal problem, though in India this problem persisted. They refused any defence for themselves on communal lines. They wanted their defence at a national level, and to be undertaken by the Defence Committee set up by the Congress.[53] This theme gave the Congress a cogent argument for its election campaign, to fight the Muslim League which had hesitated to take up the matter at its earlier stage.

Nehru also revised his view on the relations between the I.N.A. and the Japanese Army. He said clearly in a public speech on 30 August 1945 that the soldiers of the Indian National Army were misguided soldiers who tried to help a foreign government.[54] But in the beginning of December, Nehru changed his view, saying that all the evidence in the case as well as all other facts that had reached him made it clear that the members of the I.N.A. were continually resisting Japanese interference and many of them got into trouble because of this.[55]

In the defence of the I.N.A., two waves of the people's movement in Calcutta (in November 1945 and February 1946) are exceedingly important, because they brought about a change in both British and Congress policy towards the people's movement. At this stage, Nehru had to shift his emphasis, saying that the main lesson they (I.N.A.) taught us was not only love of the country and of freedom, but the discipline and organization and the unity they forged among themselves. 'How to organize and discipline ourselves' was added as a lesson to be learnt from the I.N.A.[56]

Nehru admitted that the I.N.A. trial had excited enormous attention and sympathy from all kinds and classes of people. On the eve of Calcutta riots which started from 21 November, the Intelligence Bureau of the Government of India prepared a note on the I.N.A. situation.[57] They shared the same perception albeit from the other side.

According to this note, 'The situation in respect of the Indian National Army is one which warrants disquiet. There has seldom been a matter which has attracted so much Indian public interest and, it is safe to say, sympathy.' The publications of the nationalist press were most popular and widely read even in rural areas. The Congress led this 'outcry' since its commencement, and intended to continue to do so throughout the election period. The influence of the Sikhs in the central Punjab recruiting areas was also grave, because Sikhs had formed a considerable part of the Army.

The note recorded that the politicians who were active in the election campaign had to speak of the I.N.A. 'in appreciative terms' to interest their audiences. This was attributed 'partly to a wave of anti-British feeling which is now being deliberately fostered, partly to a genuine sympathy for the I.N.A. and partly to the fact that Army men on leave from Assam and Burma had not trouble enough to make their feelings known'. The negative response of those who 'might otherwise have supported the Government openly' was disappointing to the officials.

The Intelligence report had to conclude as follows:

> One thing seems clear and that is that sympathy for the I.N.A. is not the monopoly of those who are ordinarily against Government. It is equally clear that this particular brand of sympathy cuts across communal barriers. This is explained to some extent by the fact that the thousands in the I.N.A. have many thousand relations who are anxious about their fate. There is, therefore, support for the political bodies who are helping the I.N.A. and a growing general bitterness.[58]

On the other hand, Tuker in his memoirs gives details about the attitudes of the Indian officers and men towards the I.N.A. trial.[59] The older regular Indian officers, those who had been to English public schools and had maintained their contact with English ways of life and thought, held the same view as the British officers. And those whose sole contact with the British had been with their instructors in the Indian Military Academy in Dehra Dun and who, for racial reasons, had avoided further contact, maintained that the I.N.A. were the patriots and much to be praised.

Most of the newly-joined wartime Indian officers were of the semi-educated, suburban or urban type, who had little acquaintance with the British, usually adopted the view that the accused were patriots and to be treated leniently.

Among the men, the Viceroy's Commissioned Officers (Subedars and Jamadars) and the sepoys of the Indian Army, there were the two categories, the urban-educated and the peasant from the village. On the whole, the educated supported the view of the wartime Indian officers, while the regular V.C.O. and sepoys were one and all loud in condemnation of the accused and of the whole I.N.A. The 'loyal' prisoners of war protested strongly against any leniency towards any of the I.N.A.

The simple wartime sepoys were in the main set against the three accused, even if their feelings were qualified by the fact of having or not having relatives among the I.N.A.

Tuker's is a recollection told five years later. But, it is to be noted that this analysis was done by a responsible Army leader who could say, 'we speak of discipline in the Army, and we and every citizen worth his salt know that no army can exist without discipline'.[60] Unrest infiltrated deep into the feelings of the Indian officers and men of the Army. Moreover, the 'leniency' shown by the military authorities in dealing with the I.N.A. trial had a potentially adverse effect on the feelings of the 'loyal' men.

In the meantime, Nehru emphasized the necessity of maintaining a peaceful atmosphere in the country while the trial lasted. Particularly, he disapproved of the idea of holding a demonstration at the Red Fort, Delhi on 5 November, the first day of the I.N.A. trial. Nehru warned on 3 November that it was improper to hold a demonstration there when the question of the lives of young men was to be decided and the I.N.A. Defence Committee formed by the Congress was trying its best to secure their release.[61]

But the situation took a serious turn when the students' protest against the trial led to the violent police action after 21 November. The Government records and the recollection of Gautam Chattopadhyay who participated in this demonstration are not very different in the main description of the development of this protest, though, of course, their interpretation differs.

Gautam Chattopadhyay describes these days as follows.[62] The Bengal Provincial Students Federation led by the Revolutionary Socialist Party (RSP) gave a strike call throughout Bengal on 21 November demanding the release of the I.N.A. prisoners. The Congress-CSP (Congress Socialist Party)-led Students Congress and the CPI-led Bengal Provincial Students Federation supported the call, but there was no formal joint action. Calcutta students went on strike and a huge student rally took place in Wellington Square on the forenoon of the twenty-first, where the Communist-led BPSF leaders were not allowed to speak in the rally, as they had opposed the Quit India movement of 1942. However, after the meeting all the students marched together towards Dalhousie Square along Dharmatolla Street.

Mounted police barred the path of the procession at the crossing of Madan Street and Dharmatolla Street and the students sat down en masse. This was around 3 p.m. in the afternoon.

The processionists wanted Sarat Chandra Bose, a Congress leader and elder brother of Subhas Chandra Bose, to come and address them. He refused and instead sent a courier with a letter to the students asking them to disperse. The students refused. Around 6 p.m. the police opened fire and made repeated cavalry charges, killing and injuring many students and working youth. As soon as firing started, the Calcutta tram workers went on complete strike, followed by bus workers and rickshaw-pullers.

Gautam Chattopadhyay describes the scene he witnessed:

> What followed was something unique. Conventionally squatters decrease heavily after dark and again increase next day. This time people—students, workers, citizens—started pouring into Dharrmtolla Street all night, swelling the ranks of the squatters, who had reorganised their ranks after the first police attack. No top Congress leader visited the area, nor did they go to hospitals even to see the injured people. But the honour of the tri-colour was kept high by the militant nationalist students, as also by two courageous women leaders—Jyotimoyee Ganguly and Bimalprotiva Devi. They stayed with the demonstrators all night, protecting them, tending to the injured and even scolding them—just like mothers.[63]

On 22 November *hartal* and general strike in Calcutta and suburbs were complete. Congress, Muslim League and Red flags tied together were flying on top of every road-block. British troops had taken over control of the city, but they could control only the main roads—the lanes and by-lanes were all barricaded and were virtually out of bounds for British troops. A big procession of Muslim students carrying the Muslim League flag was also witnessed. Hundreds of students rushed forward, embraced the Muslim students and tied the Muslim League flags together with the tricolour. At once, the whole rally burst into thunderous slogans about Hindu-Muslim unity.

One of the features of the movement is that the question of the connection of the I.N.A. with the Japanese Army receded completely into the background. Instead, the processionists used this movement as a symbol and a pivot of the anti-imperialist movement. To ascertain whether this scene of unity among the students could provide at once the people's alternative to the deteriorating Congress-League relations or not, it further needs the analysis of the development of the student movement in Bengal immediately after this wave of the movement. However, it can be said that this uprising released the gigantic energy of the disenfranchised people, students and labourers. It was this character of the movement, albeit limited in space and time, that attracted the serious concern of the Government and the Congress leaders.

Referring to the connection between this movement and the elections, Gautam Chattopadhyay observed the response of the Congress leaders critically:

When such was the revolutionary mood of the masses and the rank and file militants, what role did the leaders play? They were frankly opposed to a policy of a confrontation with the Raj. General elections were round the corner and a negotiated settlement with the British was in the offing. So the bourgeois nationalist leaders now wanted to keep the mass upsurge in check. That is why Sarat Chandra Bose, in a press statement issued on the night of 21 November, dubbed the call for a protest general strike as a 'Communist Conspiracy'. We have already noted that similar was the public stance of the then Congress president, Maulana Abul Kalam Azad.[64]

Patel's response was almost immediate. On 24 November, Patel wrote to Nehru to say it was unfortunate that the local organization of the Congress and the local leadership had not been able to control the students. Patel thought that, from all accounts, it appeared that the students acted against the advice of the local leaders. 'This is not a good sign. It does compromise our position and the infection of indiscipline outside is also likely to spread.'[65]

Nehru also showed his feelings of apprehension for the direction of the movement though with more reservation. On 2 December 1945 he wrote to Menon:

There is a feeling of desperation in the air and a spark may lead to a fire, as recently took place in Calcutta. There is a great deal of indiscipline about the younger people which is regrettable and yet which one can understand. It is the normal result of suppression and resistance movements, mostly underground in the recent past. It is also partly the result of the Congress organisation having become rather stale and out of date and not giving opportunities to newer elements to function through it.[66]

Nehru tried to understand the meaning of the post-War movement against the trial of the I.N.A. officers in the context of the history of the Quit India movement and its suppression, and judged that the existing Congress organizations were not in a position to cope with the changing situation. He may have implicitly criticized the condition of the Congress organization in Bengal which could not lead the enthusiastic younger people. In fact, there were many Congress men and women in the demonstration in Calcutta. Bimalprotiva Devi was a Congress worker with strong socialist leanings.[67] However, there was no direction of the movement from the side of the Bengal Congress leadership except ordering the people to disperse. In this respect, Nehru appreciated the heroic spirits of the students but apprehended that the movement would go out of control.

It is for this reason that Nehru emphasized the lesson of 'discipline' in his inaugurating speech for the I.N.A. Week in Calcutta on 9 December. He warned the crowd that sporadic violence would not pay and that it would fritter away their energies. Younger people were asked to adopt organized and peaceful methods which the Congress had so far followed.[68] The next day's speech in Calcutta had a different tone and praised the Calcutta uprising:

> What happened in the recent Calcutta firing is not an isolated instance. Nobody was aware that there was a ban on processions to Dalhousie Square. When the students were stopped they simply squatted on the ground. They were peaceful all through. I did not know the details of what happened until I came here. Bullets were showered upon them again and again. The students faced the bullets quietly. They did not move a single pace and demonstrated admirable courage and patience. Then the whole city was ablaze in indignation and various incidents followed. The students of Calcutta gave a lead to the entire people. Those who took part in this uprising are great.[69]

Nehru appears to have revised his opinion of the uprising with first hand knowledge in Calcutta. He did not think that it was an isolated incident. He knew well that this first serious wave of the post-War freedom movement might become 'a good sign' or 'a bad sign', depending on the role of the Congress leadership. At this stage too, the role of Nehru was a link between the people's movement and the Congress which was in the midst of the elections, and to divert the enthusiasm of the people into the 'right channel'. The Bengal Congress leadership could no longer play this role, and Patel was not the man for this work. Only Nehru could do this job skillfully. Hence his inspiring speech in Calcutta.

Even after that speech, however the Congress Working Committee which met from 7 to 11 December in Calcutta issued a warning to the 'unguided masses' in its resolution on non-violence.

> After the arrest of the principal Congressmen in the August of 1942, the unguided masses took the reins in their own hands and acted almost spontaneously. If many acts of heroism and sacrifice are to their credit there were acts done which could not be included in non-violence. It is, therefore,

necessary for the Working Committee to affirm for the guidance of all concerned that the policy of non-violence adopted in 1920 by the Congress continues unabated and that such non-violence does not include burning of public property, cutting of telegraph wires, derailing trains and intimidations.[70]

Not only the acts of the 'unguided masses', but also the speeches of Nehru who praised the sacrifices of the people in 1942 and the uprising of the students a few weeks before were circumscribed within the framework of this resolution. The following resolution on the Calcutta Demonstration was no exception:

The Working Committee are of opinion that the demonstration by the students of Calcutta on 21st of November, resulting in the loss of precious student life and many injured from bullet wounds, and the events thereafter demand an open and impartial judicial inquiry by the Government of Bengal. Meanwhile, the Committee record their opinion that the students of Calcutta showed the utmost bravery of the non-violent type by remaining unmoved under shower of bullets.[71]

However, it is noteworthy that the Congress did not voice overt any criticism about the Calcutta uprising in its official resolution, despite the apprehension of Patel immediately after it and the refusal of Sarat Chandra Bose to come to the spot. This means that the Congress accepted this uprising as the first big tide of the post-War freedom movement in India which, though limited in scale, would become a spearhead of the future struggle. Just because of this, the Congress emphasized non-violence as its guiding principle and the peaceful character of the Calcutta uprising.

On 23 November, Jyotimoyee Ganguli was killed in a car crash. She was the Congress leader who stood by the students all the while they faced lathi charges and police firing.[72] She was the person who told the students that she would herself go and try to bring Sarat Chandra Bose, and afterwards reported that he would not come.[73]

The clemency to the I.N.A. officers published on 1 December 1945 was not a *direct* result of the Calcutta demonstration, but it was a decision adopted in this stream of the post-War freedom movement. At the India and Burma Committee meeting on 19 November 1945, the Secretary of State for India had informed members that Indian opinion was disturbed on certain issues, e.g. the situation in Indonesia (the dispatch of the Indian Army to Indonesia) and the trial of the members of the I.N.A. He added that no effective answer had been made to the speeches of the Congress leaders. Much of what these leaders had said could be regarded as electioneering exuberance, but some of the speeches could be regarded as definitely serious.[74]

Already on 15 November, the Governor of the Punjab had decided to submit some important proposals to the forthcoming conference in Delhi.[75] Among these proposals there were the following suggestions:

1. The trials of Shah Nawaz, Sahgal and Dhillon be not stopped now as this would betray weakness and a lack of courage, which Congress would immediately exploit.
2. The crux of the matter was whether Government intend to stand firm in the event of death sentences being imposed. The agitation which would follow the execution of these three men, and the force which would have to be used to suppress it, would prejudice any hope of a settlement with India.
3. Future trials should be confined to charges of murder and atrocities. Charges of treason and waging war against the King should be dropped. Publicity should be given to this decision now.

These proposals have a particular importance, because these were suggested by the Governor of a province which became one of the chief centres of the post-War movement against the trial of the I.N.A. Many of the I.N.A. officers and men came from this area.

The meetings between the Home Department of the Government of India and certain representatives of the Provincial Governments were held in New Delhi *apparently* on 19 and 20 November.[76] Here the representatives from the Punjab were the main spokesmen of the above-mentioned view. But the Provincial representatives agreed that the charge of waging war against the King could not be dropped, because they recognized that this would amount to almost complete condonation. The legal argument also consolidated this view, as, in many cases, the charges of brutality and murder would not stand unless that of waging of war was also proved.

However, General Auchinleck, Commander-in-Chief, India, shared the opinion of the Governor of the Punjab. In fact, the views of his civil and military advisers differed widely among themselves.[77] One point of view was that no further trials should take place except in cases of brutality which could not be defended by the practices and law of any civilized people. First, the present I.N.A. trials were agitating *all sections of Indian public opinion* deeply and had also provided the Congress with an excellent *election cry*. Limitation of trials was likely to allay public excitement and soothe feelings. Second, the proposed course of action was unlikely to undermine the stability or the reliability of the Indian armed forces. With the existing armed forces recruited from *all parts and all classes of India* and modern means of communications and the growth of nationalist feeling in the country, it was impossible to isolate them from the rest of the country. There was evidence to show the absence of a general resentment in the Indian Army against the I.N.A., and reasons to believe that Indian officers of the three Services would, generally speaking, approve the proposed limitation of trials.

Thus, Auchinleck selected this course of action. In his letter to Wavell, he wrote that he was left with no doubt that from the point of view of *public opinion in general* it would be the most satisfactory. From the point of view of the Army, there was undoubtedly a risk; but it should be taken. So concluded Auchinleck.

His final decision was fashioned largely by public opinion which came from *all classes of people.* Election speeches of the Congress leaders undoubtedly contributed to the formation of this public opinion, but at the same time it is to be noted that people of all classes and men of the Army who came from these classes finally moved Auchinleck to reach his conclusion.

Significantly, Auchinleck gave priority to the political factor over the military. His appreciation of the internal situation in India confirms this:

> If there is a widespread revolt against the Government everything will depend upon the reliability of the Indian Armed Forces. This depends upon political more than upon military factors and it is essential that our political action both in India and in the neighbouring countries where Indian troops are employed, should in no way give opportunities for political agitation to subvert the loyalty to government of the Indian Armed Forces.[78]

Auchinleck thought that the Indian Armed Forces were the last apparatus to maintain the 'constitutional' framework of the Raj, and the stability of the Army had to be protected from political agitation by all means. For this purpose he could no longer stick to 'our standards'. He wrote to the Viceroy on 26 November:

> I do not think any senior British officer today knows what is the real feeling among the Indian ranks regarding the I.N.A. I myself feel, from my own instinct largely, but also from the information I have had from various sources, that there is a growing feeling of sympathy for the I.N.A. and an increasing tendency to disregard the brutalities committed by some of its members as well as the forswearing by all of them of their original allegiance. It is

> impossible to apply our standards of ethics to this problem or to shape our policy as we would, had the I.N.A. been men of our own race.[79]

As we saw, the discussion on clemency had started before the Calcutta 'riot' occurred. However, there is no doubt that this uprising promoted the final decision on the part of the British though there is no *direct* reference in the pronouncements of Auchinleck in those days so far as we can judge from the limited published documents. Auchinleck may have had no need to say much about it as R.G. Casey, Governor of Bengal, dealt with this situation only with the help of the police. Even so the lesson that Casey learnt from this 'disturbance' must have been shared by Auchinleck who already thought that it was impossible to isolate the armed forces from the rest of the country. Casey wrote in his letter to Wavell that, though the disturbances were not planned, there was a spirit of lawlessness abroad which, as in 1942, could, on a slight and sudden cause, be worked up with remarkable speed to produce over a very wide area simultaneously, manifestations paralysing the life of the community.[80]

Auchinleck was a little relieved to find that the violent tone of the speeches of the Congress leaders were curbed after the 'disturbance'. He wrote in his situation report dated 24 November:

> Anti-Government disorder on a large scale is unlikely until after the elections, that is before April, since this would not be in the interests of Congress. Moreover, most of the political leaders and big business men seem at present to be opposed to violent methods. It is possible that Congress may excite popular feeling over some issue such as that of the I.N.A. to such an extent that they may lose control. On the other hand, their most recent utterances might be held to show that they realise this danger.[81]

This perception was shared with more conviction by the Viceroy's House which analysed the speeches of Gandhi, Nehru, Azad and Sarat Chandra Bose. Abul Kalam Azad, Congress President, said on 1 December that the present policy of the Congress was to maintain peaceful undisturbed conditions in the country and to fight the elections with the Congress manifesto. Though Wavell did not deny the danger of a mass movement after the elections, he thought that the Calcutta disturbances made the Congress leaders realize that the violent language that was being used for electioneering purposes might cause premature demonstrations and riots. Also, a mass movement, as a weapon to be used at the right moment and according to a plan, was being prejudiced by the creation of an atmosphere in which disturbances might occur any time and anywhere. Wavell also agreed with Auchinleck, writing that the strong capitalist element behind the Congress was becoming nervous about the security of its property.[82]

In the face of the Calcutta uprising, a kind of *détente* was concluded at least for the moment until the elections had been completed.

Two resolutions of the Congress Working Committee should be understood in this context. The uprising in Calcutta forced the Congress leaders to reconsider to what extent the people's movement against the I.N.A. trial could go and to confirm the crucial meaning of the elections to the Central and Provincial Assemblies which had to be contested by all means.

Wavell observed two stages of the 'Calçutta riots'.[83] In the first stage, the students' procession took the form of the movement. Casey described that they were hysterical young men with whom it was impossible to reason, but who were not violent. They eventually dispersed, probably from sheer exhaustion after some 15 hours. The feature of the second stage was attacks on all forms of transport, large numbers of lorries and private cars being stopped and burned, road blocks from across many of the streets, and some of the railway lines stopped by crowds sitting on them. There was a good deal of organization behind the second phase. This phase ended suddenly. Last, the strike of the Calcutta Corporation employees was an industrial dispute and had no connection with the riots.

Casey was to write later that the procession on the first day was a deliberate act of defiance of authority by students, primarily those associated with the Forward Block. He also said that, in the trial of patience between the students and the police, the students' patience ran out first and they precipitated the riot by trying to force the cordon and attacked the police. After the second day, the stoppage of transport was enforced by the students, a number of Sikh taxi drivers, and Communist-led tramway workers. Casey guessed that the actual violence was perpetrated more often by Sikhs, 'up-country' mechanics and the hooligan element generally. He said that this was particularly true of the most affected area, i.e. Bhowanipore in South Calcutta.[84] As for the reason of the sudden collapse of the 'disturbances', Casey mentions, besides the police action and his warning in a broadcast, the effect of the fact that, throughout the morning and early afternoon of 23 November, Congress and some Communist propaganda cars toured the affected areas dissuading the students from further participation.

The role of the Communists on the third day of this great tide, however, cannot be verified from other sources. The Communists were also contesting the elections and at the same time were facing an anti-Communist campaign due to their non-participation in the Quit India movement during the war. Under this unfavorable condition, the collections which the Communists had for the defence and relief of the I.N.A. officers facing trial were sent to the I.N.A. Defence Committee set up by the Congress. The elections and the protection of the party organization may have led the party to close the movement in the streets for the moment.

Whatever the reasons for the closure of the movement, the majority of the demonstrators in November 1945 had not reached the age of voting or were workers like the tramway workers, deprived of the right to vote. 'Hooligans' was a convenient official label for unidentified social classes since the days of the Quit India movement, and needs serious analysis. The point is that disenfranchised students and workers had the means of expression of their will to freedom in these 'disturbances', even if it embarrassed the political parties. The citizens of Calcutta in November 1945 experienced the same dilemma as the peasants of Satara a few months earlier.

The people's movement against the I.N.A. trials forced the British to take prompt decisions.

On 1 December, a press communique was published, as a result of which the trial was now limited to those who 'committed acts of gross brutality, resulting in some cases in death, upon their fellow countrymen who were prisoners of war or members of the I.N.A.'.[85]

On 31 December, the General Court Martial found all three accused officers guilty of the charge of waging war against the King Emperor. Lt G.S. Dhillon was acquitted of the charge of murder and Capt. P.K. Sahgal was acquitted of the charge of abetment of murder. Capt. Shah Nawaz Khan was found guilty of the charge of abetment of murder. The court sentenced all the accused officers to transportation for life, cashiering and forfeiture of arrears of pay and allowance for waging war against the King Emperor. No separate sentence was passed upon Capt. Shah Nawaz Khan on the charge of abetment of murder.[86]

On 3 January 1946, a communique was announced in which Auchinleck, the confirming authority, declared again that it was the policy of the Government of India to bring to trial in future only such persons as were alleged, in addition to waging war against the State, to have committed acts of gross brutality. Dhillon and Sahgal were acquitted of the charges of murder and abetment of murder, and it was not alleged that they were guilty of other acts of brutality. Although Shah Nawaz Khan was found guilty of abetment of murder and the charges proved against him were serious 'prevailing circumstances have been taken into account by the confirming officer'. Therefore, the Commander-in-Chief remitted the sentences of transportation for life against all these three accused, and only confirmed the sentence of cashiering and forfeiture of arrears of pay and allowances, 'since it was in all circumstances a most serious crime for an officer or soldier to throw off his allegiance and wage war against the State'.[87]

On the same day they were released.

On 6 January, Wavell expressed his ambivalent feelings towards this announcement of confirmation:

> This was a very difficult decision to make. Auchinleck kept me fully informed, and I think that what he did was right. A 'national' government would have let out immediately any of the three who was under a term of imprisonment. Nevertheless there will naturally be many soldiers, both British and Indian, who will resent the leniency shown.[88]

Already on 19 November 1945, M. Hallett, U.P. Governor, had informed Wavell of a circular issued by Achut Patwardhan who directed the Satara activists to establish contacts with demobilized soldiers and families of the I.N.A. prisoners and civil and railway officers and their families in connection with probable terrorist activities in future.[89] Actually, Naganath Naikaudi of Valva, one of the leaders in Satara, went to Delhi to seek contact with the men of the Indian National Army for purposes of imparting military training to the volunteers. Though he got a cold response from Maniben Patel, he could get the agreement of two Sikh army youths to come to Satara. Thus, at the end of 1945 a training camp was set up in the Sahyadris.[90] Satara in 1945 and Calcutta in November 1945 were connected in the undercurrent of the freedom movement.

Meanwhile, election results of the Central Assembly were known to the public in December 1945. Elections were held on the basis of a very limited franchise in which only about one per cent of the people could vote. Still it served the role of a spearhead of the coming Provincial Elections. Both the Congress and the League could boast of their victory in the Central Assembly Election. The League won every seat reserved for Muslims, while the Congress won all the elective seats in the Assembly except those reserved for Muslims and a few of those reserved for special interests.[91]

In a Victory Day (11 January 1946) message, Jinnah said that this cent per cent success was unparalleled in the history of any country and that the establishment of Pakistan was the only solution to India's constitutional problem. He asked the Muslims to sweep the provincial polls.

On the other hand, the Central Election Board of the Indian National Congress also said, 'Congress today stands vindicated. It is the biggest and the most representative organisation in the country. . . . Congress is the single biggest party in the Central Legislature, with an overwhelming majority of elected members. . . . The most significant feature of these results is our victories in "mixed" constituencies in which Hindus, Muslims, Christians and others voted jointly. Throughout India, there are only three non-communal seats, three constituencies which have joint electorates. Here the Congress had cent per cent success.'[92]

So long as both sides boasted of 'cent per cent success', there was no room for a common approach to constitutional development.

On 22 January 1946, the Cabinet meeting in London decided to send its Mission to India in the middle of March.

When Casey, Governor of Bengal, met Auchinleck on 24 November, he could express the validity of his thesis that, by the use of troops armed with rifles, one might stifle local trouble, but create a risk of widespread conflagration. He said that he had in mind General Dyer and Amritsar of 1919, and confessed his inner feelings that, by the use of troops in the circumstances, he would in fact be relying on the judgement and good sense of a number of junior military officers, which he was reluctant to do.[93] But after less than three months, he had to call in the military in Calcutta.

The occasion of the second big tide of the movement against the I.N.A. trials was prepared by the sentence on Capt. Abdul Rashid whose trial started on 9 January 1946. He was found guilty of waging war against the King and also of acts of brutality and sentenced to transportation for life, cashiering and forfeiture of pay. The sentence was commuted by the Commander-in-Chief to seven years' imprisonment on 4 February.[94]

Gautam Chattopadhyay, who said that a 'brief but essentially revolutionary period' in Indian history (November 1945 to February 1946) had gone largely untouched by historians to the days of his writing (1986), followed the second uprising in Calcutta, using the nationalist daily ***Amrita Bazar Patrika*** and the Intelligence Reports of the Government.[95] I too have read the same Intelligence Reports to know the official view of the movement.

The C.I.O. Calcutta in a telephonic report sent the following reading of the situation:

> Procession to protest against the conviction of Abdul Rashid of the I.N.A. led to renewed disturbances in Calcutta on February 11. Those concerned were students of the Bengal Provincial Students' Federation (R.S.P.I. crowd) and the Muslim Students' Federation. The processions carried Congress and Muslim League flags side by side as a demonstration of unity. The situation got gradually worse, and by 9 p.m. lorries were being burnt in north Calcutta, over 20 being accounted for. The police had to open fire three of four times and one police station was attacked. The trouble again originated over an attempt by processionists to pass through Dalhousie Square, which was resisted by the Police with a lathi charge and they made about 27 arrests. Schools and colleges closed on the afternoon of 11-2-46.
>
> Second information is that the Muslim Leagues as a whole in Calcutta are in sympathy with all this, though they have not yet openly backed the students who began it. The Muslim League, as already reported, regard the conviction as a direct insult to the League, and have now expressed the intention of organising a *hartal* on 12-2-46, and a procession and demonstration if possible, regardless of consequences. All schools and colleges are to remain closed on 12-2-46.[96]

This report emphasized the importance of an attempt by the demonstrators to pass through Dalhousie Square, a prohibited area as the flash point which led to the disturbances. Nikhil Chakravarty, sent a wire report from Calcutta on 14 February, and recounted the details from a different angle. His observation is as follows.[97]

On 11 February, a meeting of Calcutta students was jointly called by the All-Bengal Muslim Students' League (ABMSL) and the Bengal Students' Federation (in which Communists and others worked together) to demand the release of Capt. Abdul Rashid and other prisoners. A procession of Muslim school boys on their way to the meeting was lathi-charged by the Police at Dalhousie Square and 12 arrests were made on the spot. This was the first police attack, and roused the indignation of all at the meeting which was held at Wellington Square. Suhrawardy who attended the meeting said, 'Today the great desire of my life is fulfilled, that Hindu and Muslim students have stood united under the banner of the Congress and the Muslim League.'

The students then marched in a procession, 5,000 strong, through different streets, holding the Congress and League flags and shouting slogans like 'Police zoolum bandh ho', or 'Congress League ek ho'. When the students reached Dalhousie Square from Clive Street, the Police blocked their way, but the onrush of the students pressure pushed the Police back. The people of this business centre also came out to see. The students squatted on the road. Meanwhile, a fresh contingent of the armed Gurkha Police arrived. Ananda Bhattacharya, General Secretary, BPSF, asked the Police Officer to give the processionists their right to pass peacefully. However, after a while a Police Sergeant arrested Mohammed Osman, Secretary, Calcutta City League, and thereupon the police attacked the peaceful students for nearly an hour. Over 100 students were wounded. This enraged the people all over the city. Crowds collected at street corners, and trams and buses were stopped. At two places the police burst teargas shells indiscriminately and also opened fire, and this infuriated the people all the more.

Nikhil Chakravarthy reports the complex response of the political parties towards the disturbances. On that day the League leaders contacted the Congress and Communist leaders and, after a prolonged discussion, a joint statement was issued, condemning the police action and calling a meeting of citizens the next day. But the Congress leaders signed in their individual capacity. The participants therefore, went to Sarat Bose's house to secure the official signature of the Congress. There a decision to call for a *hartal* was adopted, which included the stoppage of all vehicular traffic. Then the Communists approached the Tram and Bus Union workers for a call for strike. But after midnight information came that the Congress and the League had finally decided against the *hartal*.

Tuker, G.O.C.-in-C., Eastern Command, recollects that the intention of the 'youthful hotheads' to march through Dalhousie Square, a prohibited area for meetings and processions, was to provoke the police. According to him the students:

> . . . hoped thereby to enrage the public, always ready to side against the police, until they took up the cudgels on behalf of the squatters. This is a good example of what the Congress Party was pleased to call non-violent action; any impartial observer could see that it was willfully designed towards compelling the authorities to take forceful measures. The non-violent elements could then go back, pose as martyrs and display themselves as heroes, and write in their diaries and in newspapers of the merciless and vicious beatings

> they had experienced and of the low form of life of all police, particularly the British and Anglo-Indian Sergeants and inspectors, compared with their own innocent selves.
>
> Sensing a scene and piling up against the road block of students, an excited crowd of about three thousand now started to gather close by near Charnock Place. Armed police with tear-gas hurried to the scene. As yet there had been no violence and the police had avoided using force but the atmosphere was unbearably tense and tragedy was in the air. . . .
>
> Showers of stones came flying from the crowd at the silent, motionless police.
>
> The police at once sprang into action and delivered charge after charge with their brass-bound staves and within half an hour, before 5 p.m., the crowd was hurriedly dispersing. Soon afterwards the city was quiet and it seemed that the trouble was done with.[98]

Tuker writes that, although the city was tense, at this phase, they could not anticipate 'a night of rioting'. He ridiculed this as a typical Congress-style 'non-violent' action, but in fact the League and the Communists were trying to lead the demonstrations along with some Congress leaders who joined it in their individual capacity. Tuker's recollection is a typical example of 'imperialist historiography' that, according to the expression of S. Gopal, took 'not only the mind but decency, character, integrity and selfless commitment out of the Indian national movement'.[99]

Some of the developments on the first day of the second big tide in Calcutta need to be examined. First, though the League did not join the leadership in the first wave of the movement in November, they actively tried to lead the demonstrations this time. It may be true that Suhrawardy thought that the conviction of Abdul Rashid meant a disgrace to the Muslims and the Muslim League, and that he took advantage of this occasion to direct popular support into the electoral channel. But here at least, unlike in the election campaign, there was room for some political dialogue between the Congress and the League. The people's movement provided this chance even if success was unlikely. The Congress had already decided in November 1945 to keep aloof although it had officially appreciated the non-violent character of the student movement. Also, Nehru's declaration, 'the time has come to declare that there would be no more approach to the League' on the occasion of the AICC meeting in September 1945 proved true at this critical moment.[100]

Second, it is natural that the Government and the political parties took completely opposite views on the question of who 'provoked', but it seems true that the students and their leaders tried to remain calm at the first stage, even though they demanded their right to pass through a 'prohibited area'. This is corroborated by the development of the movement on 12 February.

The C.I.O. Calcutta in his Telephone Report No. 2 of 12 February says that the situation deteriorated considerably, and was grave. It appeared that the Muslim League was sponsoring the agitation and that groups of students of all political denominations had combined under the auspices of their parent political organizations, i.e. all political parties were united. The persons who actually started the agitation the previous day were Communist controlled Student Federation and the Muslim League. The report added,

> The present situation is as follows:
>
> Military lorries are being burnt in North and South Calcutta. Private cars in various parts of the city are being stoned and the occupants are being assaulted, and there have been several cases of police firing. A large meeting, which is being addressed by Sir Nazimuddin and Suhrawardy and other leaders, is now taking place at Wellington Square. After this a procession will probably be taken out and will be allowed by the authorities to go through Dalhousie Square.
>
> Muslim students are taking a bigger part than anybody else and the situation is serious at the moment.[101]

Casey sent his telegraphic report that night to the Viceroy, and explained how the peaceful demonstration took a turn for the worse, and why he had to call in the military:

> Protest meeting . . . . was held this afternoon. Attendance reported in evening press as 50,000. Meetings were presided over by Suhrawardy and addressed by some Congress and Communist leaders. Following meeting very large procession was allowed to pass through Dalhousie Square (prohibited area). The passage was apparently peaceful although one Head Constable was stabbed in the back by one of processionists. As procession after passing through Dalhousie Square was going past Central Police Headquarters a police lorry returning to Headquarters with injured constable forced its way through procession. This was followed by throwing brick-bats on a large scale and some tear smoke had to be used to disperse a portion of the crowd. . . . The exact cause of the worse turn taken by events soon after is not yet clearly ascertainable. The crowd appears to have split up into gangs of hooligans spreading over centre of the town including European residential area and indulging in looting shops (particularly arms-dealers') and looting and setting fire to private houses, molesting peaceful citizens etc. . . . .[102]

At 6.30 p.m. on 12 February, Casey had a meeting with the Area

Commander and the Commissioner of Police, and authorized the invocation of military assistance in aid of civil power.

Nikhil Chakravarty confirms that the basically peaceful character of the demonstrations was maintained up to the meeting in the afternoon. In the morning all vehicular traffic was stopped. Many military lorries were attacked. Peace squads of the League, Congress and Communists, and students tried to pacify the people by patrolling the streets. But firing was opened in north Calcutta, killing one person.

By 1 p.m. on 12 February a huge crowd of 25,000 belonging to all sections of the people collected at Wellington Square. Nikhil Chakravarty writes:

> It was an unforgettable scene, where scores of Tri-colour, League and Red Flags mingled together. In some cases flags were found knotted to one another. And continuous shouts of 'Hindu-Muslim ek ho', 'Down with British Imperialism' rent the sky.[103]

After the students' meeting, the meeting convened by the leaders followed at the same place with Suhrawardy in the chair. Here, Abul Hashim, Secretary of the Bengal Muslim League and a 'progressive' leader, told the people that yesterday's tragedy had been turned from a curse to a blessing since it had brought Hindus and Muslims together. He added that, through greater unity in the entire country, we should build our Azad Hind Fauj (Indian National Army). Then, Somnath Lahiri said that, if leaders took six hours the previous night to come together, it did no take six minutes for the common people, both Hindus and Muslims to unite in the face of the Police. He asked the Congress and the League to campaign unitedly for the release of the prisoners. After the meeting, a huge procession started with Suhrawardy and Satish Das Gupta, a Bengal Congress leader, at the head. It swelled into over two lakhs. Chakravarty continues,

> When teargas was used by the Police, women from houses on both sides showered buckets of water to neutralise its effect.
>
> I witnessed an interesting scene; a League volunteer soaked the green League flag in water and gave it to Satish Babu. He wiped his own face, then gave it to Suhrawardy Sahib, who after using it gave it back to Satish Babu.
>
> Despite teargas, the crowd behaved peacefully. When they returned to Wellington Square, both Suhrawardy and Satish Das Gupta exhorted the people to maintain peace and not to fall a prey to Police provocation.[104]

Here also a careful reading of Chakravarty's article, written from the standpoint of the Communist strategy of the Congress-League Unity in those years, is essential. There is no doubt that he grasped the scene of the demonstration in February 1946 as an experiment of this strategy on the part of the Communists and the League 'Progressives'. It is also true that some scenes of communication between the demonstrators and the citizens in Calcutta were similar to scenes of solidarity between the naval ratings and the citizens of Bombay, to be observed a week later.

The Bengal Muslim League which did not join the November upheaval participated in the demonstration in February 1946. The Commissioner of Police, Calcutta, reported later on the political aspects of the Calcutta 'disturbances' in April and recorded a cool and critical view of the role of Suhrawardy:

> The Muslim League was forced into an awkward situation politically by the actions of the Muslim students who defied government on the 13th. With the elections approaching, Mr Suharawardy could not afford to lose popular support. Like all other party leaders in Bengal he has no control over his rank and file. He knew that he had to agitate against the conviction of Abdul Rashid even if the agitation led to violence. He knew that the procession on the 11th through the prohibited area, declared such by the Cabinet of which he was a member, would be dispersed by force and that this would lead to serious disorder. His efforts to prevent this defiance were small and he had little of success. His knowledge that the procession on the 12th would be allowed to pass through the prohibited area enabled him to pose with safety as a hero of liberty and the protagonist of Hindu-Muslim or League-Congress unity. He also led the procession, undoubtedly in the hope that his presence would prevent unseemly behaviour, but undoubtedly, too, with the intention of not committing the error of Sarat Bose who lost much popularity by not showing himself at Dhurrumtolla on the 21st November. As a leader of the Muslim League he reviled the Police and criticized the Government of which he was confident he soon would be the Prime Minister. He organized peace squads during the disturbances. Had votes not been necessary perhaps the Muslim League would have attempted to take a stronger line with the Muslim students, but with no hope of success. Although the disturbances arose out of a Muslim demonstration against the Government the participants in them were probably more non-Muslim than Muslims.[105]

There may be some truth in the official view which concluded that Suhrawardy took advantage of the occasion of Rashid's conviction to lead the elections to victory and also to pose as a hero of Hindu-Muslim unity, just as some truth is seen in the interpretation that the Congress took advantage of the I.N.A. trial to contest the elections as a champion of Hindu-Muslim-Sikh unity. There is also some truth in the official explanation that the 'disturbances' were 'engineered' by the Communist Party, League, and to a lesser extent Congress student leaders, and were 'directed' by the Communist leaders Somnath Lahiri and Muzaffar Ahmad.[106] However, more important was the undeniable fact that those people who acted in this critical moment moved the political leaders to see the mood of the people, whatever their initial purpose. It may not be easily concluded that this unity in action could prepare a joint constitutional plan for independent India without friction, and avoid the Great Calcutta Killing of August 1946, but there was something in the demonstration which the election campaign of the political parties in Bengal could not achieve.

The Commissioner of Police, Calcutta, wrote in his final report that the Indian National Congress, whatever individual members might have done, took no part in the agitation preceding the disturbances or in the disturbances.[107]

Nikhil Chakravarty felt sad to write that Sarat Bose and Suren Ghosh, President of the Bengal Provincial Congress Committee, remained absent from the meeting though both were signatories to the joint statement calling for it. He placed particular importance on this absence because he believed that it led to the situation in which Casey could justify the use of the military. He wrote in Calcutta on 14 February as follows:

> It was most surprising to find Bengal's top Congress bosses deliberately holding themselves aloof from a demonstration, where thousands of our Muslim brothers, shoulder to shoulder with their Hindu brethren, were jointly defying the Imperialist Police.
>
> The absence of guidance and direction from top leaders left the people to themselves all over the city. The result was that their fury took spontaneous forms of mass anger and this gave a chance to rowdy elements also to come into picture.
>
> Trucks were burnt by scores; trams at Kalighat were burnt; the Kalighat Police Office was raided; European shops and hotels on Chowringhee were stoned and Europeans and Anglo Indians were roughly handled.
>
> The Police taking advantage of all this opened indiscriminate fire and used teargas and lathis brutally. Casualties include more than 20 killed and over 200 injured on Tuesday (12th) . . . .
>
> And he (Casey) handed over the city to the Military.[108]

Nikhil Chakravarty regretted this and wrote that, if only the leaders had taken their lesson from the mighty united upsurge and come forward jointly to establish peace and discipline, the Governor's game of calling in the military would have been foiled and the city brought back to normal in no time.

The absence of the top Congress leaders seems to have seriously affected the later course of history in Bengal. Their participation might have opened at least some chances of political dialogue instead of, or in parallel with the constitutional rivalry in the elections, and made impossible Tuker's comment that

> Within the agitation against the British we have seen the gnawing growth of communalism. We knew full well and for certain, and we said so at the time that this growth was the one reality of the whole body politic and that the anti-British symptom was artificial and only exhibited to sight by quack politicians in order to cover the fatal disease hidden beneath.[109]

As noted earlier, the action of Congress members was circumscribed by the resolution of the AICC session in Bombay in September 1945 and particularly by the two resolutions which were adopted by the Congress Working Committee after the uprising in Calcutta in November 1945.

Furthermore, factional bickerings were rampant among the Bengal Congress leaders. As Sudhir Chandra Roy wrote to Patel in the beginning of January 1946, 'An organisation must have a unitary leadership in a person or programme. Both of these are lacking in Bengal. None of the known leaders enjoy the confidence of all the sections or groups of workers.'[110] It was on the same day that Sarat Chandra Bose admitted that there was no contact between the Congress and the Muslim masses. Under these circumstances there was very little chance that creative initiative came from the Congress leadership in Bengal. This negative character of the Congress organization in Bengal was at least partly responsible for the deteriorating communal situation which led to the Calcutta massacre on 16 August 1946 and to the poor popular response to the discussion on 'United Bengal' on the eve of Partition in August 1947.

On 13 February, the military took up positions in various parts of Calcutta and its suburbs. The British authorities made contact with the Muslim League and the Congress leaders to induce the strikers to return to work. Congress lorries went around carrying loudspeakers and urging the crowds to disperse.

On the morning of 14 February, Casey toured all affected areas of Calcutta with the Commissioner of Police and found 'all quiet'.[111] On 18 February, he reported to Wavell that disturbances were over at least for the moment. But the impact of the 'disturbances' on later history was tremendous. It was not an isolated incident in the post-War history of the country. When Wavell received this letter from

Casey, he was already facing another crisis in Bombay and other ports.

The Royal Indian Navy on Strike

On 21 February 1946, Wavell got two telegrams, one from Pethick-Lawrence, Secretary of State for India, and one from Attlee, Prime Minister, both sending a strong complaint that they had no information about the situation in Bombay.[112] In response to the Royal Indian Navy Strike which started on 18 February, the attitudes of the Government of India, the Congress and the Muslim League towards the Freedom Movement became quite clear. Particularly, the response of Sardar Vallabhbhai Patel who was then working in the Election Board office of the Congress in Bombay was prompt and left no room for question.

B.C. Dutt who became one of the leaders of the strike, recollects how discrimination during the War and post-War days drove him to plan the Mutiny:

> Discrimination, yes. No question about ill-treatment. But, up to a point, all that served as a spur to determination. We must prove that skill for skill, courage for courage, we were better than the B.O.Rs. So we did, more than once, when we were called upon to establish communications in hilly terrains after the British signal units had failed. These areas lay beyond the sea beach and, strictly speaking, beyond the beach signal unit's area of operation. We established and maintained communications to everyone's satisfaction. Men from other units were decorated for far less achievements. We were just taken for granted.
>
> On our way back to Bombay, I brooded over this. Even on the front, the discrimination was as crude and glaring as it was back in the training camp. Transport, tents and hot meals were somehow arranged for British personnel even in deep jungle or on a distant beach. For us, often, there was nothing.[113]

> I was twenty-two. I had come through a war unscathed—a war fought to end Nazi domination. I had seen the British people defending their country. I had served alongside British sailors and others from the other Commonwealth countries in different theatres. They knew what they were fighting for. I began to question my whole existence. What did I fight for? Whose war did I fight? Was it for my country? I was a sailor, but in whose service? . . . . To the British authorities, we were servicemen. We were not supposed to think, but do our jobs with unquestioning devotion and loyalty. But loyalty to whom? To nationalist India we were mercenaries, whose closer contact with the British servicemen had thoroughly shaken my sense of loyalty to the Raj. And the association with the men from free countries had given me a sense of identity with my own country. It was up to us, I felt, to prove that we were as much sons of the soils as the nationalist Indians who were fighting for the country's independence. Without quite realising it, I became a conspirator.[114]

On February 18, 1946, the ratings of the *H.M.I.S. Talwar* were awakened as usual at 5 a.m. They gathered in the mess hall for breakfast at 8 a.m. More than 1,500 of them. Suddenly a murmur went up. No one was sure as to who started it. Soon there was an uproar from all corners. In a few minutes, the men walked out of the hall. They would not eat. The food was poor and inadequate.

Someone shouted the slogan in one of the mess halls: 'No food, No work'.

They had crossed the line! They had done it! We had now got them committed.[115]

Subrata Banerjee who wrote *The RIN Strike* in 1954, later criticized that B.C. Dutt had underestimated the role of the Communist Party in this Mutiny due to his subjective hostility towards the party. Nevertheless, Banerjee agreed that *no political party* had been prepared for the RIN revolt, though he asserted that the Communists gave valuable support and organized the masses.[116] Though there are different views on the historical significance of the Mutiny, there seems little discrepancy in the analyses of what moved the ratings to revolt. There was discrimination in all aspects of the life of the naval ratings, and a strong urge for freedom among them and the people at large. However 'innocent' their political ideas may be, their doubt about the 'noble cause of the war' came from reflections on their daily experiences. The revolt occurred in the context of the new historical experience of the people who plunged into the Quit India movement and could express their critical view of British war aims through their daily experience of rising prices and food scarcity. Perhaps the election speeches of the political parties played their role. The Mutiny made it clear that there was a serious gap between the thinking of the ratings and that of the political leaders who were facing the Provincial Elections. In Bombay, the elections were expected in March.

A minimum description of the revolt may be indispensable for understanding the response of the political parties and the thought of the people at this critical stage.

On 19 February, all the eleven shore establishments in Bombay and its suburbs and some sixty ships in the harbours were on strike. Nearly 20,000 naval ratings were involved.[117]

'To the *Talwar*!' had become a slogan of the ratings of Castle Barracks and later Fort Barracks. They marched in the city and reached the *Talwar*. On Hornby Road the ratings requested all to close their shops and support the RIN struggle. The Indian shopkeepers promptly closed. British shop-owners ignored their request, and in fury, the ratings rushed to the shop windows and smashed them. 'For a time some of the ratings fell into the grip of racial fury.' In front of the United States Information Library they hauled down the US flag and set fire to it. A few Europeans were attacked and seriously injured.[118]

B.C. Dutt discloses that, in the preparation of the operation, those who went on strike received some guidance from the leftist leaders of the Indian National Congress, militant elements of the Quit India movement, though their contact was through intermediaries.[119]

On the other hand, Banerjee describes the scene of the Remote Control Office where the ratings replied to the Flag Officer, Rear-Admiral Rattray who told them to send their representatives, 'We are not prepared to send anybody to you. We want a national leader, either from the Congress, the Muslim League or the Communist Party to negotiate between us.'[120] Also, on 18 February, when the programme for the next day was discussed in the *H.M.I.S. Punjab*, it was decided to hoist the flags of the three main Indian political parties. Next day the procession of ratings shouted 'Congress-League ek ho', and at the same time all the three flags went up at the head of the procession.[121] This reflects the influence of the Communist idea of the 'national unity' on the naval revolt.

However, it can be basically said that the revolt was started on the initiative of the ratings, particularly of the *Talwar*. On 19 February, the Naval Central Strike Committee was formed. M.S. Khan and Madan Singh were selected as President and Vice-President, respectively. This also symbolized the climate of the revolt which cut across the communal lines. At the meetings of the ratings, the following demands were approved:[122]

1. Release all political prisoners including those of the I.N.A.
2. Take action against Commander King, CO of the *Talwar*, for using insulting language against the ratings
3. Speedy demobilization and provision for resettlement in peace-time employment
4. Same scale of pay, allowances, etc., as those of RN ratings
5. Access to NAAFI canteens
6. Better food
7. No return of clothing kit at the time of release
8. Withdrawal of Indian troops from Indonesia

These demands incorporated issues of day-to-day life as well as political issues.

The revolt undeniably aimed for the Quit India and for this purpose the ratings wanted the leadership of political parties. Above all, they asked Aruna Asaf Ali, a heroine of the Quit India movement, to come and lead them. The news that she would not come brought a big disappointment to them. According to B.C. Dutt, Aruna Asaf Ali told the strike leaders that they were wrong in mixing 'political demands' with 'service demands' and promptly advised them to contact with Patel. He recollects that they lacked the political insight to understand that she too was merely a product of the larger movement and that they had gone far to glorify Aruna Asaf Ali personally.[123] This incident illustrates the spontaneous character of the Mutiny, but it is not correct to dismiss the significance of the revolt by saying that the Mutiny came 'too late' as the British Government and the Indian political leaders were going to sit together to finalize their plan for the transfer of power. It cannot be concluded that the Congress already institutionalized the wish of the people into its electoral channels and that it no longer needed the support of the people in its negotiation with the Labour Government which was ready to transfer power. As Nehru was to say later, the wall between the naval ratings and the people fell on 18 February.

The response of the Congress towards the naval revolt not only decided the destiny of the Mutiny, but also the character of the Independence of India. It is another matter whether the naval strike prepared a detailed alternative plan which could take the place of the Congress plan. The main theme at this critical moment was to what extent the Congress could assess the direction of the will of the people which was reflected in the Mutiny.

Meanwhile, on 19 February the following cipher was sent by the naval authorities:

> Mutiny has spread to all RIN establishments inside Bombay and to ships in harbour. Latter flying Congress flags. Early this morning RIN ratings invaded Fort areas and Europeans molested and shops raided and damaged. FOB met deputation and has registered mens demands and warned against violence. Situation quiet at present.[124]

At this stage the authorities could not imagine the scale of the revolt even while they were following carefully every important phase of the mutiny.

On that day, Pethick-Lawrence, Secretary of State for India announced in the House of Lords that British Government had decided to sent out to India a special mission of Cabinet Ministers to act in association with the Viceroy. He recalled the statement of policy made by Wavell on 19 September 1945 outlining positive steps to be taken immediately after the Central and Provincial Elections.[125] Prime Minister Attlee, making a similar statement to the House of Commons, added that the Mission would go to India towards the end of March. Both made these statements without any direct information from the Government of India on the situation in Bombay.[126] There was an immediate response from political leaders in India. According to V.P. Menon, the announcement was well received throughout India.[127] It is not clear how this statement reached the ratings and conditioned their and their leaders' decisions in later days. But it is certain that these new political conditions circumscribed the movement of the Congress leaders, and made it possible for the British military authorities to take prompt steps.

Already at 2.30 p.m. on 19 February, J. Colville, Governor of Bombay, called a meeting consisting of the Flag Officer Rattray, General Board, the Area Commander, Butler, the Commissioner of Police and Bristow, the Governor's Adviser, and it was agreed that this was a matter for the troops to deal with, supported if necessary by the armed police.[128]

On 20 February there was a meeting at the *Talwar*, where a song of Iqbal about the poor and the downtrodden was sung. Banerjee writes that Iqbal's song seemed to have set the tone of the speeches. On that day there was more militancy, more determination. He also adds that there was more discipline and order than on the previous day.[129] But a new development appeared on the side of the British military authorities on the same day. Admiral Godfrey, Flag Officer Commanding, RIN, reached Bombay. An order was issued that all ratings must return to their ships and establishments by 3.30 p.m. and most of them returned. A few were picked up and brought to the *Talwar* by military trucks. Godfrey agreed to meet all the demands concerning food at once, but was not prepared to discuss any other demands.[130] The Strike Committee refused this partial concession.

On 21 February, the situation took a serious turn.

A report received from Rodger, C.I.O., Bombay, said at 3.30 p.m., 'The situation deteriorated this morning and is now serious. . . . This morning they (mutineers) were fired on by the Mahrattas on guard at the gate (of the Castle Barracks). From the Castle Barracks wall the R.I.N. mutineers have fired on the police guard in the Mint. A burst of machine-gun fire was heard from this area about 2 p.m. today. . . .[131]

The situation report of the Director of Intelligence continued,

Firing was resumed at 1350 hrs. At 1430 hrs FOB met a leader of the mutineers in the Dockyard. He warned the latter that if the mutineers continued they would take the consequences and added that no condition other than unconditional surrender would be accepted; that there could be no question of a withdrawal of troops. . . . By 1443 hrs firing was reported in the Dockyard. By 1550 hrs a police report stated that a small shell had caused minor injuries to several civilians at Mallet Bunder Rd. By 1602 hrs a listening post reported heated argument amongst ratings whether to continue or not. About 12 to 15 ratings landed at Apollo Banda armed with rifles, raided food stalls and put off again. Troops were reported to have aimed arrived [sic] on *H.M.I.S. Shivaji* at 1640 hrs. The last report timed 1657 hrs stated that firing had recommenced in Castel Barracks area.[132]

This intelligence report already felt relieved to say that

A report from Bombay, which confirms information received by the Commissioner of Police on 20 Feb. 46 was to the effect that Patel had nothing to do with the mutiny; that the mutineers had acted on their own; and that Purshottam Tricumdas, a Congress Socialist leader, would have nothing to do with them.

On 21 February, the Governor of Bombay got information from Patel. Colville writes:

There were signs that the city, which had hitherto been quiet, was likely to be subjected to disturbance. The Congress leaders had decried any share in the mutiny, and had advised people to preserve order. I received a message from Vallabhbhai Patel to this effect on Thursday, together with an offer to do anything which he could to prevent bloodshed.[133]

A naval squadron was enroute to Bombay, and air reinforcements were also moving to the area. The army reinforcements were concentrating in Bombay too. Obviously encouraged by these changes in the situation, Godfrey made his well-known statement over All-India Radio:

The overwhelming forces at the disposal of Government of India at this time will be used to their utmost even if it means the destruction of the Navy of which India has been so proud.[134]

However, on 21 February, a moving scene was witnessed. Citizens came to help the ratings. B.C. Dutt recollects that people

rushed to our rescue. From every walk of life they came and crowded the seafront around the Gateway of India, with packets of food and pails of water.

The restaurant keepers were seen requesting people to carry whatever food they could to the beleaguered ratings. Even some street beggars, it was reported in the press, were seen carrying tiny food packets for the ratings. The harbour front presented a strange spectacle. The whole area was patrolled by armed Indian soldiers. British forces were kept ready at distance. Indian soldiers with rifles slung across their backs helped to load the food packets brought by the public on boats sent from the ships in the harbour. The British officers were helpless spectators. On the *Talwar*, in a few hours, we received so many food parcels sent over the wall that we had enough to eat for a few days. A lot of food reached us through the main gate of *Talwar* which was still guarded by Indian soldiers. There were 1,500 ratings on the *Talwar*.[135]

There was a prelude to this scene. In the morning the Maratha soldiers stationed near the Castle Barracks had opened fire on the ratings. The latter did not fire back, but sent their message to the soldiers over the loud-speakers, telling them that they were fighting for freedom, not only for the ratings themselves but also for the soldiers. The firing ceased, and, after a while, a signal was sent from the soldiers, communicating that they were firing blanks.[136] This meant that the Indian freedom movement had reached a new stage cutting across the barrier between the people and the military, and between the army soldiers and the naval ratings too. Though the strike leaders in the navy were 'innocent' of the logic of politics, the ratings and the people could express their will to freedom, risking their own lives despite the fact that most of them had no right to vote in the coming month. The Congress and the League were not on the scene.

The firing which started at 9.00 a.m. ceased completely by 5.30 p.m. In the evening, the NCSC issued an appeal to the political parties and the people for support:

> . . . following the example of the brothers in RIAF (the strike of the Royal Indian Air Force which preceded the RIN strike) we decided to go on strike. For the last five days we have been on a peaceful, disciplined, organised strike.
>
> The authorities, however, have refused to listen to us. Instead, they have called up the Military, particularly British troops, since naturally they could not trust our Indian Army brothers. They opened fire on us in Castle Barracks and forced us to take to arms to defend ourselves. . . .
>
> We appeal to you all, particularly to the leaders of the Congress, League and Communist Parties:
>
> Use all might to prevent a blood bath in Bombay!
>
> Force the Naval Authorities to stop shooting and threats and to negotiate with us!

Rally our people to support us, through a peaceful hartal and peaceful strikes!
We appeal to you, our brothers and sisters, to respond.
We await your reply.[137]

B.C. Dutt, one of the NCSC who wrote about the exchange of the feelings between the people and the ratings, makes no reference to this appeal of 21 February. Instead, he says that, at the moment when the reaction of the people was overwhelmingly in favour of the ratings, the strike leaders felt somewhat discredited in the eyes of the bulk of the ratings, because 'it was we who had talked of involving the national leaders. The ratings had followed us hopefully. That hope had turned into a mirage'.[138] If this was the fact, was the appeal only a shout in the wilderness? Dutt emphasized that none of the political parties were amongst the ratings, nor did they try to contact them.[139] The problem thus is how we should observe the process from the navy strike to the general strike in Bombay on 22 February. What was the role of the Communist Party which supported the demands of the naval ratings? It seems that careful analysis of the whole process is still awaited.

On 22 February the Communist Party called for a general strike, and appealed to all parties and people to observe the day as a complete *hartal* in all shops, schools, colleges and mills as a mark of disapproval of Government repression and to demand the immediate cessation of repression, the opening of negotiations and the satisfaction of the just demands of the strikers.

The same day newspapers carried the statement of Patel that there should be no attempt to call for a *hartal* or stoppage of mills or closing of schools and colleges. All possible efforts were being made by the Congress to redress the genuine grievances of the naval ratings. He asked the people to maintain strict discipline and to do nothing to disturb the peace in the city.[140] He said, 'The Congress has a big party in the Central Assembly and is doing its best to help them.'

Patel did not say that the Congress was in the midst of the Provincial Elections, but it is evident from this statement that the elections to the Provincial Assemblies and the negotiations with the British Cabinet Mission immediately after the elections were the most imminent task that the Congress had to fulfil.

On the same day, Colville received calls from I.I. Chundrigar (President of Pakistan, October-December 1957), President of the Bombay Provincial Muslim League and S.K. Patil (Minister of the

Government of India 1957-67 including the post of Food and Agriculture 1959-63), Secretary of the Bombay Provincial Congress Committee, both of whom assured him of their anxiety to stop the disturbances, and offered the help of volunteers to assist the police.[141] By now the aloofness of the Congress and the League from the strike became a reality.

Early the next day the Governor of Bombay sent the following telegram to the Viceroy:

> . . . situation appears well in hand. Mutineers mainly contained in barracks but some are in possession of several small ships which are covered by fortress guns.
>
> City has remained calm so far with little reaction except some natural alarm in area close to docks. Congress officially disowns participation in mutiny but left wing elements and Communists are trying to work up sympathy and there may be some trouble with mill hands and transport workers.[142]

In the afternoon, the Intelligence Bureau sent the following situation report:

> Last night the Communists using vans with loud-speakers etc., called for a hartal throughout Bombay; for all mills and schools etc., to close, and transport not to run. In the early hours of this morning the hooligan element started looting and burning shops. This morning only seven were working and a few more were working partially, but by 2.30 p.m. all mills were closed except for three working partially. The G.I.P. and B.B.C.I. Railway workshops have also closed down. Buses and trains have stopped running. Local trains are still running. During the morning the same type of trouble spread throughout the city and before midday four military columns which included armoured cars were sent to assist the police in dealing with the city disturbances. The situation in the whole centre of the island is extremely serious.
>
> At 1 p.m. a meeting of R.I.N. personnel observed breaking up on the Mole at the dockyard where some R.I.N. ships are alongside. About midday crowds of sympathisers with the R.I.N. ratings started disturbances in the Fort area. Rioting has never occurred there before. Europeans were assaulted and their cars burnt. This was especially bad on Hornby Road. Two armoured cars which were clearing up riotous mobs fired over their heads. The situation can only be described as grave as the disturbances are so widespread.[143]

This also confirms that the Congress was against the *hartal*, but the Communist call for sympathy with the R.I.N. ratings had won the day and the Congress Labour Union had been totally ineffective.

It is noteworthy that the telegram which reached New Delhi in the evening made an interesting analysis of the *hartal*:

Today hartal organised by Communists and students in spite of official Congress advice to the contrary. ROWDY crowds have burnt numbers of tramway and police CHOWKIES, smashed windows and committed other acts of HOOLIGANISM. Mills are on strike due to communist influence but *mill areas are so far quiet except for obstruction to train lines. Disturbances principally in business and shopping areas.* Banks closed at mid-day. (italics mine)[144]

Colville's report which was sent later on 27 February, also writes how serious a situation the police and military had to face in the centre of the city:

A *hartal* was organised by Communists and students, and hooligan elements ready to join in whenever trouble appears combined to make a very different situation for the police in several quarters of the city simultaneously. Almost all the mills came out, and looting and burning was widespread. The police had to open fire, and called on the military for assistance. A battalion went to their help at about 11.30 a.m. and by the evening two battalions were deployed. At a number of places the mob offered determined resistance, erecting road blocks and covering them from nearby buildings; any one who tried to clear the road block was stoned. Business in the European quarters of the city was affected, and banks were closed at midday. The trouble moved to the congested area in the centre of the Island, and, to a lesser extent, to the mill area of the north.[145]

Colville adds that 23 February was 'a day of considerable rioting and violence, particularly in the mill area in the northern part of the city'.

But the Communist reports emphasize that repression took the form of controlling the working class movement from the start, not curbing 'hooliganism' though they also admitted that some anti-social elements took advantage of the situation. S.A. Dange, a member of the Central Committee of the Communist Party of India and a candidate for the Bombay Provincial Assembly, made his statement on 25 February. He saw the scenes of food arriving for the naval ratings on 21 February and himself addressed a workers' meeting the next day. He explained that the exchange of shots at Castle Barracks showed the threat of the government to crush the naval strike, and that panic had seized the Fort area. In this situation some anti-social elements broke open and looted some shops. But this took place twelve hours before the *hartal* had started. Criticizing the indiscriminate shooting by the police and the military, he continued,

In the working-class areas the Military shot in all directions. We have got evidence to show that the men sitting in their houses, chawls and shops fell victims to this orgy of shooting. In one shooting in Lal Baug alone, our comrades picked up nearly fifty people and removed them to the hospital. Fifteen to twenty had died on the spot.

It is sheer dishonesty to justify this shooting as merely a consequence of 'hooliganism' on the part of the people. . . .

The mass-shootings mostly took place in working-class areas. This fact must be noticed. For this was an area which was particularly free form breaking open of shops and looting etc. No shops were looted or broken open in this area. Some tram stands were burnt, but that was done only after the brutal firing had started. . . .

No doubt in some parts anti-social elements took advantage of the situation to loot shops and carry on incendiarism against the people. This will be strongly condemned by all. But the main and dominant reality of the 22nd and after, was not the anti-social hooliganism, but the political demonstration, often resulting in pitched battles between the people and the Military. To describe it as hooliganism is to put an end to all political activities.[146]

Dange said at the press conference that those who were lying in the hospitals comprised Hindus and Muslims, 'touchables' and 'untouchables', men from Madanpura, Bhendi Bazar and Shivaji Park, in fact the whole of Bombay. 'Never had Bombay seen such a united demonstration of all communities.' 'Bird's-Eye View' in the *People's Age* also discussed the situation on 23 February and pointed out that the main storm centre was now in the Muslim localities.[147]

The movement of protest against the offensive attitudes of the Government and the military authorities covered the broadest classes of the people who came from the various parts of Bombay. Particularly in the worker's area, the Government took pains to deal with the situation. On 24 February the following report was sent from the C.I.O., Bombay:

. . . by Saturday (23rd) evening some of the previously troublesome areas, for instance Bhendi Bazar, were comparatively quiet, although the situation was extremely difficult to deal with in the more thickly populated labour areas on the northern edge of the city.

Up to midnight on Saturday reported hospital figures were 187 dead. . . .

All sections of the riff-raff of the city have been taking part in the disturbances. The Communists made capital out of the occasion by their early backing of the R.I.N. Mutineers. Two Communist women have been shot, one killed and the other wounded. This tends to show that they have been taking an active part. . . .

The night was quieter with fewer incidents. The situation is easier today. A sign of improvement is that this morning fifteen mills are open, four fully and eleven partially. . . . The looting of approved Government cloth shops was a new development yesterday evening. Kamatpina and Kala Chowki areas, where looting has been very serious, are predominantly populated by mill workers from Satara district most of whom have been taking part, and it is probable that Ninth Augusters have been inciting them to continue the disturbances. It is reported but not confirmed that violent mobs have been of such mill workers as well as Communists.[148]

It is generally believed that the workers in Bombay did not respond actively to the call for Quit India in August 1942 under the strong influence of the CPI which adopted the People's War policy. On the occasion of the sympathy strike on 22 February 1946, they earnestly supported it. To what extent 'Ninth Augusters' from Satara led the movement awaits analysis in future, but it is true that here in Bombay the spirit of Satara was alive. In this sense, it may be said that the workers in Bombay did express in their own way a call to Quit India. How the workers interpreted the meaning of the Provincial Elections in which S.A. Dange and other labour leaders stood as candidates should also be clarified, because it was this matter that forced both the Congress and the League to advise the stoppage of the naval strike and the worker's strike.

On the day when the general strike paralysed Bombay, a conversation took place over the telephone between Sardar Vallabhbhai Patel and Maulana Abul Kalam Azad. Naturally we suppose that the talk must have centered around the strike in Bombay. But in his letter the next day, Patel vented his anger on Azad in connection with the nominations and the election campaign. He wrote to Azad:

In continuation of our telephonic conversation yesterday, I feel bound to make it clear that the nomination of Sjt Pandey (C.P.) is nothing but an unexpected letting down of the Central Board and a total disregard of ordinary courtesy. If you wanted to change the decision, you should have at least consulted us... your action has lowered our prestige in the eyes of the people of that province.... They were informed that there will be no change. I had not the slightest idea that they will come to you and get a reversal of the Board's decision.... If you had taken all the power alone and disposed of all the nominations, nobody would have been more glad than myself....

From your conversation on the phone, I also understood that my coming to Lahore is likely to embarrass you and that I should rather not go there. But for Maulana Daud's invitation to go there, I would not have agreed to do so, particularly in my present state of health. In Sind also, I went there because a special messenger came to call me simultaneously when another came to Delhi to call you.

. . . But I feel from your conversation that I have lost confidence and therefore you don't want me to go there. . . .

In view of your attitude I propose to immediately tender my resignation from the Central Board as well as the Working Committee.[149]

Patel's anger was not appeased even in his letter to Azad on 6 March.[150] It is to be noted that Patel expressed his anger over the phone on the evening of 22 February, when he sent his message to the naval ratings through M.S. Khan, President, NCSC, in which he advised them to lay down arms and to go through the formality of surrender as 'the Congress will do its level best to see that there is no victimisation and the legitimate demands of the naval ratings are accepted as soon as possible'.[151] Patel was on the spot in Bombay, listening to the voices of the naval strikers while solving the complex problems of nominations in the elections. This means that the surrender of the ratings and the smooth working of the elections were matters of life and death for Patel and the Congress. At this critical moment, he was greatly irritated by the 'arbitrary' attitudes of Azad towards him in the nomination and the election campaign.

As for the response of the Congress towards the Mutiny, it was Patel's judgement which was virtually the Party's final decision. Gandhi supported it, and dismissed the general strike since he saw it as the joint violence of Hindus and Muslims at the barricades. Patel did not want Nehru to rush to Bombay, but when he arrived, Nehru ridiculed the 'seven hour gun battle' at Castle Barracks as 'more or less harmless gunfire' and criticized the barricade fights as 'eighteenth century methods of revolution'.[152] The enthusiasm of the people had not been directed into the 'proper channel'.

It was the message of Patel that decided the later course of the naval strike so long as the strike leaders sought and followed the opinions of the Congress leaders. In the evening of 22 February, M.S. Khan read Patel's message at the meeting of the ratings after he came back from his contacts with Patel and Chundrigar. At this meeting, Khan said, 'I am of opinion that, having received this assurance, we should now surrender and lay down our arms. . . . Do not think that we are surrendering to the British. We are surrendering to the people, because the whole nation is with us.'

According to Banerjee, Muslims among the ratings thereupon asked whether Khan had met the League leaders and added, 'We don't want to put ourselves in the hands of one party. We at least want an assurance from the Muslim League before we give up.'[153] Khan told them that Chundrigar had expressed his regret, saying the he was unable to give any assurance unless he got a directive from the League High Command. He was not in a position to take any initiative and kept aloof from the strike. B.C. Dutt recollects that this enquiry by the Muslim ratings was 'nothing more than the immediate reaction of people in trouble to look to co-religionists in a time of crisis'. He says that it did not in any way constitute a communal turn of the type prevalent in Indian public life of the time.[154] Nevertheless, it is also true that the idea of the League had exerted some influence on the Muslim ratings, though there may be differences in the interpretation of its extent. This is why the message of Jinnah brought by a rating on the early morning of 23 February was decisive in finally closing the naval strike. Jinnah's message confirms the fact that he basically believed in the 'constitutional' means both immediately after the First World War and after the Second World War:

> No civilised Government or responsible man in this country can treat their feelings and grievances lightly.
>
> I offer my services unreservedly for the cause of the RIN men to see that justice is done to them. If they will adopt *constitutional, lawful and peaceful* methods and apprise me fully of what will satisfy them, I give them my assurance that I shall do my best to see that their grievances are redressed.
>
> I appeal to all RIN men not to play into the hands of those who want to create trouble and exploit those on strike for their own ends. . . . I, therefore, appeal to the men of the RIN and to the ratings to call off the strike and to the public in general not to add to the difficulties of the situation. Particularly, I call upon the Muslims to stop and to create no further trouble until we are in a position to handle this very serious situation. (italics mine)[155]

This call had a special message for the Muslims.

The naval strike came to an end with a message of the ratings to the people that for the first time the blood of men of the armed services and of civilians on the streets flowed together in a common cause. It is now known that the draft of this message was prepared by Mohan Kumaramangalam, a Communist.[156]

On 25 February Colville's Secretary sent a telegram to the Viceroy's office:

> Bombay had a quiet day, and no incidents have been reported. His Excellency toured the affected parts again.
>
> No further telegram will be sent from this Office on this subject unless the situation deteriorates.[157]

Colville's report of 27 February mentioned earlier estimated that the civilian casualties to date amounted to 228 killed, and 1,046 injured while 24 police officers and 67 men were injured, and 3 constables were killed.

The following is an appeal in the bill prepared by the Congress for the election campaign in Bombay:

> Quit India—
> was the battle cry—
> Let us not forget the perils
> Millions have shared—
> the price they paid for Freedom
> the danger they dared—the brave men
> and women whose battle cry was
> Quit India—
> Quit India is again the battle cry—
> Onwards, soldiers onwards—
> Speed up the job—
> the call has come
> Who will not answer it?
> It is a mighty vision before us.
> Let it not fade—[158]

It is not clear when this was distributed. But at the end of the bill appeared 'Vote for Congress—Vote for the Freedom of India'. If the elections were the battle cry for Quit India, what did the Naval Strike mean to the Congress?

After the end of the Second World War, the provision of voting rights for the members of the armed services had been one of the main concerns on Nehru's mind. It is noteworthy that he said in October 1945:

> For some time past I have been receiving complaints from persons serving in the army and allied defence services to the effect that *facilities for voting at the coming elections were not being given to them*. I understand that the Viceroy gave an assurance some time ago that these facilities would be given. But complaints continue and servicemen demand for themselves in India and overseas the same facilities as were given to British servicemen for enrolment as voters, for free propaganda, and approach to political parties and for voting. They complain that many authorities are ignoring their representations for enrolment on voter's lists. The Congress fully supports this demand.

> It is improper and unfair to deprive our men in the Army, the Navy and the Air Force of their right of citizenship. (italics mine)[159]

Nehru correctly understood the meaning of the restriction on the voting rights of the persons in the defence services under the Government of India Act, 1935. On 24 October 1945, the Indian Franchise Act, 1945, was passed to make temporary provision for the inclusion in electoral rolls in India of persons who had returned from war service, to relax residence qualifications for these persons and to extend certain Indian franchise qualifications which depend on service in His Majesty's Forces or on the award of a pension.[160] Under this Act, in case a person satisfied a residence qualification but for his absence on war service, that qualification was treated as satisfied.

But there was no change in the fact that the naval ratings in Bombay were not provided their franchise. For instance, besides the residential qualification, an elector for the Bombay Legislative Assembly was required to fulfil another condition. The qualification by reason of service in His Majesty's forces meant 'being a retired, pensioned or discharged member of His Majesty's naval, military or air forces.'[161]

The Congress asked the ratings to surrender as the party was doing its best to help them. The League asked them to adopt *constitutional* methods. However, most of the ratings were in their teens.[162] Those who reached twenty-one years were not provided their franchise. In fact, no political leaders advised them to express their will by means of the 'ballots instead of the bullet'. What kind of *constitutional* methods were available when they had no right to vote?

In this sense, the Royal Indian Navy Strike represented the 'Mutiny' of the people who had no right to vote. Although there is a view that the strike was limited in its scale and impact, there is no doubt that it brought to light the limited character of the Provincial Elections of 1946.

NOTES

1. Zaidi, op. cit., pp. 398-9.
2. Ibid., pp. 401-2.
3. Gail Omvedt, 'The Satara *Prati Sarkar*', Gyanendra Pandey (ed.), *The Indian Nation in 1942*, Calcutta, 1988, p. 260.
4. Ibid., p. 241.
5. Ibid., pp. 247-8.
6. D.G. Tendulkar, *Mahatma—Life of Mohandas Karamchand Gandhi*, Vol. 6, Delhi, 1962, p. 252.
7. Ibid., p. 270.

8. Omvedt, op. cit., p. 251.
9. *Extract from Bombay Weekly Letter No. 22,* dated 2 June 1945, MSA.
10. Ibid., No. 30, dated 28 July 1945.
11. Ibid., No. 31, dated 4 August 1945.
12. Omvedt, op. cit., p. 254.
13. *Weekly Confidential Report for the week ending Aug. 24, 1945,* MSA.
14. Ibid., 30 August 1945.
15. *Extract from the B.S.A. for the week ending Sept. 1, 1945,* MSA.
16. *Weekly Confidential Report for the week ending March 14, 1946,* Satara District, MSA.
17. *Confidential Letter*, DSP, Satara to DM, Satara, 4 May 1946, MSA.
18. D.D. Kosambi, *Exasperating Essays—Exercises in the dialectical Mathod,* Poona, 1957(?), p. 18.
19. Nehru, op. cit., p. 85.
20. Nehru to Patel, 31 October 1945, ibid., p. 114.
21. Nehru to Menon, 3 September 1945, ibid., p. 80.
22. Patel to Nehru, 4 November 1945, Das, op. cit., p. 68.
23. Patel to Azad, 1 January 1946, ibid., p. 49.
24. Nehru, op. cit., p. 213.
25. Nehru to Cripps, 27 Jeanuary 1946, ibid., p. 141.
26. P.N. Chopra, *Quit India Movement,* New Delhi, 1987, p. 13.
27. Ibid., p. 21.
28. *Report for the first half of September 1945,* Bombay, NAI.
29. *Report for the second half of September 1945,* Bombay, NAI.
30. *Report for the first half of October 1945,* Bombay, NAI.
31. *Report for the second half of October 1945,* Bombay, NAI.
32. *Report on the event in Bihar during the first half of July 1945,* NAI.
33. *Report on the event in Bihar during the second half of July 1945,* NAI.
34. G.P. Singh (ed.), *Sardar Patel—The Working of His Mind,* Delhi, 1949, p. 39.
35. *Report on the event in Bihar during the second half of September 1945,* NAI.
36. T.G. Rutherford to R.F. Mudie, 26 Setpember 1945, *Home Dept. Poll (I), File No. 101/45,* NAI.
37. R. Tottenham to All Provincial Governments and Chief Commissioners, 12 October 1945, ibid.
38. Nehru, op. cit., p. 218.
39. Ibid., p. 226.
40. Sucheta Mahajan, 'Post-War National Upsurge', in Bipan Chandra *et al.* (eds.), *India's Struggle for Independence 1857-1947,* New Delhi, 1988, pp. 474-5.
41. Moon, op. cit., p. 178.
42. *TOP,* Vol. 6, pp. 451-4.
43. Ibid., p. 452.
44. Nehru to Menon, date unknown, Nehru, op. cit., pp. 96-7.

45. *Sardar Patel's Correspondence 1945-1950,* Vol. 5, Ahmedabad, 1975, p. 325 cited by Gyanendra Pandey, op. cit., p. 15.
46. Sir Francis Tuker, *While Memory Serves*, London, 1950, pp. 63-4.
47. Sumit Sarkar, 'Popular Movements and National Leadership 1945-47', *Economic and Political Weekly*, Annual Number, April 1982.
48. Tuker, op. cit., p. 54.
49. Ibid., p. 70.
50. Nehru, op. cit., p. 331.
51. Zaidi, op. cit., p. 405.
52. Nehru to Azad, 31 October 1945, Nehru, op. cit., p. 115.
53. Ibid., p. 208.
54. Ibid., p. 173.
55. Nehru to Menon, 2 December 1945, ibid., p. 359.
56. Ibid., p. 367.
57. *TOP*, Vol. 6, pp. 512-15.
58. Ibid., p. 514.
59. Tuker, op. cit., pp. 64-6.
60. Ibid., pp. 58-9.
61. Nehru, op. cit., p. 195.
62. Gautam Chattopadhyay, 'Post-War Upsurge in India (1945-46)', in Jagannath Sarkar *et al.* (eds.), *India's Freedom Struggle—Several Streams*, New Delhi, 1986, pp. 220-4.
63. Ibid., p. 221.
64. Ibid., p. 223.
65. Patel to Nehru, 24 Novmeber 1945, Das, op. cit., p. 79.
66. Nehru to Menon, 2 December 1945, Nehru, op. cit., pp. 358-9.
67. Sarkar *et al.*, op. cit., p. 221.
68. Nehru, op. cit., p. 366.
69. Ibid., p. 253.
70. Zaidi, op. cit., p. 489.
71. Ibid., p. 493.
72. *People's Age*, 23 December 1945.
73. Renu Chakravarty, *Communists in Indian Women's Movement,* New Delhi, 1980, p. 97.
74. *TOP*, Vol. 6, p. 501.
75. Ibid., pp. 535-6.
76. Ibid., p. 531.
77. Auchinleck to Wavell, 24 November 1945, ibid., pp. 530-4.
78. Ibid., p. 583.
79. Auchinleck to Wavell, 26 November 1945, ibid., p. 545.
80. Casey to Wavell, 2 January 1946, ibid., p. 726.
81. Ibid., p. 577.
82. Wavell to Pethick-Lawrence, 5 December 1945, ibid., pp. 602-3.

83. Wavell to Pethick-Lawrence, 27 November 1945, ibid., p. 553.
84. Casey to Wavell, 2 January 1946, ibid., pp. 724-5.
85. Wavell to Pethick-Lawrence, 1 December 1945, ibid., pp. 586-8.
86. Moti Ram (ed.), *Two Historic Trials in Red Fort*, Delhi, n.d., p. 303.
87. Ibid., p. 305.
88. Wavell to Pethick-Lawrence, 6 January 1946, *TOP*, Vol. 6, p. 740.
89. Hallett to Wavell, 19 November 1945, ibid., p. 507.
90. Omvedt, op. cit., pp. 250-1.
91. E.W.R. Lumby, *The Transfer of Power in India 1945-7*, London, 1954, pp. 68-9.
92. *Home Political (I)—51/2/46*, NAI.
93. *TOP*, Vol., 6. p. 539.
94. K.K. Ghosh, *The Indian National Army—The Second Front of the Indian Independence Movement*, Meerut, 1969, pp. 202, 220-1.
95. Gautam Chattopadhyay, op. cit., pp. 224-7.
96. *Home Poll (I)—5/22/1946*, NAI.
97. Nikhil Chakravarty, 'Calcutta Students' Demonstration Grows into Big Tide of Hindu-Muslim, Anti-Imperialist Unity', *People's Age*, 24 February 1946.
98. Tuker, op. cit., pp. 101-2.
99. Bipan Chandra *et al.*, op. cit., p. 20.
100. Nehru, op. cit., p. 91.
101. *Home Poll (I)—5/22/1946*, NAI.
102. Casey to Wavell, Telegram, 13 February 1946, ibid.
103. Chakravarty, op. cit.
104. Ibid.
105. *Home Poll (I)*—5/22/1946, NAI.
106. Ibid.
107. Ibid.
108. Chakravarty, op. cit.
109. Tuker, op. cit., p. 100.
110. Das, op. cit., p. 387.
111. Casey to Wavell, Telegram, 14 February 1946, *Home Poll (I)—5/22/1946*, NAI.
112. *TOP*, Vol. 6, pp. 1034-5.
113. B.C. Dutt, *Mutiny of the Innocents*, Bombay, 1971, p. 72.
114. Ibid., pp. 76-7.
115. Ibid., p. 111.
116. Subrata Banerjee, *The R.I.N. Strike*, New Delhi, 1981, p. xii and p. xiv.
117. Ibid., p. 14.
118. Ibid., pp. 18-19.
119. Dutt, op. cit., p. 79.
120. Banerjee, op. cit., p. 10.

121. Ibid., p. 18.
122. Ibid., pp. 21-2.
123. Dutt, op. cit., pp. 132-4.
124. HQ108 (Bombay) Area to SOUTHCOM, 19 February 1946, *F. No. 5/21/46—POLL (I)—1946*, NAI.
125. Bose, op. cit., pp. 101-2.
126. Cf. note 112.
127. V.P. Menon, *The Transfer of Power in India*, Princeton, 1957, p. 234.
128. Colville to Wavell, 27 February 1946, *TOP*, Vol. 6, p. 1080.
129. Banerjee, op. cit., p. 31.
130. Dutt, op. cit., p. 143.
131. Secraphone Message received from Rodger, C.I.O., Bombay, 21 February 1946, *F. No. 5/21/46—POLL (I)—1946*, NAI.
132. Director of Intelligence, *Situation Report No. 2*, 21 February 1946, NAI.
133. Colville to Wavell, 27 February 1946, *TOP*, Vol. 6, p. 1081.
134. Dutt, op. cit., p. 159.
135. Ibid., pp. 156-7.
136. Ibid., pp. 147-8.
137. Banerjee, op. cit., pp. 59-60.
138. Dutt, op. cit., pp. 165-6.
139. Ibid., pp. 146-7.
140. Banerjee, op. cit., pp. 62-3.
141. Colville to Wavell, 27 February 1946, *TOP*, Vol. 6, p. 1082.
142. Colville to Wavell, Telegram, 22 February 1946, *F. No. 5/21/46—Poll (I)—1946*, NAI.
143. Intelligence Bureau, *Situation in Bombay*, ibid.
144. Bombay Special, Bombay to Homein, New Delhi, Telegram, 22 February 1946, ibid.
145. Colville to Luavell, 27 February 1946, *TOP*, Vol. 6, p. 1082.
146. 'S.A. Dange's Press Conference on Bombay Hartal—Indiscriminate Military Shooting', *People's Age*, 3 March 1946.
147. 'Bombay's three Days of Heroic Battle—Bird's Eye View', ibid.
148. Secraphone Call from Rodger, C.I.O., Bombay, received on 24 February 1946, *5/21/46—POLL (I)—1946*, NAI.
149. Patel to Azad, 23 February 1946, Das, op. cit., pp. 59-60.
150. Patel to Azad, 6 March 1946, ibid., pp. 63-5.
151. Banerjee, op. cit. pp. 67-8.
152. G. Adhikari, 'Where are the Congress, League leaders taking us?—Ignoble Surrender or Joint Struggle?' *People's Age*, 10 March 1946.
153. Banerjee, op. cit., p. 68.
154. Dutt, op. cit., p. 178.
155. Ibid., pp. 182-4, and Banerjee, op. cit., pp. 71-2.
156. Banerjee, op. cit., p. xiii.

157. Governor's Secretary, Bombay to PSV., New Delhi, 25 February 1946, *5/21/46—POLL (I)—1946*, NAI.
158. *File No. 5/1945-1946*, AICC Papers, NMML.
159. Nehru, op. cit., p. 212.
160. For the full text of the Act, see Appendix I.
161. N.C. Narasimha Acharya, *A Manual of Elections in India—Being an up-to-date and comprehensive Study of Franchise and its exercise*, Bombay, 1946, p. 79.
162. Bishwanath Bose, *Rin Mutiny: 1946 (Reference and Guide for All)*, New Delhi, 1988, p. xx.

III

The 1946 Provincial Elections

Elections and Political Parties

At its meeting in September 1945 the AICC resolved that a manifesto containing the policy and programme of the Congress should be prepared by the Working Committee and placed before it for consideration and adoption at a subsequent meeting.[1] But the resolution indicated that, in the event of the election for the Central Assembly taking place before the AICC meeting, the Working Committee might issue a brief manifesto for the election, leaving the principal manifesto for the Provincial Elections. In fact, a draft manifesto for the Central Assembly Election was prepared by Nehru, and sent to Patel on 10 October. Changes were made by Gandhi and the manifesto appeared in the newspapers on 27 October. At the stage of preparation of the draft, Nehru anticipated that the Muslim League would avoid mentioning any of the country's problems and would harp on Pakistan in its manifesto. He also thought it quite probable that the League would not issue any manifesto at all.[2]

In December 1945 the Congress Working Committee issued another election manifesto for the Provincial Elections without giving a chance to the larger body to comment on it.[3] Many parts of the earlier manifesto remained in this version. Here we will concentrate on the later document.[4]

According to the manifesto the Congress 'envisaged a free democratic state with the fundamental rights and liberties of all its citizens guaranteed in the constitution. This constitution, in its view, should be a federal one with autonomy for its constituent units, and its legislative organs elected under universal adult franchise'.

In connection with the constitutional structure of the State, three points should be noted. First, the later manifesto specifically clarified the federal structure. 'The federation of India must be a willing union of its various parts. In order to give the maximum of freedom to the constituent units there may be a minimum list of common and essential federal subjects which will apply to all units, and a further optional list of common subjects which may be accepted by such units as desire to do so.'

Second, this manifesto, while stating that the Congress stood for the unity of all communities and religious groups and for tolerance and goodwill between them, emphasized that the state should observe 'neutrality in regard to all religions'.

Third, it provided that the State would help in the development of the people of the tribal areas in a manner most suited to their genius, and in the education and social and economic progress of the *scheduled classes*.

The Congress reminded the people of the relevance of the 'Quit India' resolution of 1942 and stressed that 'in these elections, petty issues do not count nor do individuals, nor sectarian cries—only one thing counts: the freedom and independence of our motherland, from which all other freedoms will flow to our people'. The leading principles of the Constitution of India were already written in this manifesto.

In the field of economic policy both manifestos confirm that the most vital and urgent problem was to remove the curse of poverty and raise the standard of the masses. But the manifesto prepared for the Provincial Elections specified the Congress policy in more concrete terms. In its industrial policy, the Congress proposed that the State must own resources, railways, waterways, shipping and other means of public transportation to prevent the concentration of wealth and power in the vested interests. Most remarkable was its land policy because, the Congress ministries once formed had to tackle it immediately. (Actually after the elections these Congress provincial governments prepared the *zamindari* abolition and similar bills in various parts of India).

> The reform of the land system, which is so urgently needed in India, involves the removal of intermediaries between the peasant and the state. The right of such intermediaries should therefore be acquired on payment of equitable compensation. While individualist farming or peasant proprietorship should continue, progressive agriculture as well as the creation of new social values and incentives require some system of co-operative farming suited to Indian conditions. Any such change can, however, be made only with the goodwill and agreement of the peasantry concerned. It is desirable, therefore, that experimental co-operative farms should be organised with State help in

various parts of India. There should also be large State farms for demonstrative and experimental purposes.[5]

The removal of intermediaries between the peasant and the state, on payment of compensation, was officially declared in the Congress document. Simultaneously, the reference to cooperative farming later reappeared in a resolution adopted at the annual session of the Congress held in Nagpur in 1959. We can thus observe the impact of the idea of socialism in India in the 1930s.

At a public meeting in Calcutta Nehru criticized the lack of a League manifesto:

The Hindu Mahasabha is hardly a force to be counted, as has been seen in the Central Assembly elections. There can be no truck with the Muslim League, which is a reactionary body, and which has always opposed the Congress struggle for freedom. Have you ever heard of any manifesto of the Muslim League? It has only one thing to say—Pakistan. It is impossible for it to issue any other manifesto. It can only frighten our Muslim countrymen by raising the false cry of danger to Islam. It never talks of industrial labour, food or agricultural distress. The leadership of the League is dominated by landlords and aristocrats.[6]

Nehru emphatically repeated that the League had no economic and social programmes, and even referred to the meaning of the appearance of the atomic bomb to refute the idea of Pakistan. He said in Karachi,

Old ideas and thoughts have gone. The atom bomb has revolutionalised the outlook of the people. No country can be strong unless it is large and powerful and has resources to make itself self-independent. The withdrawal of foreign rule by itself will not make India a strong nation. It has to develop its resources after becoming free. It may take years before India will be powerful in the modern sense of the term.

Division of India is neither economically nor politically a sound proposition. The Muslim League has mentioned Pakistan as its goal. It has not defined its economic or social objectives. . . . The Muslim League is not a fighting organisation. It is an electioneering body with Pakistan as its election cry. If India should be strong, it should prevent internal conflict within its units.[7]

When the Second World War ended, Nehru said at a press interview, 'There are many ominous signs, not the least being the atomic bomb, which indicate the disastrous way that modern civilization is following. No sensitive individual can view this prospect without dismay.'[8] But, as the days passed, he seems to have inclined to think there were alternatives, destruction of this world or construction of a new world. In Allahabad in 1946, he declared,

> If the atomic energy behind the atom bomb is utilised for constructive power, it will very much develop the entire structure of the world. The world is bound to change within the coming few years and I hope that atomic energy will be used in constructive power to uplift mankind.[9]

At that stage Nehru was basically optimistic about the possibility of science, and envisaged India in future as a strong modern State that would adopt the socialist way of economic reconstruction 'with the goodwill and agreement' of the people. From this view of a 'modern state', the idea of Pakistan had to be refuted. This does not mean that Nehru did not take the challenge of the League seriously. Already after the AICC meeting in Bombay, Nehru wrote to Menon, 'The Hindu Mahasabha and the Ambedkarites do not count for much in the long run. The Muslim League of course counts.'[10]

Nehru's criticism of the League and its lack of manifesto led to his condemnation of the Communist Party of India which 'supported' the Muslim League and its Pakistan demand. For instance, Nehru said in the public meeting in Calcutta cited earlier,

> The Congress has not turned out the Communists. When they have openly opposed the Congress and even set up candidates against the Congress how can we take them into executive positions? Their leader (P.C. Joshi) has replied to the Congress statement in an insulting way. Every week their papers abuse the Congress. There are many fine young men in this party, but they do not think for themselves. When the Congress leaders were arrested and the people rose in revolt, the Communists acted in a manner which was anti-national. The Communists now support the Muslim League and their Pakistan demand. The leadership of the League is a reactionary one. How can a revolutionary party attach itself to the reactionary Muslim League? It passes my comprehension. The League is openly opposing India's freedom, yet the Communists associate themselves with it. I urge the kisans and the mazdoors (workers) to realise the harm the Communist Party is doing to the country.[11]

This is one of the main reasons why we will now take up for discussion some cases of the elections for separate seats, contested between the Congress and the League, and elections for the general rural seats and special labour seats which were contested between the Congress and the Communist Party of India.

The Muslim League did not publish its own election manifesto, and there is no sign that its Working Committee took any important policy decision during its election campaign. Though the League adopted *constitutional, lawful and peaceful* methods during this period and Jinnah still had to face the serious challenge from various quarters on the provincial level, Jinnah's speech took the place of a manifesto. It was imperative for the League to connect the complex and antagonizing demands of the broadest social classes and strata among Muslims under the slogan of Pakistan. Jinnah told the Muslims of the North-West Frontier Province that every vote in favour of the Muslim League candidate would be a vote for Pakistan. Every vote against the League meant Hindu Raj. 'That is the only choice and only issue before us.'[12]

Within this framework, Jinnah sometimes revealed his idea of Pakistan though it did not yet have the formal approval of the League organization. In his interview with the representative of the Associated Press of America in November 1945, he clarified that geographically Pakistan would embrace all of the North-West Frontier, Baluchistan, Sind and the Punjab in the north-west and Bengal and Assam in the east. Politically Pakistan was planned as a Muslim State and a democracy which would oppose one party rule.[13] The component states or provinces of Pakistan would have autonomy, but economically, Pakistan, divided into two separate zones, was just as sound an undertaking as if it were a country with all its states in one contiguous area. Essential key industries would be controlled and managed by the State.

Jinnah was conscious of the Congress view that the League was only composed of the upper strata of the society.[14] He said that it was the common people who were behind the Muslim League, though an earnest change-over on the part of any Muslim was welcome.[15]

So far as industrial policy was concerned, there seemed little difference between the League (or Jinnah) and the Congress though Jinnah was not as insistent about the nationalization of key industries.

Very often Jinnah emphasized that the Muslim League wanted to fight the forthcoming elections constitutionally and lawfully and that the League wanted a verdict by means of free and fair elections.[16] This position was fully utilized by Jinnah to advise the naval ratings to surrender in February 1946. He knew the crucial importance of the elections of 1946. As he said at the meeting of the Frontier League, 'Elections are the beginning of the end. If the Muslims decide to stand for Pakistan in the coming elections, half the battle would have been won. If we fail in the first phase of our war, we shall be finished.'[17]

This was more than mere rhetoric. It had to be proved

constitutionally in these elections that the League was the only representative organization of the Muslims in India. Recent historical studies in India positively appreciate that the Congress adopted both constitutional and extra-constitutional methods in its struggle for freedom, and in the later stages, took its constitutional approach from its understanding of Indo-British ralations.[18] Yet it was Jinnah who correctly understood the 'constitutionalism' on which the British and the Congress leadership staked their destiny. The lack of an election manifesto at the central level of the League came from this strategy.

On the provincial level, there were efforts to publish a League election manifesto. In its manifesto the Bihar Provincial Muslim League intended to promise the nationalization of key industries, mines and banks, promotion of cooperative methods in farming, in the sale of agricultural products and in purchase of seed, manure and other necessities and also an original draft containing clauses for the abolition of the *zamindari* system and for guaranteeing full Trade Union rights and adequate minimum wages to workers. But this had to be dropped by pressure from the 'reactionaries'.[19] The *People's Age* explains that only those issues which related to the nationalization of key industries, mines, banks, were retained as the feudal reactionaries were not directly affected by these promises. This paper also adds that the manifesto was silent on the demands of weavers who formed a major section of poor Muslims in Bihar. The Communists expressed their dissatisfaction with the fact that the 'progressives' like Jafar Imam (member of the Bihar Provincial Muslim League Parliamentary Board) who was well-known for his progressive and democratic view had abandoned the fight for a popular democratic programme.

According to the explanation of the same correspondent, some 'reactionary elements' were even working to shelve the manifesto altogether and prevent its publication. These elements said that the All-India League leadership did not want any such manifesto to be issued by the provincial units and that this was proved by the fact that the central leadership had themselves not issued one. It is not clear whether this manifesto of the Bihar Provincial Muslim League was even published, but this episode tells us how seriously the slogan of the *only issue,* i.e. *Pakistan* affected the activities of the Provincial League in the province which was not demanded as a part of Pakistan, and almost killed the initiative from 'progressives' that the Communists were expecting.

As for the Bengal Provincial Muslim League, Harun-or-Rashid analyses that on the eve of the Provincial Elections the League emerged as a kind of Bengal Muslim nationalist movement and that even the poor peasants and day-labourers came to take an active part in organizing the League.

> the poor Muslims began to consider the League as their own organization. Indeed, on the eve of the Assembly elections the BPML had emerged as some kind of Bengal Muslim nationalist movement. The Muslim students formed 'the vanguard of the army of voluntary workers' of the League in the elections. Whereas in 1937 they remained divided between the KPP (Krishak Praja Party) and the League Parliamentary Board, in 1946 they were united under the banner of the All Bengal Muslim Students League—the only organised student body with 75 sub-divisional branches. The League workers also included the Muslim National Guards, a special volunteer force. During the elections, the Jamiat-i-Ulema-i-Bangla, a pro-League ulema organisation, took an active part in support of the League.[20]

He further explains that, though the Hashim-Suhrawardy group most probably envisaged two independent states of Pakistan in the north-east and the north-west of India, the Bengal League leaders urged the voters to vote on the issue of Pakistan without reference to this ideal. For the election issue was either Muslim independence through partition or Akhand (undivided) Hindustan.[21] In other words, the closure of discussion on the details contributed to Muslim unity. But this made it difficult for the Bengal leaders to present their own ideas, if any, immediately after the elections as the proceedings of the convention of the League legislators in April 1946 were to show.

In the election campaign of the Bengal League, slogans such as 'Abolish Zamindari without compensation' and 'Land Belongs to the Plough' were heard.[22] In this connection, we should recollect the destiny of the draft manifesto of the Bengal Muslim League, prepared by its 'progressives' (one that was not, however, specially drafted for the elections). This manifesto was not placed before the Working Committee of the Bengal League, but directly *before the people*. When it was published on 24 March 1945, Suhrawardy questioned the authority of Abul Hashim to publish it and demanded disciplinary action against him.[23] It was not possible even for 'progressives' like Abul Hashim to make their political and economic ideas a part of the programmes of the Provincial League.

On the other hand, the Muslim League in the Punjab, another key province for the scheme of Pakistan, was the organization which the

Communists expected to be the force 'fighting for the day-to-day demands of the people'. Romesh Chandra, a Communist leader, highly appreciated the manifesto of the Punjab Muslim League which appeared on 8 November 1944 as 'a charter of rights' for the working class and the peasantry.[24] Later, he was to write how the Punjab League, which parted with the Unionists in 1944, grew to be a political force with a membership of one lakh. According to his review, most of the city Leagues had grown in one year from the later half of 1944, taking up the day-do-day demands of the people such as the problems of food, clothes, sugar and kerosene. He also mentioned that the League was actively concerned with the demands of the workers.[25] He said that the Muslim League in the Punjab took up the demands of the hosiery and textile workers as well as the demands of the municipal sweepers in Ludhiana, and that every member of the Khewra Salt Miner's Union, Jhelum, joined the Muslim League under the leadership of Haji Dost Mohammad, himself a miner. He added that a Joint Secretary of the Amritsar District League organized the Weavers' Union with a membership of 5,000. Also, the League in the Central Punjab tried to study the problems of the Kammins, village artisans. In Lahore District, there were fifty-nine Primary Committees and a whole group of 'well-trained Muslim Kisan Congressmen' joined the League to help fight police repression. Besides, the League in Jalandhar and Hoshiarpur was ready to cooperate with the Kisan Sabha and agitate for the Doaba Canal.

Romesh Chandra concluded that the Punjab League manifesto had opened the doors of the League to every *progressive* Muslim. The entry of Mian Iftikhar-ud-din into the League can be understood in this framework of analysis.

Simultaneously, Romesh Chandra had nevertheless to admit that the League had no activities among the peasantry, the 'largest and most-oppressed section' in west Punjab. This was the 'biggest weakness' in the Punjab League, and there was no mention of their demands in the League Manifesto. He wrote that in the awakening of the tenants would lie the true path forward for the League and the only true hope for the freedom of every section of the people of the Punjab.

It needs careful investigation to confirm whether or not Romesh Chandra's analysis depicted the position of the Punjab League correctly. Meanwhile it may be true that it was the reflection of changes occurring in the Punjab League. At the same time it should be asked why Romesh Chandra did not explain that the Muslim League, not the Communist Party of India which claimed to be a party of workers and peasants, could succeed in penetrating Muslim workers and peasants.

The manifesto was drafted with the help of a Communist, but it is another matter whether it could work in an election in which League candidates like Feroz Khan Noon (who had just left Government Service) or many landlord politicians (who had left the Unionist Party only recently) were the League candidates. During the Second World War, the League strengthened its activities in the rural areas, criticizing the Unionist Government's unpopular policy for military recruitment and the requisitioning of foodgrains. Students toured the rural areas exploiting war-time discontent. In May 1945, membership of the Punjab League is said to have reached 150,000. Mian Mumtaz Daultana and Shaukat Hayat, landlord politicians who left the Unionist Party and joined the League, contributed to the growth of the League in the countryside during the latest phase of the War.[26] Under these circumstances the slogan of Pakistan and the anti-Unionist stance could be unifying factors.

The Communist Party of India published its election policy or 'blueprint of election programme' under the name of P.C. Joshi in the *People's War* on 14 October 1945.[27]

This stated that the policy was not to expose the Congress and the League but popularize among the electorate a vision of Free India that would ensure freedom to all and would not become the domination of some over the others. Two basic principles were established. One was a constitution-making body based on universal adult franchise. The other was based on the Communist view of the national self-determination. The constituents of the constitution-making body should be the sovereign Constituent Assemblies of Pathanland, Baluchistan, Sind, Muslim Western Punjab, Sikh homelands of Central Punjab, Hindustan, Bihar, Rajasthan, Assam, Orissa, Andhra, Tamilnadu, Kerala, Karnatak, Maharashtra, Gujarat and Bengal with previous agreement of plebiscite of Hindu and Muslim areas.

According to the statement, this was the only democratic solution of Congress-League differences and met the just demands of both, because it met the essence of the League demand for Pakistan by giving sovereign rights to Muslim homelands while repudiating the 'unjust claim' of some leading Leagues to the whole of the Punjab or to Assam. Also, the Congress was told that it met the Congress objection that they could not agree to the League claims without the verdict of the people. There was a possibility that the leaders of the Sikhs and Muslims might preserve the unity of the Punjab by coming to an agreement among themselves, while the entire people of Bengal could decide through a prior plebiscite whether they would preserve the unity of their homeland or split. However, the CPI was convinced that the majority of the delegates to the Constituent Assemblies based on universal adult franchise would not only guard the freedom of their own homeland but voluntarily agree to set up a *common Indian Union* for defending and advancing common interests.

The Communist theory of homelands and national self-determination was voiced with conviction. Within this framework even the partition of the Punjab or Bengal was approved. In the case of Punjab there was the probability of it being divided into three parts according to 'national' or communal factors. We will separately examine the Communist theory of 'Sikh homeland'. But there was distance and discontinuity between their faith in the full application of the principle of self-determination and their optimistic expectation of a common Indian Union under the post-War situation.

Though the Communists were full of conviction in presenting their ideas and devoted most of their statement to this theme, the problems of daily lives of the people were not closely analysed. They proposed the idea of a People's State but did not explain it in detail. The demands of the Communist Party for the abolition of landlordism and the nationalization of land with large-scale cooperative farming were theoretical rather than based on an analysis of the prevailing situation. Above all, this policy statement did not anticipate that the 'national' upsurge of the freedom movement and the organized or spontaneous movements of workers, peasants and other sections of the people would play such a crucial part in the destiny of the subcontinent.

The demand for universal adult franchise was clear, but it was not clear whether the Communist participation in the elections on limited franchise would affect the realization of the original policy or how the interests of the disenfranchised section could be guarded.

Later in December 1945, the Central Committee of the Communist Party revised its view. Its new resolution said that the strategy of the Party would now aim for a new United National Front in the form of a Congress-League-Communist joint front and to represent the freedom and unity urge of the common people behind the two great organizations, Congress and League, despite the prevailing sectarian policies of their leadership.[28] Anti-Communist steps taken by the Congress leadership and the cold rebuff of the League leaders to the theory of national self-determination had forced them to revise policy. The Communist Party was now distinguishing the masses supporting the Congress and League from their leaders.

The change of view was clearly shown in the approach to the mass upsurge which had not come into the picture in the earlier blueprint. The resolution of the Central Committee said that the Party must take the foremost lead in organizing not only particular struggles of workers and peasants but also anti-imperialist mass protest actions, and that it must fearlessly intervene and participate in every spontaneous outburst of popular fury against British rule and police terror and thus endow the newly rising spontaneous mass upsurge with a sense of its true direction and effective organizational leadership and prevent the factional game of the Congress and League leadership. The movement against the I.N.A. trial in November 1945 must have been one of the main factors which forced the CPI to revise its policy, and also its attitudes towards the Royal Indian Navy Strike must have been directed by this decision. In this resolution stress was laid more on mass upsurge than the theory of national self-determination, though the Communists still recognized the urge for freedom behind the Pakistan demand.

The Party still stood for a voluntary union of sovereign national states, while guaranteeing the Sikhs their right of self-determination, and providing Bengali Muslims and Hindus the same right. There was no radical change in this aspect.

As for the elections, the Communists stated that the decision to contest the elections was sound, but the party had not grasped the importance of the election battle correctly:

> The Party leadership however notes that the Party membership yet considers the election battle as an organisational battle for its existence and not yet the issue of life and death for the Party as a political force and as leader and organiser in the working class and peasant movements and as the main lever for building the United National Front in the new period.[29]

Though the party clarified that the election was only the first round of the battle, the meaning of participation in elections on limited franchise was not examined. But Communist policy towards the kisan movement was more specific: '. . . strengthen its own Kisan Sabha base by expanding Sabha enrolment both ways from middle-peasant downwards to embrace the entire mass of poor peasants and landless labourers and to bring in the majority of middle-peasants and the best of the rich peasants'.[30]

The main strategic aim of the Party was to isolate even those toady anti-national parasites and profiteers who wore a patriotic mask, and rally the vast majority of the village people from the small zamindars and rich peasants up to the landless 'untouchable labour'. This reference to the small zamindars and rich peasants may be related closely to the Communist strategy of the elections.

But the heated discussion on the character of the Government of India Act, 1935 which was observed in 1936-7 was no longer heard in 1945-6 among either the Congress leadership or the Communists. Despite its demand for the Constituent Assemblies under universal adult franchise, the Communists did not talk much about the serious implication of the limited franchise system except in the first stage of its election campaign.

The Election Campaign

The Congress, and Jawaharlal Nehru in particular, were conscious of the prospects of losing Muslim seats. Nehru wrote to Frances Gunther in January 1946 that there had been no real contest so far as the general seats were concerned. The real contest was over Muslim and certain special seats.[31]

In the first stage of his election campaign Nehru was optimistic because of his conviction of the Congress as the mass organization:

> There is no doubt that as a rule city Muslims are for the League, especially the rougher elements. But it is also clear, especially in the U.P. and Bihar, that the Momins (chiefly weaver class) and the Muslim peasantry are far more for the Congress because they consider the League an upper class organisation of feudal landlords etc. An unknown factor, however, creeps in when God and the Koran are used for election purpose.[32]

Nehru had predicted that in U.P. the Congress and pro-Congress candidates might win 25 Muslim seats at the most, more than one-third of the seats. Though he had some reservations he did not lose his original hope. He wrote to Azad:

> In the Meerut division and elsewhere I have found an extraordinarily favourable response from the Muslim masses. Whether we win these seats or not on this occasion, I have no doubt in my mind that we can win quite a

number of Muslim seats in the Provincial Elections in the U.P. especially in the rural areas. I was surprised to find how popular the Congress was among the Muslim peasantry. In fact the Jamiat (Jamiat-ul-Ulema-i-Hind) did not go far with them, it was the Congress that counted. In the cities, the Jamiat influenced people more. On the whole, however, it was obvious that the Congress counted. It is pretty clear that we have long neglected the Muslim masses. The fault lies with us, not with them.[33]

But Rafi Ahmad Kidwai, Convener of the U.P. Congress Parliamentary Board who contributed to the birth of a Nationalist Muslim Parliamentary Board consisting of the representatives of all non-League Muslim parties in U.P., feared that the Congress and Nationalist Muslim candidates would not fare well in most of the constituencies, largely on account of open official patronage to the League and threats to Muslim peasants.[34] M. Hashim Kidwai, his biographer and one of the founders of the U.P. Nationalist Muslim Students Federation, writes:

Moreover, the malicious League propaganda had done havoc with Muslim masses during the absence of the Congress and Nationalist Muslims in jail and the official patronage of the League had put it in an advantageous position. As such the Nationalist Muslims found themselves greatly handicapped in many ways. Muslim peasants, artisans and working classes had been excluded from the voters' list as they were the vote-banks of the Congress and Nationalist Muslims. Rafi Ahmad succeeded in getting the electoral roll of U.P. revised and thus those who had been excluded were included in it. It was also brought to his notice that the police and the Muslim officials were openly supporting the Muslim League candidates against which he strongly protested.[35]

At least it may be said that the message of Quit India did not have the desired effect on the Muslim peasantry in U.P. In his speech in Kaiserganj, Bahraich District, Nehru appealed to the people, saying that the district should be proud of sending Mr Kidwai, a valiant freedom-fighter, from its constituency and that Mr Kidwai was responsible for enacting the Tenancy Bill for the benefit of kisans.[36]

On the other hand, Chowdhry Khaliq-uz-Zaman, a member of the Central Parliamentary Board of the Muslim League, said in Meerut in the beginning of October 1945 that he was not sorry for the Congress or its leaders for their challenge of the Muslim mass contact. What pained him most was that 'some of us, who are Muslims, are stabbing the Muslim Nation in the back and they are helping the Congress and Hindus to disrupt Muslim solidarity for reasons best known to them'. He asked the Muslim youth not only of Meerut District, but all over India, to go to the villages and educate ignorant Muslims villagers. Chowdhry Khaliq-uz-Zaman apprehended that the Congress would influence the Muslim tenants through Hindu landlords to vote against the League.[37]

Later, on 20 December 1945, Jinnah said that the Central Assembly Election delivered a knock-out blow to those who masqueraded as 'Nationalist Muslims but who were really the henchmen of the Congress'.[38]

Though the Provincial Elections in 1946 were held under limited franchise, the contest for Muslim seats was critical for the controversy over a united India or Pakistan.

The following episode narrated by Riaz-ur-Rahman Kidwai gives an instance of how Nehru, who was secular-minded, was forced to respond to the unfavourable situation:

> After the Second World War fresh elections for the U.P. Assembly were held when Jamil Sahib (Jamil-ur-Rahman Kidwai) stood as a Congress candidate. His rival was Maulana Jamal Mian, a religious leader of local Muslims from the famous institution of Firangi Mahal. . . . Since Jamil Sahib was a candidate against that of Muslim League, he was always on the disadvantage due to religious feeling brought in during the elections. Jamil Sahib refused to accept the services of Muslim Ulemas who were especially sent by All India Congress Committee for meeting Muslim League's communal challenge and to pay their outbursts in their own coin. Even Nehru could not convince him on this strategy. On Panditji's insistence to make use of the Ulema, Jamil Sahib replied that he would not do anything against which he was ideologically opposed and if the voters wanted to elect a person who prayed more than him, they were welcome to do so. He is not going to the Assembly to compete with Moulvis on religious matters.[39]

This aspect of Muslim League politics was noted by the Raja of Mahmudabad, who was once closely associated with Jinnah and whose advocacy of an Islamic State had brought him in conflict with Jinnah.[40] Though he did not specifically refer to the election campaign of the League, the Raja admitted that the League leadership at the top was secular-minded and trained in modern political methods, but at the lower level, and especially among the field workers, propaganda on religious lines was the general practice. The episode shows that even Nehru could not ignore this aspect of the election politics.

Though friction and even physical assaults were reported in the U.P. elections, it was in Bengal that mode of campaigning became the main issue of an open controversy between the Congress and the League.[41] Maulana Azad, Congress President, said in his statement on 4 April 1946 that the elections in Bengal were reduced to a mockery.[42] In his words, they were 'hardly an election in the normally understood meaning of the term. It was more in the name of a crusade in which worst religious passions were excited than an election in the modern age where political parties placed before their constituencies alternate programmes to be carried out through the legislatures.'

Azad pointed out that the League was able to secure the help of the Pirs in order to arouse religious fanaticism on an unprecedented scale. 'Instead of raising or discussing any political issue the elections were turned into a religious crusade. Fatwas were issued that to vote against the League would lead to eternal damnation. Non-League candidates were branded as heretics and infidels and it was stated that their return would lead to the banishment of Islam form India. Verbal exhortation of these Pirs and Moulvis were beyond the Fatwas.'

Along with this criticism Azad remarked that the Government had failed to control violence during the elections and that in many cases officials had openly sided with the League. He mentions various instances of intimidation and violence, and of official interference.

However, Suhrawardy challenged this statement, saying that if there had been any official interference in Bengal, it had been on behalf of the Congress as Muslim officers in position of responsibility were few in Bengal. According to his counter statement, the camp followers of Azad among the Muslims gathered round them a band of *lathials* and ruffians who roamed the country and made Muslim League meetings impossible. It was entirely incorrect to say that the Congress instruction to the Muslims was to practice non-violence.

Suhrawardy retorted, saying that there had not been a single case in which the Muslim League had sought votes or captured any vote by holding up the terror of religious condemnation.

The controversy between the leader of the Congress which confessed it had lost touch with the Muslim masses and the leader of the League which claimed to have become the mass organization of the Bengal Muslims could not proceed on the same grounds. Humayun Kabir later participated in this battle of words. (He had just been defeated by Jyoti Basu, a Communist candidate in the Labour seat).[43]

Humayun Kabir had his doubts about the extraordinarily heavy polling. He said that in most seats in Mymensingh, Noakhali and Dacca, over 60 per cent of the electorate were reported to have excercised their franchise. In some cases the numbers of votes polled represented 80 per cent of the electorate. He argued that with the beginning of the season for cultivation, peasants who constituted over 90 per cent of the voters in the rural areas had hardly any time to catch their breath let alone cast their votes.

He also pointed out the 'constant fanning of religious fanaticism' in addition to the physical obstacles that the League and its supporters placed in the way of its opponents, and to the malpractices on the day of polling:

> Another feature of the present Bengal elections was the constant fanning of religious fanaticism. On behalf of the League it was preached in meetings and through pamphlets that anybody who voted against the League would incur divine displeasure. The effect of such propaganda on the illiterate masses can be easily understood. In many cases, the electors lost their freedom of judgment on account of interference by their religious teachers and threats of divine displeasures and punishment in the afterlife.[44]

It may be true that the Maulvis and Pirs had a decisive role in mobilizing the Muslim peasantry in favour of the League. But it is also true that the Congress and the Krishak Praja Party could not break through the election tactics of the League, which might have depended on the influence of the religious leaders on the masses. The strength of the Krishak Praja Party which was once in power had been gradually eroded during and after the Second World War. However, Humayun Kabir, an independent candidate, attributed the success of the League exclusively to intimidation by the League workers:

> It is true a section of the Muslim middle class has become intensely League-minded but the peasantry who constitute over 90 per cent of the voters are strong supporters of the Krishak-Praja Party. It was only hooliganism, intimidation and threat of Divine displeasure which contributed to the astonishing and suspicious success of the League. Whenever the threat of Divine displeasure and/or League hooliganism was checked, candidates belonging to other camps have been returned. Maulana Shamsul Huda in Mymensingh, himself a religious teacher of standing, came out successful with a thumping majority against the League.

In his conclusion, Humayun Kabir threw doubts about the validity of the elections. He said,

The present Bengal Elections have therefore been a mockery. Real voters have not voted in many cases. False voters have recorded votes without check or hindrance. The real opinion of the people of Bengal has not been expressed. The elections have a strange resemblance to the plebiscites conducted by Hitler, Mussolini and other dictators in both the methods followed and the results achieved.

So far as the abolition of the *zamindari* system was concerned, there were few differences among the official statements of the Congress, League and Krishak Praja Party. Therefore their election campaigns were consciously directed towards the 'Unity of India' or the 'Unity of Muslims'. Jamiat-i-Ulema-i-Banga played an important role in support of the League candidates.[45] Pakistan was expected to remove radically the present difficulties that the Bengali peasants were facing.

Kamruddin Ahmad, who belonged to the 'progressive' group of the Bengal Muslim League recollects his talk with Muzzaffar Ahmad, a Communist and President of the 9th Session of the All-India Kisan Sabha which was held at Netrakona, Mymensingh District, from 5 to 9 April 1945. Explaining why the Communists could not enlarge their influence among the Muslim peasantry, he told Muzaffar Ahmad how deep was the influence of religion on rural Muslim community through *namaz*, Id celebrations and untouchability.[46] The role of the Maulvis in the elections of 1937 was also cited. Muzaffar Ahmad of course did not agree. The slogan of Pakistan attracted the Muslim peasantry whether or not the impact of the words of religious leaders was decisive. Simultaneously, the electoral scene in Bengal showed that the 'constitutional' procedure was not necessarily 'peaceful'. And the majority of the people who have already reached voting age were outside this 'constitutional' drama. If the validity of the elections had to be questioned, first of all this aspect should have been asked.

The controversy on the 'malpractices' in the election campaign was very heated. The *Amrita Bazar Patrika* which continued to condemn the 'gangster tactics of the fanatical adherents of the Muslim League and its leaders' challenged Suhrawardy and said, 'if he is so sure about the immaculate behaviour of Muslim officers and Leaguers, why does he not join with Maulana Azad and Mr Huq in demanding an independent enquiry?'[47] Furthermore, 'Maulana Azad's statement is revealing and we make a present of it to Lord Pethick-Lawrence and the other members of the British Cabinet Mission.'

The present to the British Cabinet Mission was not the statement of Azad, but the election results which the British wanted.

Besides the serious conflict between the Muslim League on the one side, and the Congress and Krishak Praja Party on the other, there were crucial fights between the Congress and the Communists in the elections for the Labour seats.

Moni Singh, a Communist leader of the peasant movement in Bengal who stood as a candidate in Mymensingh District recollects that the middle class generally thought that the Communists supported the British and did not join the Quit India movement: the Congress fought for India's Independence, the Communists for bread and cloth. The fight for Independence took precedence over the fight for bread and cloth in the logic of the Congress. Moni Singh writes that this kind of logic exerted a considerable influence on the people in those areas where there were no organized movements. He admits that during this confrontation a Congress volunteer, Mahendra, a son of a *dhobi* (washerman) working in the house of a zamindar, was killed by a Communist volunteer. He also mentions that on the day of polling Mahendra's mother was forced to go to a polling station to vote 'on behalf of' the woman of the house who generally did not stir outside. Mahendra's mother appeared as a false voter at another polling station too. Moni Singh thought that everything was possible for the realization of class interests.[48]

Jyoti Basu, later Chief Minister of West Bengal, who stood in the Railway Labour constituency against Humayun Kabir, President of the B.A. Railway Employees' Association (who got the support of the Congress leaders like Azad and Aruna Asaf Ali) writes in his memoir that in this election the ballot papers which should have been sent to the voters by registered mail did not reach them and instead were sent to other persons. Then there was a movement for the correct distribution of ballot papers in railway stations, post-offices and other places. He recollects that through the elections of 1946 he came to know that in bourgeois elections there was no meaning for policy: the only purpose of elections was to win by any means (money and violence included).[49]

Officialdom in Bengal reported for the first half of March 1946 that the Communists were recruiting volunteers, 'Red Guards', among workers in the industrial areas. 'Already there have been fights between the partisans of the Congress and the Communists and each party is determined to meet the use of force by its opponent with force'.[50]

The report for the second half of March 1946 noted that on the whole general election for the Bengal Assembly passed off smoothly in most places and produced much less trouble than was apprehended.[51]

This report, however, noted that on the day of polling there were numerous cases of rioting, injury, arson and looting in the elections for Muslim seats. It also added that the contest between the Communists and the Congress for the Labour seats and a few rural seats produced more trouble than the fight between the League and other Muslims. Though Maulana Azad indicated the intimidation and violence on the part of the League, Nikhil Chakravarty also reported that the trouble between the Communists and the Congress was due to a pre-planned terror prepared by the Congress against the workers stretching from their *bustees* right up to the polling stations, in most cases located inside the factories.[52]

Let us consider the case of Howrah where Sibnath Banerji, a Congress candidate, and Bankim Mukherjee, a Communist, contested. According to the official report,

> A major flare-up in Howrah due to the senseless action of some Congress volunteers in attacking a mosque where some Communists had taken shelter was averted by the tact of local officers who persuaded the rival candidates and some Muslim leaders to appear together on the scene and pacify their followers. A Congress youth was killed in this area by a gun-shot fired by an unknown person; another Congress volunteer was murdered by Communists in a rural constituency.[53]

Nikhil Chakravarty's explanation of the same scene is partly the same, but is different in its interpretation of the role of the police. He writes that the Congress launched an offensive on the second day of polling, feeling that the Communists got a good poll on the first day. The Congress Committee in Burra Bazar (Central Calcutta) sent lorry-loads of *lathials*. Congress loud-speakers blared out abuse at the Communists and attacked them as '*dalals* (agents) of Muslims'. There was a communal fight because Muslims were angered, and many Red Flag volunteers were wounded in the melee. But Congress *goondas* pursued them into a nearby *bustee* and looted a number of Muslim huts and even began battering the door of a mosque, injuring those who resisted. This set the whole area aflame. The police fell on the *bustee* folk and the Communist Volunteers, the Congress *lathials* captured the polling station at Dinabandhu Institute and physically debarred everybody from approaching the booth.

All of a sudden, a shot rang out, a man died instantly and was removed to hospital, and another man was wounded in the firing. As the tension mounted, the District Magistrate and Police Superintendent called Bankim Mukherjee, Sibanath Banerji, and the local Muslim League leader, Sharif Khan and appealed for help in controlling the situation. All of them later toured the area, but the District Magistrate did nothing to stop Sibanath's lorries, full of *lathials*, parading the streets. Instead, the police did all they could to extract false 'evidence' from the injured men in hospital, trying to place the blame on the Communists.

However, *The Statesman* which reported on the 'incendiarism' in Calcutta and Howrah concluded that the incidents occurred as a group of workers of different parties (Congress and Communist Party) attempted to lead voters to the polling booths, each claiming them as its supporters. Following the war of words, a clash ensued, in which *lathis*, knives, aerated water bottles and brickbats were freely used.[54]

Concerning the description of the initiative of the officials and the appeal of the political leaders to the people, the official explanation does not differ from the writings of Nikhil Chakravarty. But the latter impressed that the District Magistrate did nothing to disarm the Congress supporters and that the police wanted to put the blame on the Communists. From these scenes before and on the day of the polling, we know how the policy of the Communists on the Quit India movement and Pakistan movement provided the Congress a chance to attack them ideologically and with force of arms. Just as the 'secular-minded' leadership of the League could not control the 'Islamic' factor in their election campaign, so also the Congress leaders who adopted the resolution on 'non-violence' in Calcutta three months earlier could not control the use of violence on the part of their supporters.

In this connection Patel's will to 'demolish' Communist strongholds on the labour front should be recollected. In his letter to V.V. Giri, a labour leader and later President of India (1969-74), Patel remarked that in Madras (including a part of the present-day Kerala and Andhra) the Communists had established a strong foothold and that it had to be demolished.[55] The scuffle in the election for the Labour seat in Calcutta was a part of the rivalry for the hegemony of the all India Labour movement which finally led to the birth of the Indian National Trade Union Congress on the initiative of Patel in May 1947.

The elections of 1946 also eroded the 'friendly' relations between the Muslim League and the Communist Party in Bengal. Hashim writes that he told the Bengal Communist leaders that, if both the League and the Communists contested the Muslim seats, friendly relations would be damaged. Hashim assured then that the League would support the Communists for the Labour seats, but asked them not to contest the Muslim seats. The Communists did not concede and fielded some candidates for the Muslim majority areas where they were convinced of their victory. He concludes that this was the beginning of the deterioration of the League-Communist relations.[56]

We can have a glimpse of the gulf between theory and reality that the Communists were experiencing in the elections through the words of P.C. Joshi who led their election campaign. On 31 January 1946, he addressed a public meeting in Chittagong where Kalpana Dutt, a revolutionary of the Chittagong Armoury Raid in 1930, stood against a Congress woman candidate. He told the people that the Communists respected both the Congress and the League, because they had aroused in the people the spirit of freedom, and appealed that a vote for Kalpana was not a vote against the Congress, nor for Communism, but a vote for Congress-Communist unity, a vote against the British Government. He was at great pains to explain the reason;[57] but was it easy for the people to understand his logic?

> We respect the Congress intensely, for it is the organisation that had fought most for the freedom of our country. We have fought for the same goal inside the Congress and *today, even though outside it,* we are continuing to do so.
>
> . . . While the Congress goes on its own way, the Muslims go out of the Congress more and more. Think how appalling is this tragedy. If Hindus and Muslims go apart, then all talk of freedom is a vain, empty boast. (italics mine)[58]

P.C. Joshi also emphasized that they supported the demand of the Muslim League, because those who were oppressed and poor must have their freedom, but criticized the demand of six provinces of Bengal, Assam, the Frontier, the Punjab, Baluchistan and Sind for Pakistan:

> We say that this is an unjust demand. How could they demand Assam where Muslims form only one-third of the population? How could they deprive the Sikhs of their own freedom when Muslims are only in a minority in their land?
>
> To claim justice for oneself and inflict injustice on others betrays the mentality of the zamindar who tries to grab other people's land: such cannot be the attitude of a true fighter of freedom.[59]

Joshi's speech clearly shows that the theory of 'a Free India as a family of free nationalities' placed special importance on Hindu, Muslim and Sikh communities and their sense of identity. In this respect, his optimistic prediction that the Congress and the League would finally take the right course seemed baseless. There was undoubtedly some truth in his presentation that, unless the Hindu and the Muslim kisans stood together, not a single struggle could be successful against the zamindars. Also there was enthusiastic support for a Communist candidate in some pocket areas like Dinajpur where the Kisan movement had roots among the peasants. The Communist report on the Dinajpur (Bengal) Scheduled Caste Primary Election, for example, gives us some information:

The elections came in the harvesting season, but whole batches of kisans kept away from the fields, busy on election work, going from *hat* (market) to *hat*, village to village. The best-educated among them are barely literate. But they spotted out all the names on the voter's lists, slowly and deliberately spelling out the names and repeating aloud to themselves. . . .

On polling day, the scenes at the booths were symbolic and unforgettable. . . .. There were Rajbansis, the Palias, batches of Santals with their bows and arrows. Batches of women too came to vote. . . . for the first time in history in any noticeable strength.

Slowly, the small bands swelled into a sea of humanity. They walked all the way, from villages 12, 14 or even 18 miles away. They had no food and no money, yet they stuck on to the polling booths all day. Large numbers who had come to vote had to go back disappointed because their names were not on the electoral rolls.

The crowd was so big and the arrangements at the booths so inadequate that many voters waited right up to midnight and still did not get the chance to vote.[60]

This enthusiasm reflects the earnest desire of the *adhiars* or share-croppers for the reform of their conditions. In this connection, it should be examined whether the Communist theory of the Congress-League unity did not affect the strength of the Kisan movement in Bengal.[61] *Tebhaga* (two-third of the crops to the share-croppers) had already been proposed during the Second World War, but actually the Kisan movement started on a large scale only in the autumn of 1946.[62]

Alec Johnson, an Englishmen who visited the small towns and the villages in Bengal during the days of the elections, observed how the situation was heated in small towns:

In England, even at election times, it is sometimes difficult to fill a public hall and party workers complain the people are so apathetic! Yet the comparative excesses of Indian politics are easy enough to understand. India is a subject nation under alien rule. The consciousness of foreign domination colours the whole lives and outlook of the people, its effects are felt on every hand. . . This tremendous latent feeling in India against British rule is particularly captured by Congress with its cry of 'Quit India'. I was in a Bengal town when reports came through of police firing on the students in Calcutta. One could feel the tenseness in the atmosphere, see the little knots of people in the streets and sense the news being passed around in every home. Next day this burst out into protest and demonstrations, even some amount of rioting, against the British raj. There was a 'hartal' all day long when not a shopkeeper took down his shutters or a rickshaw appeared on the streets.[63]

Johnson also noticed the difference in the atmosphere between the town politics essentially dominated by the middle class and the feelings of the villagers:

How different in the villages is all this politics! There the elections seem unreal while the town is in a fever. The peasant feels his immediate oppressors to be the zamindar and the hoarder—Bengalee oppressors. The town student feels that by the British quitting India or by achieving Pakistan all will be solved. How real is this difference between the town and country?[64]

Johnson expected the possibility of the Kisan movement in Bengal. However, the following comment by a Commissioner, though it is similar to the observation of Alec Johnson in its contents, is only cited for the justification of British rule. There was but one step between the observation of this Commissioner in 1946 and the words of the foremost imperialist, Lord Curzon, who could claim that he represented the voice of the 'silent' peasants in the later part of the nineteenth century and the beginning of this century:

Commenting on the general attitude of the rural population towards elections, one Commissioner remarks, 'I am sure that what excitement and heat there has been for the most part artificially whipped up and engineered; but for the aggressive attitude and efforts of Muslim League and Congress volunteers the amount of interest actively shown in the elections everywhere outside municipal areas would be so little that one would have judged the electorate as being apathetic in this matter. This feeling is confirmed by the observations of certain touring officers to the effect that the ordinary villager still feels very little interest in politics and that he is much more interested in the problems of obtaining for himself and his family two reasonably good meals a day and two cloths each for their bodies.'[65]

In another key province, Punjab, the Congress was still faction-ridden and could not rise beyond middle class interests as it lacked a basis in rural Punjab, particularly among the Muslims, on the eve of the Provincial Elections. This despite the campaign for officers and men of the Indian National Army, many of whom came from the Punjab.[66] The Nawab of Mamdot, President of the Punjab Provincial Muslim League, characterized the leadership of the Congress in the Punjab as 'reactionary', and was more hopeful about the 'progressive' sections in the Sikh and Jat parties in September 1945.[67]

For the Punjab League, it was the Unionist Party and not the Congress which was the main opponent in the contests for the Muslim seats.[68] The League propagated its own 'anti-imperialist' image in a big way against the Unionist Ministry under Khizr Hayat Khan supported by the Punjab Governor, Glancy and his bureaucracy. Already in the War years the Punjab Muslim League had strengthened its activities in the rural areas and attacked the unpopular policy of the military recruitment and the requisitioning of foodgrains adopted by the Unionist Government. Students toured the rural areas, exploiting the wartime discontent. Primary League branches were established in various parts of the Punjab. We have already noted that the membership of the Punjab League was said to have reached 150,000 though Mian Mumtaz Daultana and Shaukat Hayat Khan, its leaders, were landlord politicians who left the Unionist Party and joined the League.[69]

In this situation, Feroz Khan Noon, a bureaucrat turned Muslim Leaguer, thought it his mission to pit himself against the bureaucracy to prove his *bona fides*. He said in Rawalpindi that it was in fact the bureaucracy that was fighting the Muslim League in the Punjab under the mask of the so-called the Unionist Party.[70]

On the eve of elections in the Punjab, the *Dawn* appealed to the Muslims and said that in the Punjab elections a war was on between the Muslim freedom-fighters and a British Misgovernor bent on keeping Punjab tied to the chariot wheels of British Imperialism.[71]

This 'anti-Imperialist' image of the Punjab League led the Communists to welcome the Leaguers in their mass organizations. For instance, Romesh Chandra wrote a report of the annual session of the Punjab Kisan Sabha in a village named Jia Bugga, Lahore District, on 29 and 30 September 1945.[72] In this report he proudly announced that this was the first Provincial Kisan Conference in the Punjab in which the League workers participated as delegates, and joined the Congress and Communist kisan workers in preparation for the conference. Mian Mumtaz Daultana, General Secretary of the Punjab League, attended the meeting on the first day and left this message: 'The Muslim League stands for self-determination of all nationalities. We fight for the Sikh's right of self-determination with as much zeal as for our own.' This report placed hope on the appearance of new League workers:

> Themselves leaders of the district, with a proud record of service in the kisan movement, *these workers of Punjab's new Muslim League have taken the message of Pakistan deep among the peasant masses.* But, the message they teach is not one which separates the Muslim kisans from his Sikh and Hindu brothers, but on the contrary, unites him with them. (italics mine)[73]

This shows how League activities penetrated even into the kisan movement under the leadership of the All-India Kisan Sabha with the support of the Communists, although careful investigation is required as to what extent the League took up the day-to-day demands of the Muslim peasants. It should also be clarified whether the election campaign of the League did not contribute to the separation of the Muslim peasants from other peasants. It seems that the rout of the Communists in the Provincial Elections of the Punjab was mainly caused by their incorrect judgement of the situation.

In fact, though *Dawn*, the paper created by Jinnah, carried detailed reports on Mian Iftikhar-ud-din and his resignation from the Congress membership, his 'spirited' speech as a Muslim Leaguer and his victory in the Provincial Elections, it did not discuss the Communist idea of 'national' self-determination.[74] Jinnah himself was very cautious about the Communist influence. For instance, finding that in the training camp in Bagwanpura, Lahore, Communists like Hamid Hashmi, Abdullah Malik, and Daneil Latifi were included among the trainers for the League workers, Jinnah was worried and advised that the League should impart its own training.[75]

Above all, Iftikhar-ud-din was well aware of the social classes who supported the League. Replying to critics that the League was a body of Nawabs and Khan Bahadurs, he answered that this was correct. But he added, 'What about the Congress of some 50 years back. The Congress was founded by the Knights and Government men.' And, he said, 'the Muslim League is still passing through that stage. We are not ashamed of it. A time will come when our leadership will pass into the hands of the masses. Even today the Muslim League is more progressive than the Congress. The latter is a friend of British Imperialism, while the former is being considered as the enemy No. 1.'[76] Here is a mixture of correct observation and his image of the League of his own making, even while he considered that the League was not led by the masses.

As is well-known, G. Adhikari submitted his report on the resolution, *On Pakistan and National Unity* before the enlarged Plenum of the Central Committee of the Communist Party of India in September 1942, and approved the 'right of self-determination' of the 'Muslim nationality of Western Punjab' while he stressed that Sikhs and Hindus in the eastern districts of the Punjab could easily come to a settlement with the Muslims of the western districts, on the basis of self-determination and guarantee of cultural rights. But at this stage stress was more on 'a united autonomous Punjab, with the right to secede from the rest of India'.[77]

Punjab was the area where the Communist theory of national self-determination was tested in history; the theory of 'Muslim nationality' forced the Communists to reconsider the position of Sikhs in the Punjab. In December 1945, the CPI published a special policy statement which clarified the Communist solution for a free Sikh homeland in a free India.[78] This plan had three parts: separation of the Hindustani-speaking zone of the Punjab consisting of the Himalayan states and Ambala Division with necessary adjustments; creation of a Punjabi-speaking Central Punjab State with Amritsar as its capital; and demarcation of western Punjab with all the Muslim-majority districts, and Lahore as its capital. In the central Punjab the Sikhs and Hindus together made up 65 per cent of the population and most of the Sikh population in the Punjab would be included here. It would give the Sikhs an autonomous province. Also, the demarcation of the western Punjab would guarantee self-determination to the Muslims there. There would be two separate Constituent assemblies, and Central Punjab was to be free to join either Pakistan, *remain an independent state,* or join the Hindustan Union as its Constituent Assembly decided. But the Communists still thought that the road was open to reunite the Punjabi-speaking Punjab on the basis of autonomy to Sikh homelands, and of fraternal relations between the Muslims, Hindus and Sikhs so that Punjab's common people may build a democratic and happy Punjab bereft of landlordism and profiteering capitalists.

The Communists reappraisal of their own theory in the context of the growth of the Pakistan movement, the partial Congress-Akali Pact for seat readjustment, and the results in the Sikh seats of the Central Assembly Elections seemed to have led them more and more to the theory of Sikh homelands to overcome their isolated position. But this policy only endangered their scope for their own independent mass movement, without expanding their expected support.

In the present work the problem of election funds has not been examined, but I wish to point out that the letters exchanged between Jinnah and M.A.H. Ispahani, and also between Patel and Azad showed that the elections needed colossal amounts of money.

Before concluding, a few words about the response of the people and the leaders of the Indian states to the Provincial Elections of 1946.

Many of the political leaders of the Princely States were carefully following the election campaign and the election results in the neighbouring provinces and were even ready to support the Congress, the League or other political forces.

The report from the Mysore Residency claimed that some of the leaders of the Mysore State Congress including K.T. Bashyam intended to help the election campaign in British India, particularly in the areas of Karnataka.[79] The same report also notes that the Mysore State Muslim League issued an appeal to the effect that although these questions did not directly affect the state, the Muslims in the state should support the League's demand for Pakistan and help its candidates in the British Indian elections. Later, the official report confirmed that Bashyam visited Cannanore (Madras Presidency) to inaugurate the election campaign.[80] In Jaipur, it was reported that collections were being made for the election fund of the All-India Muslim League.[81] In Kashmir, people were watching the rising election fever in the neighbouring provinces, Punjab and the North-West Frontier Provinces.[82]

There was also a move for an All-India Convention of the members of the States legislatures (who were also members of the All India States' Peoples' Conference) and of the representatives of the states which had no legislative bodies for the purpose of discussing the position in the future constitution of India.[83] This move must have been promoted by the Provincial Elections of 1946. The mutual influence between political developments in the Princely States and in British India and the integrating process thus encouraged, is an important theme which is unfortunately not examined here.

Polling and Polling Stations

Here the technical side of the Provincial Assembly Elections will be investigated, taking up the case of Bihar.

The Indian Christian, Labour and University rolls which were freshly prepared were published by 10 January 1946, and the lists of amendments in respect of all other rolls of the Assembly by 27 December 1945. Electoral rolls and lists of amendments were prepared in English and 'the vernacular'.

The total electorate for the Bihar Assembly was 2,844,171, representing about 7.8 per cent of the total population of Bihar enumerated in the 1941 Census. Scheduled caste electors in the fifteen reserved constituencies were 68,015 in 1942. The amendment of rolls increased their number by only six, which appears strange. While the number of electors in Women's (Urban) constituencies increased from 41,883 in 1942 to 44,553 as a result of the amendment of the rolls, the total number of women electors in the General and Muhammadan electoral rolls was 359,987 (13.1 per cent of the total electorate). The meaning of this percentage also must be examined. The total labour electorate was 58,347 including 2,326 women.[84]

Primary elections were held in December 1945 in the fifteen General rural constituencies of the Assembly in which seats were reserved for the members of the scheduled castes. This was for the purpose of electing a panel of four candidates for each reserved seat by the votes of the scheduled caste electors. Actually a poll at the primary election did not arise in any constituency, because, in seven of them only one qualified candidate was nominated and declared elected unopposed and in one constituency three, and in each of the seven remaining constituencies, two qualified candidates were nominated and were at once declared to have been duly elected to the panel to be selected finally by the 'General' electors including the scheduled caste voters. The Election Officer admitted that the expectation of the 'Poona Pact' of 1932 which stuck to the joint electorate system while giving consideration to the wishes of the scheduled castes, did not seem to have been realized.[85]

Votes were recorded by post in only two constituencies of the Legislative Assembly, namely the Indian Christian and the Bihar Chamber of Commerce. Votes were recorded at polling stations in the General, Muhammadan, Women's, 'Landholders' and Labour constituencies.

The number and location of the various polling stations and booths were determined at the time of the preparation of the electoral rolls in 1941-2 in connection with the General, Muhammadan, Women's and Landholders' constituencies. It is to be noted here that preparations for elections continued even during the War days. There were in all 475 polling stations and 657 polling booths. In rural areas nearly all the polling stations were located at police stations, while in urban areas district and subdivisional court buildings, sub-registry offices, district board and municipal offices, etc., were commonly used for this purpose. The polling stations and booths for the Labour constituencies were selected at the time of the preparation of the new rolls. They were all located at police stations except at Monghyr Town Hall and another at Jamalpur municipal office.[86]

In the Patna City Muhammadan Urban constituency special polling booths were provided for all women voters, and staffed exclusively by women, except for inspecting officers and police constables, no males were allowed inside. As a result a good deal of confusion and congestion occurred at most of these polling booths; and the lady presiding officers and their assistants had a most strenuous task in conducting the poll. At most of the urban polling stations and at a few rural polling stations a lady assistant presiding officer was appointed to give advice and help to women voters.[87]

At most polling stations the polling was spread over eight days, including two days on which no voting took place. All Government offices and courts were closed for the eight days covered by the polls, except in four districts. Schools and colleges also remained closed. This shows how big an event the elections were despite the restricted franchise system.

All the ballot papers are printed on yellow paper, except those for use in the special Women's constituencies which are printed on pink paper.

The method of voting was as follows: On entering the enclosure the voter went first to the table of the polling officer, who ascertained his/her name in the electoral roll. In case the voter had been provided with a slip containing his/her number on the roll by an election agent, there was no problem. If the voter had no such slip, the polling officer had to ask for the name and address and then search for it in the roll.

If the voter was entitled to vote, the polling officer handed him/her a ballot paper and directed him/her to proceed with it to the presiding officer's table. There the polling officer read out his/her electoral number, name and address, and the official stamp was impressed on the back of the ballot paper by the presiding officer.

The voter then proceeded into the polling compartment and placed his ballot paper in the box of the candidate for whom he/she desired to vote.

In the polling stations at Patna City, Muzaffarpur town and Bhagalpur town votes were recorded simultaneously for two different constituencies, that is, the special Women's constituency and the ordinary urban constituency. At such polling stations each voter was given one pink ballot paper and one yellow paper. The polling booths at these polling stations was divided into two sub-booths.[88]

The Election Officer, Bihar, reports that 53.9 per cent of the registered electors recorded valid votes. The percentage of male voters was 58.3 per cent. It would have been a little higher but for the fact that in several constituencies one of the rival candidates announced his withdrawal from the contest, with the result that the poll in such constituencies was comparatively small.

The total number of women voters in the Assembly Elections was 48,436, which represents only 22.5 per cent of the registered women electors in the contested constituencies. The percentage of women voters was highest in Patna Women's General urban constituency which returned a woman member, and here 69.3 per cent of the registered electors went to the polls. In the remaining three women's constituencies the members were returned without any contest. In other urban areas the percentage of women voters was 60, the Muhammadan figure being distinctly lower than the General. But in the rural constituencies only about 1 woman in 9 went to the poll for the General seats, and only about 1 woman in 7 went for the Muhammadan seats.[89] Though these statistics are rarely recollected, they are one of the decisive factors that conditioned the character of constitution-making in India. It was the role of women that led the well-known peasant *satyagraha* under the leadership of Jadunandan Sharma in the village Reora in 1939 to remarkable success. We cannot have a complete picture of the peasant movement in Bihar of the 1930s without referring to the participation by women. This under-current within the people's movement also contributed to the making of modern Bihar even as women were deprived of their voting rights under various political and social compulsions.

The Election Officer of Bihar felt satisfied to report that throughout the province polling on the whole was carried out successfully and with a minimum of disturbance. There was no serious breakdown in the arrangements anywhere. Nevertheless, he had to add that the atmosphere was tense almost everywhere.[90] Tension at Laheriasarai polling station in the Tiruhut Division Muhammadan urban constituency was particularly serious, and the continuous presence of the District Magistrate and other senior officials was necessary in order to keep the situation under control. Special vigilance was also called for in South Sadr, Monghyr and Khunti General rural constituencies. Serious disturbances occurred at the Subdivisional Officer's court building and the Victoria Memorial Hall polling stations in Bihar Sharif on the first day of the poll. Bihar Sharif, Patna District, was the area where a communal riot had raged in 1941. And, in eight months after the Provincial Elections of 1946, north Bihar was again in the grip of communal disturbances. At this point we must ask ourselves whether the elections promoted the worsening of the communal relations or not. Also in Bihar the constitutional process was not necessarily a peaceful process.

In the elections, numerous cases of deliberate impersonation were reported from various polling stations. One Returning Officer reported that women were produced in veil to impersonate women electors and that in one case the same women impersonated several, one after another, by changing *saris* on every occasion. Many Presiding Officers complained about the difficulty experienced in the identification of female voters. The Election Officer felt it difficult to find a quick solution to this problem:

> One of them (Presiding officers) suggests that the presence of a female polling officer at the polling booth may help to remove the difficulty to a certain extent. The remedy suggested seems impracticable because it will not be easy to find so many suitable female polling officers. It is also not likely to serve the purpose. The fact is that the *pardah* and the poll go ill together. A candidate or a candidate's agent had the indefensible right of challenging the identity of an elector: he cannot possibly do so unless he can see her face.[91]

The Returning Officer, North-East Palamau General Constituency, reported that only 37 female electors excercised their franchise though lady Presiding Officers were provided in most of the booths to facilitate the casting of vote by them.[92]

In Motihari Sadr, voters arrived in long processions with well decorated elephants, camels and band parties, etc. But the Sub-Divisional Officer wrote that the interest taken by female voters was negligible.[93]

The Sub-Divisional Officer, Khunti, who reported on the constituency where Jaipal Singh, the leader of the Chota Nagpur Adivasi Mahasabha was a candidate wrote that at the Bundu polling booth two women bowed low before the Congress box and prayed for the victory of Gandhiji and also prayed that rain should be sent to avoid famine.[94]

Despite the facts that the Government officers provided, it must be noted that the history of Bihar, or the history of the women in Bihar, was not limited to the sphere of constitutional history though the latter played a crucial part in deciding the destiny of the people there..

The Fortnightly Reports from almost all provinces joined the same chorus, singing the peaceful end of the constitutional ritual:

> In spite of some gloomy predictions the Provincial Elections have passed off without any serious clashes or widespread acts of violence. (North-West Frontier Province)[95]
>
> The elections concluded without any serious incident and with fewer disturbances than had been anticipated. (Punjab)[96]
>
> The elections in the General and Indian Christian Constituencies which were held on the 11th and 15th instant passed off peacefully. (Bombay)[97]
>
> Polling in many constituencies except Labour ones was dull. . . . (Madras)[98]
>
> On the whole elections passed off more peaceful than was originally apprehended. (Bihar)[99]
>
> Polling for the Orissa Legislative Assembly took place between the 4th and 9th April. There were contests in nineteen constituencies. There was a good deal of excitement in some of these constituencies, but in the majority the election was a dull affair. (Orissa)[100]

The report on Bengal was not an exception as we have already seen, though it referred to a violent confrontation between the Congress and the League, and also between the Congress and the Communist Party.

At least, the British Government found the way to a 'peaceful transfer of power' and now, 'constitutionally', could shift responsibility for Congress-League conflicts to the Indian side.

However, it was an ominous sign that the report on U.P. had to add that 'with mounting communal unrest, threatened food shortage, discontent among labour, unrest spreading to the police and other bodies of public servants and a general under current of anarchy the new Ministry is faced with the problems as difficult as, if not more difficult than, the province has ever known.'[101]

NOTES

1. Zaidi, op. cit., p. 409.
2. Nehru, op. cit., p. 104.
3. Zaidi, op. cit., p. 488.
4. For the text of the Election Manifestos for the Central Assembly, Nehru, op. cit., pp. 105-9, and for the Provincial Assemblies, Pattabhi Sitaramayya, *The History of the Indian National Congress*, Vol. 2 (1935-1947), Bombay, 1947, Appendix, pp. i-v.
5. Sitaramayya, op. cit. Appendix, pp. iii-iv.
6. Nehru, op. cit., p. 259.
7. Ibid., p. 320.
8. Ibid., p. 445.
9. Ibid., p. 231.
10. Nehru to Menon, date unknown, ibid., p. 96.
11. Ibid., p. 259.
12. Jamil ud Din Ahmad, op. cit., p. 247.
13. Ibid., pp. 230-3.
14. Ibid., p. 267.
15. Ibid., p. 202.
16. Ibid., p. 226.
17. Ibid., p. 242.
18. Bipan Chandra *et al.*, op. cit., pp. 25-6.
19. 'Nationalisation of Industries, but not Abolition of Zamindari!', *People's Age*, 30 December 1945.
21. Harun-or-Rashid, op. cit., p. 215.
21. Ibid., pp. 216-17.
22. Ibid., p. 222.
23. Hasim, op. cit., p. 80.
24. Romesh Chandra, 'Punjab League Manifesto Confounds Khizar-Chhoturam Combine', *People's War*, 19 November 1944.
25. Romesh Chandra, 'One Year's Growth of League in Punjab', *People's War*, 17 June 1945.
26. Talbot, op. cit., p. 18.
27. This election policy is reproduced in T.G. Jacob (ed.), *National Question in India—CPI Documents 1942-47*, New Delhi, 1988, pp. 106-18.
28. Ibid., pp. 159-78.
29. Ibid., p. 165.
30. Ibid., p. 174.
31. Nehru to Frances Gunther, 12 January 1946, Nehru, op. cit., p. 135.
32. Nehru to Menon, date unknown, ibid., pp. 96-7.
33. Nehru to Azad, 27 November 1945, ibid., p. 124.
34. M. Hashim Kidwai, op. cit., p. 108.
35. Ibid., pp. 108-9.

36. Nehru, op. cit., p. 239.
37. *Dawn*, 7 October 1945.
38. Ibid., 21 December 1945.
39. Riaz-ur-Rahman Kidwai, *Biographical Sketch of Kidwais of Avadh—with Special Reference to Barabanki Families*, Aligarh, 1987, pp. 100-1.
40. Raja of Mahmudabad, 'Some Memories', in C.H. Philips and Mary Doreen Wainwright (eds.), *The Partition of India—Policies and Perspectives 1935-1947*, Cambridge, 1970, p. 389.
41. As for the controversy concerning the elections in Bengal, and particularly the statement of Humayun Kabir which appeared in the *Amrita Bazar Patrika*, I could get the useful information from an unpublished Ph.D. dissertation written by Sachhidananda Banerjee, 'M.A. Jinnah and Muslim League Politics in Bengal' (1936-1947), Jadavpur University, 1988.
42. *Amrita Bazar Patrika*, 5 April 1946.
43. Ibid., 14 April 1946.
44. Ibid.
45. Harun-or-Rashid, op. cit., pp. 215, 227.
46. Kamruddin Ahmad, *Banglar Madyavitter Atmavikash*, Khand 2, Dhaka, 1382 (Bengal Calender), pp. 48-9.
47. *Amrita Bazar Patrika*, 6 and 8 April 1946.
48. Moni Singh, *Jiban Sangram*, Dhaka, 1983, pp. 73-4.
49. Jyoti Basu, *Janaganer Sange*, Calcutta, 1986, pp. 25-7.
50. *Secret Report on the Political Situation in Bengal for the first half of March 1946*, NAI.
51. *Secret Report on the Political Situation in Bengal for the second half of March 1946*, NAI.
52. Nikhil Chakravarty, 'Planned Terror against Working Class', *People's Age*, 7 April 1946.
53. *Secret Report on the Political Situation in Bengal for the Second Half of March 1946*, NAI.
54. *The Statesman*, 25 March 1946.
55. Patel to Giri, 2 March 1946, Das, op. cit., p. 232.
56. Hasim, op. cit., pp. 101-2.
57. 'For Hindu-Muslim Unity to fight New British Partition Plan', *People's Age*, 17 February 1946.
58. Ibid.
59. Ibid.
60. 'Communist Candidate tops Poll', ibid.
61. Kosambi, op. cit., p. 18.
62. Hiroshi Sato, 'Tebhaga Undo no Tenkai to sono Haikei—Dinajpur ken o chusin ni (In Japanese; Development of the Tebhaga Movement and its Background—with Special Reference to the Movement in Dinajpur)',

Azia Keizai, October 1970. Also, cf. Muhammad Abudullah Rasul, *Krishak Sabhar Itihas*, Calcutta, 1969, pp. 104, 148.

63. Alec Johnson, *Another's Harvest*, Calcutta, 1947, pp. 108-9.
64. Ibid., p. 109.
65. *Secret Report on the Political Situation in Bengal for the second half of March*, 1946, NAI.
66. Rai, op. cit., p. 276 and pp. 311-13.
67. *Dawn*, 4 September 1945.
68. Cf. Bedal Malik, *Faislahkun Markah—1945-46 ke Intikhabad aur Islamia College ka Kirdar*—Lahore, 1987. This book traces in detail how the college students left their studies and spent their time as *Razbakars* (volunteers) for the Muslim League and against the Unionist candidates not only in Lahore City but also in the remotest villages of the Punjab (now Haryana Province in India).
69. Talbot, op. cit., pp. 93-5.
70. *Dawn*, 13 January 1946.
71. Ibid., 29 January 1946.
72. *People's War*, 21 October 1945.
73. Ibid.
74. *Dawn*, 30 September 1945, 5 November 1945 and 20 February 1946.
75. Malik, op. cit., p. 57.
76. *Dawn*, 5 November 1945.
77. Jacob, op. cit., p. 67.
78. G. Adhikari, 'In a Free India Free Sikh Homelands—Communist Solution', *People's Age*, 16 December 1945. This is reproduced in Jacob, op. cit., pp. 127-57.
79. *Fortnightly Report of the Mysore Residency for the second half of October 1945*, NAI.
80. *Fortnightly Report of the Mysore Residency for the first half of December 1945*, NAI.
81. *Fortnightly Report of the Rajputana Agency for the fortnight ending 15th November 1945*, NAI.
82. *Fortnightly Report of the Kashmir Residency for the fortnight ending 31st October 1945*, NAI.
83. Circular No. 1, The Regional Councils, Jaipur Praja Mandal, 17 March 1946, *Praja Mandal Records*, RSA.
84. Nandalal Sinha, op. cit., pp. 10-11.
85. Ibid., p. 12.
86. Ibid., pp. 15-16.
87. Ibid., p. 17.
88. Memorandum of Instructions for Presiding Officers at Elections to the Bihar Legislative Assembly, pp. 5-6, *File No. Elec. 32/45*, BSA.
89. Nandalal Sinha, op. cit., p. 22.

90. Ibid., p. 18.
91. Ibid., pp.18-19.
92. Returning Officer, North Palamau General Rural Constituency & Sadar Sub-Divisional Officer, Dalton Ganj, Palamau, to the Election Office, Patna, March 1946, *Election Branch (Legislative Department) Files 1945-52*, BSA.
93. A. Mohammad, SDO, Motihari Sadr to the Election Office, Patna, 23 March 1946, ibid.
94. C.R.W. Webster, SDO, Khunti to the Election Officer, Patna, 18 March 1946, ibid.
95. *Report on the internal situation in the North-West Frontier Province for the first half of February 1946*, NAI.
96. *Report on the situation in the Punjab for the second half of February 1946*, NAI.
97. *Report for the first half of March1946*, Bombay, NAI.
98. *Fortnightly Report for the second half of March1946*, Madras, TSA.
99. *Report on the events in Bihar during the first half of March 1946*, NAI.
100. *The Orissa Report for the first half of April 1946*, NAI.
101. *Fortnightly report for the second half of March, 1946*, U.P., NAI.

IV

Election Results

General Review

On 22 March 1946, just before the British Cabinet Mission arrived in Delhi, Viceroy Wavell wrote to the King that it was unfortunate that elections had to be spread out over so long a period from November to April.[1]

Yet in the context of the prevailing political and economic situation it was a wonder that the elections passed off 'peacefully'.

In early 1946, India was facing a serious food scarcity as was Japan immediately after the War. The rainfall of 1945 was irregularly distributed. It was both irregular and inadequate in the south and the prospects for the Punjab wheat crop early in 1946 were also poor. In March 1946, the Government of India announced a Five Point Plan in which the statutory ration which had been so far 16 ounces a day for the each adult was reduced all over India to 12 ounces. Madras was one of the first provinces to act upon the Government of India's directive. The British Government had promised 760,000 tons of foodgrains for the calendar year 1945 and by January 1946, 621,364 tons had arrived. Also a quota of 75,000 tons of rice was allotted and received from Burma for the last quarter of 1945.[2]

The food position was not different in the Indian states. In Jodhpur a meeting between Jai Narain Vyas, President of the Marwar Lok Parishad and the Maharaja created a misunderstanding among the people about its motive. Vyas had to apologize in writing that he did not go to the Maharaja for any other purpose but for discussing the grain situation, which could not be solved without popular co-operation. But the Lok Parishad element was carefully excluded[3] from the Committee convened for the special purpose.

The *Dawn* reported on 2 February 1946 that famine on a scale surpassing the Bengal disaster of 1943 was foreseen by Government quarters in Delhi unless preventive measures proved successful. The food position in each province affected the political and electoral situation. We can say that 'smooth' working of the 1946 elections was made possible mainly by the political will of the Congress, the Muslim League and the Communist Party of India, which decided to contest them in spite of the critical political and economic situation.

The Indian National Congress won the support of 80.9 per cent of the voters in the General constituencies gaining 927 seats including the Muslim and special seats (Table XI). Many of its candidates were returned uncontested: in Madras 40 per cent, in U.P. 42 per cent, in Bihar 40 per cent and in Orissa 60 per cent. The impact of the Quit India movement on the two Ganga plain provinces can be easily confirmed. In Satara (north and south), Bombay Province, which was a centre of the movement that survived even after the end of the War, the Congress secured all General seats for the Bombay Provincial Assembly.

But in the Muslim constituencies, the Congress fared very badly. In U.P. where Nehru once expected that the Congress and pro-Congress candidates might win 25 seats, the Congress could get only 3, and the Nationalist Muslims backed by the Congress 7 seats.

In the Punjab where the percentage of the General seats to the total was small, the Congress had a tough fight. According to the AICC analysis, only 9 of 83 Congress candidates were elected unopposed (11 per cent). None of the 9 Congress candidates who stood in the Muslim constituencies could win. The Ahrars who stood for the Muslim seats and were supported by the Congress, cast in their lot with the Congress. Patel who was then occupied by the Royal Indian Navy Strike was disappointed with the results in the Punjab, stating that 'all our efforts and resources there have been wasted and all hopes given were false and the calculations and expectations were wrong'.[4] Patel thought that the results in the General constituencies in India had already been expected and the contests in the Muslim seats, particularly Punjab, were crucial to the unity of India.

Also in Bengal, the Congress and the Nationalist Muslims could not win any of the urban and rural Muslim seats. The Krishak Praja Party under the leadership of Fazlul Huq could get 4 seats.

The Muslim League won the votes of 74.7 per cent of those Muslims who voted in the Muslim constituencies. It won all Muslim seats in Madras, Bombay and Orissa. Its success in Bengal was also remarkable, and in the Punjab the ruling party, the Unionists, were reduced by them to a minority. The League became the single largest party in the Assembly. But the results in Sind were not satisfactory for them though the *Dawn* reported that Syed Party was routed in the elections.[5] In the North-West Frontier Province, the Congress could capture more seats in the Muslim constituencies than the League.

The only other parties to win some seats in the elections were the Akalis and the Communist Party of India.

The Akalis appeared as the third largest party in the Punjab, getting the support of 43.1 per cent of those who voted in the Sikh constituencies. The results reflected the delicate political situation in this key province. Conversely, the Communists lost all their contests including 4 seats which they had held before the elections in the Punjab.[6] The Communists had the support of 7.3 per cent of those who voted in the Sikh constituencies.

But the Communist Party captured two seats in Madras, two in Bombay and three in Bengal besides one in Orissa. From Bombay, S.A. Dange, and from Bengal, Jyoti Basu were elected, both from the Labour seats. The Communists were able to procure the support of 24.3 per cent of the voters who polled in the Labour constituencies, but could get only 0.2 and 0.5 per cent of the votes polled in the General constituencies in U.P. and Bihar.

Despite these results, Asoka Mehta warned the Congress that the Communist votes were the third largest in the country. If there were proportional representation, the Communist would have got 51 instead of 8 seats.[7]

Of the remaining political forces, the Hindu Mahasabha won only 3 seats, one each from Bengal, Bombay and C.P. The Mahasabha ceased to be a major political force. The Scheduled Castes Federation (SCF) under the leadership of B.R. Ambedkar (Chairman, Drafting Committee, Constituent Assembly of India 1947-9) won only one seat in C.P. The SCF won the support of 216,464 voters in Bombay from a total of 262,326 scheduled caste voters, but could capture none of the reserved seats for the scheduled castes.[8] Unlike the separate electorate system for the Muslims which worked favorably for the Muslim League, the General electorate system with the reservation for the scheduled castes badly affected the SCF.

It was in the beginning of August 1945 that the Governors' Conference was in favour of the General Election, and on 28 March 1946, these Governors reported the election results albeit incomplete, along with their view on the provincial political situation to the Cabinet Mission.[9] The general impression was that, though the Muslim League was successful in securing most of the Muslim seats, Jinnah's hold on the organization and the Muslims was not complete and the idea of Pakistan could be reasonably repudiated by substantial concession on the side of the Congress. B.J. Glancy, Governor of the Punjab and a strong supporter of the Unity of India confessed that he could not see how Pakistan could work. He suggested that the Mission should try to persuade the Congress to make the maximum possible concessions. John Colville, Governor of Bombay, said that Pakistan was a war cry, but doubted whether the Bombay Muslims considered they had anything to gain by the birth of Pakistan. Francis Wylie, U.P. Governor, did not believe that the Muslims in the province (including their political leader Chowdhry Khaliq-uz-Zaman) really believed in Pakistan. Also, F. Mudie, Governor of Sind, reported that the Sind Muslims did not believe in Pakistan in the sense of a Muslim State completely separate from the rest of India. Neither the Governor of the Punjab and nor the Governor of Bengal believed that all of the Punjab or Bengal could be included in Pakistan.

The meeting of 28 March 1946 was a ritual of taking over the constitutional procedure by the Cabinet Mission on the basis of the main election results already known. In later stages of the negotiations between the Mission and the Indian leaders, the former did not refer to the election results very often, but this implied that the conclusions drawn from the results were obvious. The Cabinet Mission concluded that voters were solidly behind two all-India organizations, the Congress and the League.

On the other hand, the Muslim League thought the results of the Provincial Elections to be 'a victory for which there is no parallel in the world' (Jinnah's speech on 7 April 1946).[10] The *Dawn* wrote in its editorial, 'The Nation's Elect':

> Those who have been elected this time to the Legislatures have been charged by the voters with the duty not of 'working the constitution' but of winning Pakistan. Within and outside the Provincial and Central Assemblies and Councils that and that alone is now the 'priority job'. —The time for decision is over; the time for action has come.[11]

It is also true that the constitutional system was most fruitfully utilized by the Muslim League. A Convention of the 500 newly elected Legislators to the Central and Provincial Assemblies was held in the Anglo-Arabic College, Delhi from 7 to 9 April 1946. It was this Convention that passed the resolution which clarified the scheme of Pakistan as 'a sovereign independent State comprising Bengal and

Assam in the North-East zone and the Punjab, North-West Frontier Province, Sind and Baluchistan in the North-West zone'. H.S. Suhrawardy, leader of the League Party in the Bengal Legislative Assembly moved this resolution and Abul Hashim was one of the members of the Subjects Committee which approved it. Now there was no room for further interpretation on 'Independent States' in the Lahore Resolution.

Also, Feroz Khan Noon was vocal at this Convention. He declared:

> If our actual course is to fight, and if in that fight we go down, the only course for the Muslims is to look to Russia, and there is a big movement in the Punjab in favour of Communism, as they say that that is the only way to freedom in view of *Akhand* Hindustan. If we have to win our freedom that way, I will be the first to lose every rupee I have in order that we may be free in this country.[12]

It is quite likely that Feroz Khan Noon was well aware of Mian Iftikhar-ud-din and his 'progressive' group, and the Indian Communists who supported the Muslim League in the elections. Iftikhar-ud-din was a member of the Subjects Committee too.

If we use the expression of the *Dawn*, in the 1946 Provincial Elections, 'The Muslim nation has spoken in unmistakable terms and it has spoken with one voice.'[13] The Muslim League got what they wanted in the elections.

P.C. Joshi who had been a top leader of the Communist election campaign was disappointed with the election results and, while observing the post-election political situation, concluded that the elections had settled nothing and in fact accentuated every problem facing the freedom movement.[14] The Communist perspective proved wrong and the theory of nationalities and national self-determination was put to severe trial in later political developments in India.

As for the Indian National Congress, it did not pass any official resolution on the election results. It secured the predominant support in the General seats but the results in the Muslim seats were far from encouraging.

Results in the Provinces

(i) Madras

On the eve of the elections, Madras Presidency was in the grip of food scarcity. The Government had to reduce the scale of food rations from 1 lb. per head per day to 12 oz. in all the statutorily rationed areas on 17 February 1946.[15] Labour unrest, including a threat of a strike by the Posts and Telegraphic Union, was serious. After the elections, in Madras city the men of the Armed Reserve of the City Police and a majority of the men in the Civil Divisions refused to draw their pay on 1 April. On 16 April, 235 out of 508 men of the Malabar Special Police stationed in Madras city refused to work. The worst affected company was disbanded. The local Non-Gazetted Officers Association also set up a demand for more dearness allowance. Discontent spread to the village officers in many districts.[16]

The Fortnightly Report for the first half of March 1946 stated, 'The Justice Party (Non-Brahmin Party) is now definitely out of the picture as far as the elections are concerned . . . . The Dravidian Federation is also taking no part in the elections . . . .'[17]

In his talk with the Cabinet Mission on 17 April, P.T. Rajan, a leader of the Justice Party and a minister of the Provincial Government 1930-7, had to confess that the party had not contested any seats in the recent elections, because owing to their support of the British Government in the past they had been dubbed as traitors by the electorate.[18]

The Communist Party which had its mass base in some parts of Andhra and Kerala also had to suffer. The Communists had two winners, P. Venkateswaralu in West Godavari *cum* Guntur Factory Labour seat, and K. Ananda Nambiar in Railway Trade Union seat. P. Sundarayya, E.M.S. Namboodiripad and A.K. Gopalan who took prominent part in post-Independent politics and peasant movements were defeated by the Congress candidates respectively in the General Rural seats of Bezwada, Malappuram and Calicut. Sundarayya got 33,714 votes. The Communists nominated 31 candidates in General seats and lost all the contests, though in the scheduled caste primary elections the Communists won in some constituencies, the substantial support of the agricultural labourers against the mirasdars or zamindars. This is apparent in the elections of Mannargadi-Tiruthuraipundi Taluks (Tanjore District) where the Communists and pro-Communist candidates won more votes than the Congressmen, and in the election of east Kistna (Andhra) where a Communist candidate swept the polls.[19] Despite the crucial issue of 'Pakistan or Not' the reality of the rural scene and peasant movement was partly reflected in the election results. Nambiar who won the seat was later arrested in the strike of the South Indian Railway in September 1946.[20]

Thus, in Madras Presidency, distant from the areas demanded for Pakistan, the basic character of the 1946 Provincial Elections was clearly observed. The Justice Party which was in office before 1937 was out of the picture. In the General constituencies the Congress won all the seats, and in the Muslim constituencies it was the League which performed a similar feat. The local character of the politics in 1946 was submerged under the crucial issue, 'Pakistan or Unity of India'.

The Muslim League was particularly satisfied with its hundred per cent success in the Muslim seats of the Muslim minority provinces outside the areas for Pakistan like Madras and Bombay. They interpreted these results as 'the most convincing evidence of nationality' as the Muslims regarded themselves with the feeling of oneness wherever they lived in the subcontinent.[21]

However, the urban and rural scene in Madras Presidency after the elections showed that these contests could not reflect the discontent of the people who were observing the elections from outside the polling stations.

(ii) Bombay

Just as in Madras, the League captured all Muslim seats in Bombay. I.I.Chundrigar who later became Prime Minister of Pakistan in 1957 was elected from a Muhammadan Urban constituency in Ahmedabad, defeating a Nationalist Muslim candidate by 22,873 votes to 487.

Bombay was a centre of the Quit India movement and its impact on the election results was evident both in Satara and north Karnataka. Here we will pick up the results in these two areas and check the political careers of the winners before and after the elections (* = scheduled caste constituency):

(a) Satara north

B.J. Shinde, Congress, 44,315, Elected

Details unconfirmed yet

G.D. Tapache, Congress*, 43, 961, Elected

Arrested in the individual *satyagraha* (1940), participated in the meeting at Satara on 9 August 1942, engaged in underground activities.

G.E. Sinhasane; Congress, 42,727, Elected

Arrested in the individual *satyagraha*, attended the AICC in August 1942, elected as a leader responsible for the north

Satara area, surrendered to the police in August 1943.

D.K. Gosavi, Congress, 41,474, Elected

Called 'Buva Gosavi', met Gandhi in July and October 1944, and was told that guerilla activities should be ended.

K.S. Sawant, SCF*, 14,010, Runner-up.

S.V. Medak, Hindu Mahasabha, 6,483, Runner-up

(b) Satara south

K.D. Patil, Congress, 64,797, Elected

Pleader, attended the AICC in Bombay, one of the convenors of a public meeting on 7 September 1942 who appealed to the people to march to the Islampur Kacheri, elected as the dictator for Satara District, arrested on 27 September 1943.

P.P. Gokhale, Congress,, 64,797, Elected

Gandhian, participated in a reception to the guerilla leaders at Konegaon on 5 May 1946.

V.P. Pawar, Congress, 59,605, Elected

Journalist, President of the Satara District Congress Committee, 1945, arrested in April 1945 on the ground that he published 'misleading articles' on the Satara situation and other apprehensions.

Y.B. Chavan, Congress, 59,375, Elected

Attended the AICC session in Bombay, a leader in the earlier stage of the underground activities, arrested on 17 May 1943, Chief Minister of Bombay (later Maharashtra), held many posts in the Congress-led Central Government.

K.R. Inamdar, Independent, 11,043, Runner-up

Though some of the prominent guerilla leaders like Nana Patil, Kisan Veer and Pandu Master appeared in the open only on 5 May 1946, the impact of the Satara struggle on the election results is unmistakable, and conversely the 1946 elections promoted the closure of the movement.[22]

In north Karnataka where the Quit India movement was at its height, many leaders who led the movement consolidated their steps for their post-Independent political activities on the occasion of the elections.[23]

(a) Dharwad, north

T.R. Nesvi, Congress, 65,216, Elected

Participated in the Civil Disobedience movement of 1930-1,

Advance Arrest in 1942, Lok Sabha member.

A.G. Dodmeti, Congress, 61,674, Elected

Advance arrest, Minister, Karnataka Government

K.B. Dundur, Congress, 61,303, Elected

Leader of the Quit India movement in north Dharwad, later arrested.

R.S. Hukerikar, Congress, 53,177, Elected

One of the five-man Committee which led the movement, later arrested, Member of Legislative Council, Bombay, participated in the activities of the Janata Shiksha Samiti and the Bharat Sevak Samaj.

(b) Dharwad south

K.F. Patil, Congress, 29,652, Elected

Led the Non-Tax movement of 1930-1, again led the Quit India movement in the southern part of Dharwad, Member of Legislative Assembly, Bombay, Minister of B.D. Jatti's Government in Karanataka, founded the Grama Sevak Mantappa

V.V. Patil, Congress, 29,318, Elected

Advance arrest, MLA, engaged in Harijan work and founded the Teachers' Training College in Hubli.

Mrs. Sambrani, Woman's seat, Congress, 7,815, Elected

(c) Belgaum north

A.B. Latthe, Congress, 55,787, Elected

Diwan of Kolhapur, Finance Minister of Bombay Government 1937-9

R.A. Kulkarni, Congress, 50,759, Elected

M.P. Patil, Congress, 49,867

Advance arrest, Minister, Bombay and Karnataka.

S.N. Mane, scheduled caste seat, Independent, 27,682

Vallabhbhai Patel understood that he stood as an independent candidate, Member of the Constituent Assembly.

(d) Belgaum south

N.B. Dalvi, Congress, 40,296, Elected

S.N. Angadi, Congress, 40,062, Elected

MLA (Bombay).

S.B. Kutre, Congress, 39,419, Elected

(e) Bijapur north
Maganlal Shah, Congress, 23,083, Elected
G.S. Sajjan, Congress, 20,838, Elected
B.R. Huzare, SC seat, Congress, 16,059, Elected

(f) Bijapur south
C.J. Ambli, Congress, 21,661, Elected
President of Bijapur District Congress Committee, Chairman of the five-man Committee, engaged in subversive activities, MLA (Karnataka), President of Karnataka Provincial Congress Committee.
S.R. Kanthi, Congress, 21,654, Elected
Advance arrest, MLA and Deputy Speaker, Bombay, and Speaker, Mysore, Chief Minister of Mysore in 1962.

(g) North Kanara
S.S. Shastri, Congress, 35,863, Elected
Advance arrest, Parliamentary Secretary (Bombay).
S.P. Gaonkar, Congress, 30,244, Elected
MLA (Bombay)
R.M. Prabhu, Congress, 27,618, Elected
MLA and Parliamentary Secretary (Bombay).

In the 1946 elections, the Congress fully utilized the will of the people for freedom. Therefore, there was continuity in the process from the Quit India movement to the participation in the constitutional process on the part of the Congress leaders though in north Karnataka there were conflicts over the selection of a candidate who was critical of the Quit India movement and these were mixed with Brahmin-Non-Brahmin rivalry.[24]

But it is also a fact that the Congress had to discard some parts of the movement, as was shown in the attitude of the new Congress ministry in Bombay towards the guerrilla leaders. Morarji Desai, Home Minister, was not so lenient to the experiment of the Parallel Government in Satara.[25] Guerrilla leaders like Nana Patil and Kisan Veer feared that the Congress would only praise the genius of the people while, in fact, subjugating all aspects of the experiment of the self-government to the main framework set by Patel and other Congress leaders. Colville, Governor of Bombay, told the Cabinet Mission that he had formed the impression that the Congress was willing to work on the constitution as it stood. According to him 'The Right Wing of Congress is in the ascendant; the Left Wing is very vocal and is especially strong in Satara but is unlikely to oust the Right Wing.'[26] There was enough reason for Colville to be satisfied with the new tendency inside the Congress.

The official report for Satara in the second week of March 1946 said that

> Election day passed off quietly, and there was no trouble at any of the polling stations. It is reported, however, that there was a lot of intimidation of the scheduled classes, many of whom were not allowed to leave the village to record their votes and were also threatened with social boycott if they went and voted for the Ambedkarite candidate.[27]

The *Dawn* also reported on the 'Patri Sarkar's threats to Muslim voters: Reign of Terror at Satara':

> Reports received from Satara are painfully disquieting. Congress volunteers resorted to all the nefarious means, including undue influence, pressure, coercion, intimidation and threats of violence, to the Muslim voters. The Election staff was also not impartial. The Congress underground organization, known as 'Patri Sarkar' served notices of heavy reprisals on the supporters of the Muslim League, says General Secretary of Provincial Muslim League, Bombay on Monday (1 April).
>
> Threats of social boycott were put into practice. At several places, the voters were prevented from exercising the right of franchise. Thus the reign of terror and goondaism prevented large number of voters from going to the polling booths or having gone there, were forced against their wishes to vote against the Muslim League.[28]

'Intimidation' and 'social boycott' appear in both reports. It needs to be checked whether this kind of intimidation was in fact done by the Prati Sarkar movement or how the leaders of the movement themselves construed the meaning of the 1946 elections and the role of the scheduled caste and Muslim constituencies. Future studies on the Prati Sarkar movement must cover this aspect too. At least it may be said that though there was continuity from the movement to the constitutional process, its transition was not so smooth.

There is another aspect of the Bombay elections which needs to be noted. In the same talk, Colville said that the scheduled castes (meaning here Scheduled Castes Federation) who had previously held some 7 seats had fared badly in the elections.

This was conspicuously shown in the results in Bombay city. In the primary elections to select a panel of four candidates, SCF candidates topped the poll.

General Urban

1. Bombay City north and Bombay Suburban District:
   (1) R.D. Bhandare, SCF, 12,889
   (2) S.G. Sogaonkar, Congress, 2,088
   Following candidates were omitted here.
2. Bombay City (Byculla and Parel):
   (1) B.J. Deorukhkar, SCF, 11,334
   (2) N.S. Kajrolkar, Congress, 2,098

But in the final elections when the General electorate including the scheduled castes voted, the results were reversed.

1. Bombay City north and Bombay Suburban District:
   (1) S.G. Sogaonkar, Congress, 59,646, Elected
   (2) R.D. Bhandare, SCF, 42,510
2. Bombay City (Byculla and Parel):
   (1) N.S. Kajrolkar, Congress, 43,251, Elected
   (2) B.J. Deorukhkar, SCF, 39,498

This was also true in the case of east Khandesh (General Rural) seat. These results were a rude shock to Ambedkar and the Scheduled Castes Federation. Ambedkar and his organization kept aloof from the Quit India movement, because he thought that it was madness to start an open rebellion when the Japanese were at the gates of India.[29]

In his meeting with Wavell and the Cabinet Mission, Ambedkar reminded them of two points in the resolution adopted by the Working Committee of the SCF on 2 April 1946.[30]

First in many cases the Congress scheduled caste candidates, though outvoted by the Federation candidates in the primary elections, had beaten them in the final elections. Second, this showed how small the number of scheduled caste voters was in comparison with the total of general voters. He added that even so the Congress had resorted to loot and arson to ensure the success of their candidates. He produced a volume of photographs to show what they had done.

From 31 March to 5 April, Bombay faced terror in the B.D.D. Chawls, Worli, a working class area. When Gandhi came to stay there, the workers of the Scheduled Castes Federation went to stage a black flag demonstration; the police took precautionary measures; and workers' *chawls* were attacked by the *goondas.*[31] Many scheduled caste workers were arrested.

The Communist Party which laid stress on the solidarity between the SC workers and other workers reviewed the election results in Bombay:

> Thus the Poona Pact of 1932, when Gandhiji's 'fast unto death' forced Dr Ambedkar, the leader of the Untouchables, to agree to joint electorates with reserved seats for the Untouchables, lost all its real meaning. The Congress could, on the strength of the Caste Hindus, smother the real voice of the Untouchables.[32]

The final election results do not seem to have reflected correctly the spirit of the Poona Pact which tried to connect the will of the scheduled caste voters with that of the other voters in the General constituencies. The Provincial Elections of 1946 which seem to have succeeded in persuading the leaders of the *Prati Sarkar* Movement in Satara and the Royal Indian Navy strikers, failed to accommodate the demand of one strong stream of thought which represented the scheduled castes within the constitutional framework.

The Communist Party of India which appealed to the citizens of Bombay to act with the naval ratings won two seats, one in the constituency for Railway Unions and another in the constituency for the Bombay City and Suburban Textile Unions. In the latter constituency the Bombay Girni Kamgar Union provided the stable support base for a Communist candidate, S.A. Dange, while M.Y. Nurie who had been elected in 1937 from the Ahmedabad Muslim constituency was transferred to the Trade Union constituency, expecting to be selected as a Congress Muslim. After 11 March 1946 when the elections for the General seats in Bombay were over, an intense election campaign was made for this single seat. However, S.A. Dange got 4,742 votes while Nurie lost the contest by a margin of 723.[33]

Despite the Communist victory, an integrated view of the surrender of the naval ratings in February and the success of the election battle in March 1946 does not seem to have been made and this forced them later to develop a radically new approach. It is not accidental that the Communist Party had not yet understood the serious meaning of the critical stage through which the *Prati Sarkar* movement was passing before and after the elections. Basically, in both urban and rural areas of Bombay the people's movement was curbed to adjust to the constitutional setting prepared by Patel and other Congress leaders.

(iii) Bengal

We have already noted the serious controversy over 'hooliganism'. and 'intimidation' in the election campaign and the conflicts between the Congress and the League, and also between the Congress and the Communists in Bengal. Sir Frederick Burrows, Governor of Bengal, wrote in his letter to Wavell,

> but so far there seems to be little disposition, on the part of those who are loudest in complaint, to see judicial confirmation of their allegations by filing election petitions. We must, I suppose, expect a few of these but generally majorities were so sweeping that unsuccessful candidates may well feel they have little to hope for from by-elections so soon after the general elections.[34]

In Bengal, no party could register remarkable results in 1937. The Congress was the single largest party with only 60 seats out of a total of 250 seats. The Muslim League won 40 seats, the Krishak Praja Party 35 and independent Muslims 41 seats.[35]

In 1946, the will of the voters was divided into two sides. In the general seats the Congress could win 71 seats out of 74, and in the Muslim seats the League occupied 110 seats out of 117. The results showed the eclipse of the Krishak Praja Party from the political scene, which won only 4 seats. The KPP actually won 5 seats, but one seat had to be vacated as its leader, Fazlul Huq was elected from two constituencies, Bagerhat and Bakarganj south.

The Nationalist Muslims who had the backing of the Congress fared even worse winning no seats at all. The KPP which was a member of the Nationalist Muslim Parliamentary Board that came into being as a result of the conference in Delhi on 18 September 1945 may be called Nationalist Muslims.[36] Many election analyses do so. But it is to be noted that the AICC analysis separated the KPP from the Nationalist Muslims.

Fazlul Huq had already become vocal against the Two-Nation Theory publicized by Jinnah, and proposed 'to modify the Pakistan

Scheme so as to enable the Muslims of Bengal also to assert their self-determination along with the Muslims of other Provinces and also members of other communities in all the Provinces'.[37] He tried to assert the right of self-determination of the Bengal Muslims without denying the idea of Pakistan. The following episode in the elections shows that Huq became more inclined towards the soil of Bengal though he did not openly negate the idea of Pakistan:

> On the occasion of the elections of 1946, he [supporter of Huq] visited the place of a learned leader in a village and said, 'We understand that we need Pakistan and for this purpose we have to vote for the Muslim League. We already decided to give one vote to Huq Sahib and another vote to the Muslim League.' When the old leader said that he had only one vote, not two votes, he answered, 'Oh, my God, why so? How is it possible for you not to vote for Huq Sahib? Is it possible for you not to vote for Huq Sahib for whom your father and again your brother voted?'[38]

However, in 1946 Huq's idea was overridden by the enthusiastic campaign led by the Muslim League with the help of students and Pirs. A Bangladeshi writer says that in 1946 the Bengali Muslims could not understand that Huq was not mistaken, but in 1954 they voted for Huq for they felt that he was now taking the right course.[39] In the latter elections the United Front under the leadership of Fazlul Huq which demanded complete autonomy for East Pakistan won a sweeping victory, defeating the Muslim League. The 1946 elections were an incomplete chapter for the people of East Bengal.

In Bengal, the Communist Party could win 3 seats. Jyoti Basu from the Railway Trade Union constituency, Ratanlal Brahmin from the Labour (Factory and Colliery) in Darjeeling Sadar constituency and Rupnarayan Roy in the General Rural seat of Dinajpur. Ratanlal Brahmin was a tea garden labourer in Darjeeling and a founder of the Communist Party there.[40] Rupnarayan Roy was a Rajbansi peasant who up to his thirtieth year lived 'the life of an average tiller of the soil'. In 1930-40, he took an active part in the Kisan movement which covered north Bengal, and during the War led it against food crisis. We have noted how the kisans in Dinajpur tried to participate in the elections.[41]

Dinajpur was one of the centres where the *Tebhaga* struggle was developed from the autumn of 1946. Whether this kind of election campaign had become assets for the later development of the movement or delayed the struggle, needs to be examined. In spite of the election policy of the CPI, here also they had to face stiff opposition from the Congress.

As for the Muslim seats, two Communists stood as candidates in Bengal and both lost their contests. P.C. Joshi made a review of their position in Bengal:

> In the Muslim seats we fared much worse at the hands of the League than at the hands of the Congress. This is primarily because the peasant movement is much weaker and political awakening new and, therefore, more elementary.
>
> The figures of Bengal are no true index of our strength among the Muslim peasantry in Mymensingh and Comilla because of the mass terror organised by the League, which was as bad as, and in some ways worse than, that adopted by the Congress in Monghyr and Aligarh villages . . . .[42]

The elections in Bengal also showed that the constitutional process was far from peaceful. Bengal was the province where the CPI had found a mass-based League organization led by the 'Progressives'. However, the Congress and the CPI had to admit that they had no strong support base among the Muslim peasantry.

(iv) U.P.

In U.P. where the Quit India movement was intensely fought, the Congress was relatively well organized in rural areas and its victory in the General seats was complete. The Congress candidates were elected unopposed from 73 seats and won another 67 seats by a clear margin. In the Muslim seats, the Muslim League won 54 seats of the total reserved seats of 66 including two women's seats, but the percentage of votes polled for the League was 71.4 per cent in the Muhammadan Urban constituencies and 62.4 per cent in the Muhammadan Rural constituencies. The Congress and the Nationalist Muslims could get the support of 33.2 per cent of those who actually voted. Consequently, though the League candidates were elected from 43 seats by a clear margin of more than 20 per cent to their runners-up, 6 winners were elected by a margin of less than 10 per cent. This is partly due to some support which the Congress had among the Muslim peasantry.

However, Rafi Ahmad Kidwai, of the Congress who stood from Rae Bareli, Gonda and Bahraich constituencies was not successful in any of these contests, but was elected unopposed from the University constituency.[43] A biographer of Kidwai wrote

> that he neglected his constituencies and did not pay any visit to them. On account of malpractices such as tampering with ballot boxes, open voting at

many polling booths, false propaganda, open interference in election and partiality for the League candidates by the district authorities, Rafi Ahmad and the majority of Congress and Nationalist Muslim candidates could not win.[44]

The *Dawn* took a different interpretation in the editorial titled 'U.P. and Bihar', and said 'The triple defeat of Mr Rafi Ahmad Kidwai, the star "Muslim" Congressman of the United Provinces, has conclusively proved, if proof was needed, that in the eyes of the Muslims a Muslim Congressman is an unwanted "pariah", whatever his status and qualifications may be in the eyes of Hindus', and concluded,

> One of the factors which strengthens the case for Pakistan is the support which Muslims in the Hindu majority provinces have consistently given to it, and the elections in U.P. and Bihar have now proved beyond the shadow of a doubt that such support exists to an overwhelming extent.[45]

In Kanpur City, the Congress could win both the scheduled caste and non-scheduled caste seats, but there was a violent scene in the city on the eve of the polling day, 13 March, for the General seats. The official Fortnightly Report referred to a 'serious riot on 12th' without giving details.[46]

O.P. Sangal, a Communist, explains the background. At a meeting in the Tilak Hall on 11 March Congress leaders delivered 'poisonous speeches' against the Scheduled Castes Federation, the League and the Communist Party. According to his understanding, the polling was in favour of the SCF candidate, and therefore the Congress used desperate methods to prevent it. He wrote that the Congress supporters began to tear the SCF voters' lists, pull down SCF tents and pelt them with stones. Such things took place at almost every polling station.[47]

As in Bombay, the spread and strength of the Quit India movement was institutionalized skillfully by the Congress in the form of the election results, but the Congress refused to accommodate the constitutional demands of the SCF.

The Communists stood for 3 Labour seats and lost all the contests. Raja Ram Shastri, a Congress leader, won his seat in Kanpur Factory Labour constituency. He was once Librarian of the Dwarkadas Library, Lahore, which was established by Lala Lajpat Rai. He taught Bhagat Singh, a young revolutionary of the 1920s, what to read. Raja Ram Shastri defeated Sant Singh Yusuf, a Communist who was General Secretary of the Kanpur Mazdur Sabha in the late 1930s.[48]

At that time, Hari Har Nath Shastri was President of this Union, and in 1946 he also won the seat for the Trade Union, defeating a Communist. Hari Har Nath later became a member of the Constituent Assembly and President of the Indian National Trade Union Congress founded by the Indian National Congress in 1947.

The Provincial Elections of 1946 was the first step towards the recovery of the influence lost by the Congress in the field of the labour movement during the War. It was not so successful in Bombay or Bengal, but realized its purpose in Kanpur under the strong favourable wind of the Quit India movement.

P.C. Joshi made a review of the results in U.P., stating that voting in the U.P. and Bihar were unexpectedly low and that this was primarily because the terror used against the Communists was worse than even in the Calcutta Labour area.[49] In fact, the Communists failed to assess correctly what the Congress and the League were trying to consolidate in the elections.

(v) Punjab

We saw that Patel was disappointed with the election results in the Muslim seats of the Punjab. This news had reached him when he was occupied with the critical phase of the Royal Indian Navy strike in Bombay. His great disappointment was due to the severe reality that the 1946 elections on which he spent most of his time did not prove to be the best alternative to the 'violent' act of the naval ratings. This led to his strong complaint to Maulana Azad who wanted to deal with the election campaign of the Congress in the Punjab at his own discretion.

In his letter to B.S. Gilani, Patel repeated his disappointment and added that the strength of the Unionists, was considerably crippled and their existence was almost precarious.[50] He was sceptical about the political behaviour of Master Tara Singh, an Akali leader; Congress was weak and not united in the Punjab. Therefore he thought that, if the Unionists were weakened, it would be bad for the Congress too.

Of a total of 86 Muslim seats, the Muslim League won all 11 Urban seats and 64 out of 75 Rural seats, though in the elections of 1937 it had procured only two seats.

Many of the League winners had been Unionists. In his work on the 1946 Punjab elections, Talbot writes that the use of religious appeal by Pirs and the traditional channels of political mobilization through the *biradari* system was decisive in communicating the message of Pakistan to the villages and in forcing landlords to change their political labels in the post-War situation.[51] The Hayats, the Noons and the Daultanas from which the Unionist Party had traditionally drawn its leadership are mentioned as the families which later gave a crippling blow to the party.

At the end of 1945 Punjab faced a food crisis and wheat, maize and gram disappeared from the open market. No grain came to the *mandis* from the small zamindars of the East Punjab. The Unionist Government was forced to requisition grain from the villages in these areas and incur resistance in the form of the disturbances in Ludhiana, Hoshiarpur and Ferozpur districts in the midst of elections. Meanwhile, the Muslim League started its movement to meet the War-time and post-War economic difficulties by helping the peasants in the villages.[52] The Communists may have interpreted this as the League becoming the mass organization in the Punjab too.

The *Dawn* reported the victory of Mian Iftikhar-ud-din over a Unionist candidate, K.S. Alla Dutta by 6969: 2118 in the Kasur Mohammadan constituency with a headline, 'Big Majority For Iftikaruddin'.[53] However, the position of Mian Iftikhar-ud-din or his 'Progressive' group among the legislators in the Punjab seems to be an isolated one.

The Muslim League was quite satisfied with the election results in the Punjab and the *Dawn* congratulated the people on the downfall of the Unionists with the caption 'Well Done Punjab', but warned the readers that, 'Although the verdict of Muslim Punjab may be unmistakable and the Muslim League may emerge finally as not only the largest single group in the Assembly but also as the only authoritative and representative party enjoying the confidence of the Muslims, the enemies of the Muslim nation comprising heterogeneous elements may try to flock together with the common purpose of cutting Muslim Punjab's throat'.[54] Ministry-making in the Punjab in later days did not proceed favourably for the League.

So far as the election results were concerned, the Congress, the Unionists and other Nationalist Muslims like the Ahrars could not realize even their slight hope of securing some meaningful results.

The support of the Muslim electorate behind the League slogan also strengthened the movement of the Akali Dal under the leadership of Master Tara Singh which maintained that the Punjab was not only the homeland of the Sikhs but their holy land. Though the Akali Dal was in favour of a single constitution-making body, it reserved its right to claim a sovereign Sikh State against the growth of the Pakistan movement. There was some contact between the Congress and the Akali Dal concerning the League, but it finally failed. However, a pact was concluded around their attitudes towards the Communists.

Of 31 separate Sikh seats the Akali Dal won 22 and the Congress 9. The Congress captured most of the General seats, but the poor results in the separate constituencies, both in the Muslim and Sikh seats, were discouraging for the Congress. The total of the General seats including 8 scheduled caste seats was only 42 in the Punjab. The disunity inside the provincial leadership, and also between the central leaders with the lack of the mass support for the Congress seriously affected the results.

'Another noteworthy point is that the Communist Party which put up 24 candidates has failed to secure a single seat, stalwarts like S. Teja Singh Swatantra and S. Sohan Singh Josh having been unseated by fairly big majority.'[55]

The details of the results in case of two Communist candidates are as follows:

Sikh Rural

(1) Amritsar North
Sardar Ishar Singh Majhail, Akali Dal, 7,464, Elected
Sardar Sohan Singh Josh, Communist, 4,546

(2) Gurdaspur North
Sardar Siva Singh, Congress, 5,467, Elected
Sardar Iqbal Singh, Independent, 2,664
Sardar Teja Singh Swatantra, Communist, 1,423

In 6 Sikh Rural constituencies the Akali Dal, the Congress and the CPI had their three-cornered battles, but there was some electoral adjustment between the Congress and the Akali Dal, which the Communists sharply criticized. Maulana Daud Ghaznavi, President of the Punjab Provincial Congress Committee wrote to Patel:

> We came to the following agreement with Baldev Singh. Some 16 or 17 Communists are contesting Sikh seats, out of which four are serious candidates. We agreed that the Akalis should contest two seats against the Communists and we would put up no candidates and that we should contest the two other Communist seats and the Akalis would not put up their candidates for these two seats. The agreement was accepted by the Akalis and was brought into action.[56]

The Communist organ writes differently. From three seats the Akalis would withdraw their candidates and support the Congress, and similarly from another three seats the Congress would do likewise and support the Akalis.[57]

Already in the Central Assembly Elections the Congress candidates had been defeated by the Akalis in the two Sikh seats of East Punjab and West Punjab. Against this background the Communists thought that the Congress was forced to change their line and to pursue the possibility of Congress-Akali-Unionist unity against the League though Congress-Akali unity was only partially realized in the constituencies where strong Communist candidates were contesting. Before this pact appeared, there had been long discussions in Bombay between Patel, Ghaznavi and Baldev Singh, Akali leader and Minister of the Unionist Government.

P.C. Joshi wrote in his election review that each MLA (Member of Legislative Assembly) meant a lot in the game of ministry-making that was part of Punjab politics.[58] He said that formerly the Congress and Communists used to ally against the Akalis to keep them out. This time the Congress fought the Communists and appeased the Akalis. The result was victory for the Akalis.

Also, P.C. Joshi admitted that in the Punjab the working class movement was 'new, weak and at a very elementary stage'. The CPI naturally lost all the three Labour seats.

The Communist theory of self-determination which granted such rights to the Muslims and the Sikhs could not exert any effective influence on the League and the Akalis. At least they failed to prove the correctness of their theory as demonstrated by the election results. No chance of re-examination of this theory came for the moment.

(vi) C.P. and Berar

In this province the Congress won most of the general seats and the Muslim League all the Muslim seats except one.

Patel was disgusted with the trouble around the nominations, saying that Nagpur was perhaps the only place in the whole of India where such protests and demonstrations were staged against selections by the Central Board.[59]

But his basic view of the Congress election policy was clearly shown in this province. When R. S. Shukla wrote that the Nationalist Muslims had formed a joint board for all the Congress provinces with headquarters at Nagpur and that they were working on our instructions and in co-operation with us, Patel gave his blunt answer, 'About the independent Muslims contesting the League candidates, I do not feel much interested.'[60]

Instead, Patel had a keen interest in the scheduled caste constituencies.[61] He agreed with Shukla that Congress should not take its interest in the primary elections in which it had no chance of winning but should instead concentrate on the final elections which were to be decided by the General voters. It was at this stage that candidates sought Congress help, and then the Congress could select the best of the lot.[62]

The Scheduled Castes Federation could win only one seat.

Also, on the day of the election for the Nagpur Trade Union constituency, a clash occurred between the Mahars and the members of the party supporting Mr Ruiskar's candidature. A curfew order was imposed.[63]

In C.P. too, the question arose whether holding the primary elections separately from the final ones would suit the spirit of the Poona Pact.

(vii) Assam

In this province, the Congress monopolized all the General seats and the League won 31 seats in the elections for the 34 Muslim seats. The results only seem to have reflected the all-India phenomenon, but the elections were related closely with the complex problems of the province.

One of the problems is that of 'immigrant Muslims' or the movement against the 'line system' in which a line was drawn in the districts under the pressure of the immigration of landless peasants from Bengal in order to settle these immigrants in segregated areas separated for their exclusive settlement.[64] Maulana Bhasani who was elected in the 1937 Provincial Elections became President of the Assam Provincial Muslim League and simultaneously a leader of the anti-line-system movement. On the occasion of the Third Conference of the Assam Muslim League in April 1944, he emphasized that Muslims in Assam would support the Pakistan movement.[65]

On the other hand, the Assam Provincial Congress Committee stood for Assam nationalism and said in its election leaflet,

Unless the province of Assam be organised on the basis of the Assam language and Assamese culture, the survival of the Assamese nationality and culture will become impossible. The inclusion of Bengali-speaking Sylhet and Cachar (plain portion) and the immigration or importation of lacs of Bengali settlers on wastelands has been threatening to destroy the distinctness of Assam and has, in practice, caused many disorders in its administration. For an appropriate solution and redress of this big problem, the Congress party should be installed as the Majority party in the Assembly.[66]

The election results basically reflected the stance that both parties took towards this problem. Only 3 Muslim seats were won by the Jamiat-ul-Ulema under the influence of Hussain Ahmad Madani, a Deoband leader.[67] It is to be noted that the Assam Congress like the Communists, used the phrase 'Assamese nationality'. But at this stage the All-India Congress leadership was not in a position to provide a solution to this problem which would acquire a serious character after the Independence of India and Pakistan.

The Council of the All-India Muslim League adopted a resolution on 10 April 1946 asking the Governments of India and Assam to take immediate steps to withdraw the 'invidious and illegal line system prevailing in Hindu areas of Assam'.[68]

The CPI contested 3 labour seats and 3 general seats, and lost all. Said P.C. Joshi,

In Assam there was no organised working-class movement and we decided to contest the elections because the Congress leaders themselves wanted us to fight the European planters, which they themselves dared not do. To begin with, they promised neutrality, but later a secret deal was negotiated between the Congress top and the European planters and the balance was turned against us.[69]

The Communists controlled the only central working-class organization, the provincial branch of the All-India Trade Union Congress, on the basis of the railway workers' movement. But during the War there were very few plantation strikes. The contest of the Communists with the support of the Congress in the 3 tea labour seats was not forthcoming.[70] Conversely, the Congress got the chance to enter this section of the labour movement after the elections.

There was another aspect to the elections in Assam. The Ahom Association lost the contest to the Congress. The Ahom Association had its own attitudes towards the British and the Congress, and its view of the problem of the Muslims did not appear directly in the election scene. According to the study of Hiren Gohain, in Sibsagar District, the stronghold of the Ahoms population-wise, immigrants had not posed a serious threat to the local peasantry. In Nowgong and Darrang districts where passion against the immigrants was strong among the sizeable Ahom communities, the Association was not in the hands of the leadership of the Ahom masses. In the elections the problem of the aspirations of the 'sub-national groups' gave way to the 'Assamese national solidarity' and the subcontinental question.[71] On the occasion of the 1946 elections there was little chance to bridge the gap between the different views and solve the local problems with the wisdom of the people of the area.

(viii) North-West Frontier Province

Tendulkar, a biographer of Abdul Ghaffar Khan, writes that Ghaffar Khan did not want to work for the elections, and Gandhi supported his attitude. But, the Frontier Gandhi later changed his mind:

> When I saw the English men and women actively participating in the elections I changed my mind, and for one month before the voting I plunged in the campaign . . . .
>
> The Pakhtuns were not like the Muslims in India. They had political sense and they could not be misled by empty slogans, such as 'Islam in danger'. They know what Islam really means. Their active participation in the national movement and their services to the people aroused in them political consciousness.
>
> At the time of polling, the British authorities and their henchmen put all their weight on the side of the Muslim League and they worked against Khudai Khidmatgars. But, with God's grace, the Muslim League was defeated and our party came out victorious.[72]

The North-West Frontier Province was the only province where the Congress could win the majority of the Muslim seats. It got the support of 22.2 per cent of the urban voters and 41.1 per cent of the rural voters in the Muslim constituencies, while the League got the support of 43.6 per cent of the urban voters and 40.7 per cent of the rural voters in the same constituencies. There were only two Muhammadan urban constituencies including the dual constituency of Peshawar city. The Muslim seats were predominantly rural, and the Congress won 18 out of the total of 33 rural seats, while the League won 13 seats. At this stage, the League in the NWFP still remained 'the party of the towns and of the non-Pathan Hazara districts'. But, it is also to be noted that the League got a slightly larger percentage of the total Muslim votes.[73]

Therefore, as Amit Kumar Gupta points out, the victory of the Congress was not as spectacular as was apparent. The crucial Muslim electorate in the Frontier, while rejecting the Pakistan idea, had not full accepted the nationalist standpoint.[74]

Because of this position, Khan Abdul Qaiyum Khan who joined the League after leaving the Congress claimed, 'If an independent body was to conduct a plebiscite in N.W.F.P., there is not the least doubt that an overwhelming majority of Muslims will vote for Pakistan.'[75]

Talbot analyses that both the Congress and the League had the support of the Pirs and Khans, but those members of the traditional rural elite who supported the Congress were disciplined and loyal to their organization, while this was not the case with the League supporters. Many of the large Khans lost their traditional influence, and their place had been taken by younger men drawn from the junior branches of the Khan families which were well represented in the Congress.[76] Local politics worked in the elections. This meant that the Muslims there had not yet conceived the idea of 'their being subjected to Hindu domination', and the Congress under the leadership of Abdul Ghaffar Khan was still strong. But now its strength was not decisive.

Sir Olaf Caroe, Governor of the North-West Frontier Province, told the Cabinet Mission that if the Province were not subjected to interference from outside the Governor would be able to keep control, but he would find that very difficult if there were serious disturbances in the Punjab.[77] The situation in this province became precarious after the proposal of the Cabinet Mission on 16 May 1946 and worsening communal relations in north India in the later half of the year.

(ix) Orissa

The Congress contested the elections under the leadership of H.K. Mehtab, the member of the Congress Working Committee, and Bishwanath Das, the former Premier of Orissa.[78] It won 43 of the total of 45 general seats and 31 candidates, 69 per cent of the total, were elected unopposed. The official Fortnightly Report says:

> Polling for the Orissa Legislative Assembly took place between the 4th and 9th April. There were contests in nineteen constituencies. There was a good deal of excitement in some of these constituencies, but in the majority the election was a dull affair. There was considerable heat between the followers

of the Communists and the Congress party at Brajrajnagar in the Sambalpur district, and between Andhras and Oriyas in Ganjam and Koraput, but there was no serious incident.[79]

In the labour constituency, Baidyanath Rath, a Communist, defeated his Congress opponent, Maulvi Muhammad Hanif by 2,234 to 1,690.[80] This official report added the information that the League gave considerable assistance to the Communist candidate in the shape of lorries and loud-speaker equipment.

Hawthorne Lewis, Governor of Orrisa, told the Cabinet Mission that the Congress leader Mehtab belonged to the right wing of the party, was diffident, admitted his administrative inexperience, and had already asked for the retention of the Governor's advisors and for more senior I.C.S. officers. He was supported by the landholders and capitalists. The Governor also stated that Patel had told Mehtab that as communal trouble was almost non-existent in Orissa, the province should concentrate on becoming a model of good administration, and thus an advertisement for the Congress rule.[81] The severe attitude of the Congress leaders towards the bureaucracy during the election campaign disappeared in this province where the Congress had suffered factionalism, but they were now expected to show 'a model of good administration' with the help of civil servants.

(x) Sind

The Muslim League got the support of the 58.9 per cent of the votes polled in the Muhammadan rural constituencies and occupied 28 seats in total, but failed to have the majority in the Assembly. G.M. Syed Group won 4 seats. The Congress won 22 seats, but its plan to 'bury Pakistan in Sind' was not successful.[82] Even if it had got the co-operation of the Syed Group and Nationalist Muslims, it failed to reach the majority.

The League was for the moment satisfied that the Syed Group was routed.[83] However, though Jinnah had some influence in Sind even after the death of Abdullah Haroon in 1942, the outlook of the official League candidates was much closer to the 'Sindhi Pakistan' scheme espoused by Syed.[84]

As for the future of Sind, F. Mudie, Governor, told the Cabinet Mission that the Sind Muslims did not believe in Pakistan in the sense of a Muslim State completely separate from the rest of India, but as one remaining in association with the rest of the country though on a new basis which would ensure to its inhabitants freedom from Hindu domination. He said that their leaders were large zamindars.[85]

It was on 9 December 1946 that the League got a clear majority, winning 34 out of 60 seats in the Assembly Elections.

A Case Study of Bihar

Bihar was one of the strongest centres of the Quit India movement. The Congress won the support of the 95.3 per cent and 86.5 per cent of the votes polled in the General urban and the General rural constituencies, respectively. In the Muslim constituencies the Congress set up 9 candidates and got only one seat, though it claimed that 5 Nationalist Muslims who were elected worked, to all intents and purposes, as party members.

The Muslim League got the support of the 83.7 per cent and 71.8 per cent of the votes polled in the Muhammadan urban and the Muhammadan rural constituencies. The League won 34 seats. In U.P., the Congress and the Nationalist Muslims won the support of the 34 per cent of the votes polled in the Muhammadan rural constituencies, while in Bihar it was 26 per cent.

The general tendency was reflected in the results in this province too. but the impact of the Quit India movement on the elections is worth examining. It will also indicate some of the important trends in the post-Independent history of Bihar.

(i) General Constituencies

'Jaya Hind'
Angrezon Bharat chor do. Angrezon Bharat chor do!
Kangres ke Lal aur Ujra Baks men hi Vote den,
Bhaiyo!
Yad rahe, dusre Baks men Vote dena Angrezi Sarkar ko Vote dena hai.
Dusre Baks men Vote dena apni Gulami ko kayam rakhna hai.
Dusre Baks men Vote dena apni Garibi ko badhana hai.
Dusre Baks men Vote dena Jhulmiyon ko nyotha dena hai.
Is liye
Yadi aap chahte hein ki Videshi Sarkar se, Gulami se,
Garibi se aur Jhulmiyon se Chutkara paye to
Lal Ujla Baks hi men Vote den.
Inquilab Zindabad. Hindustan hamara hai

The Official translation of this bill distributed by the Congress is as follows:

Britishers, Quit India.
Cast your vote in the red and white box of the Congress,
Brothers!

Please vote for the Congress. To vote against it is to perpetuate dependence for ever, to add to your poverty, and to invite oppression.

If you want freedom from British domination, poverty and oppression, please cast your vote in the red and white boxes.

Inquilab Zindabad (Long Live Resolution)! India is ours![86]

Quit India was the main theme of the Congress campaign. It was most typically reflected in the campaign carried by the former Premier of Bihar, Shri Krishna Sinha. We have already referred to the response of the bureaucracy in September 1945. Even in February 1946 there was no change in the tone of his speeches:

Mr S.K. Sinha continues his attack on Government servants for alleged atrocities in 1942 and in a speech delivered in Bankipore on the 12th February he asked whether the British did not feel ashamed . . . . He accused Government of giving advancement to those who committed atrocities and said that they should be arrested, tried in open court and, if they are found guilty, should be publicly hanged before an audience of 10,000. In another speech he urged that they should be hanged in Buxar Central Jail.

These threats, coming from one who is likely to be Prime Minister of this province in a few weeks' time, naturally have their effect on morale in the services, particularly when many of the allegations of atrocities bear no resemblance whatever to the actual facts.[87]

Whether Shri Krishna Sinha really meant to do what he said is another matter. Already we saw how Patel dealt with this. However, it is unmistakably true that the Congress tried to utilize the spirit of Quit India to the maximum extent in its election campaign. Murli Manohar Prasad who protested against press controls at the earlier stage of the Quit India movement as the editor of the *Searchlight*, was elected unopposed in the General Urban constituency (Tiruhut Division).

However, Shri Krishna Sinha's appeal received a response from an unexpected corner. On 3 April 1946, the policemen in Bihar went on strike after learning their lesson from Delhi police strike of 21-2 March. Their demands included an increase in pay to Rs. 100 per month, and in the quotas of the cloth and food rations, better service conditions and the right to form their own organization. It is noteworthy that the right to vote in the General Election was included. The policemen carried the same slogans as the Congress, 'Inquilab Zindabad', 'Jai Hind', and 'Britishers, Quit India'. Just as the naval ratings in Bombay expected, the policemen too welcomed the advent of the new Congress ministry. But the Government forced the policemen to resume work and threatened reluctant strikers with dismissal.[88] This strike occurred on the frontier of the constitutional system. The police system, of course, formed an important core of the colonial administration, but the Indian constables demanded their minimum human rights and expressed their will to freedom including their right to vote. At this moment, the new Congress Government had to get the cooperation of the 'high-handed' officers to find its way out of this crisis. This drama showed how Quit India was inherited in different ways in different quarters. The Congress policy took a radical turn after it took office.

In its election campaign the Congress turned more fire on the Communists. In the South Sadar Monghyr constituency, Shri Krishna Sinha faced a Communist candidate, Karyanand Sharma. Sharma had been working in the Congress since 1920, and his Chittaranjan Ashram was opened by Gandhi in 1927. He led a famous peasant *satyagraha* in Barahiya Tal (Lakhiserai) in the later half of the 1930s. Since his election campaign started, Shri Krishna Sinha carried a tirade against the Communists for 'trying to mislead the poor and betraying the struggle in 1942'.[89] Karyanand Sharma was a 'traitor'. The Communist meetings were very often obstructed. On 4 February 1946, the first election meeting which was to have been addressed by P.C. Joshi was broken up, and Karyanand Sharma was assaulted. He had to be moved to the Patna General Hospital due to a serious injury.[90]

The official explanation is as follows:

> In Monghyr district a clash occurred between the Congress and the Communists. The occasion was a meeting which was to have been addressed by P.C. Joshi which the Congress wished to be disturbed. Lathis were freely used on both sides and 14 persons were taken to hospital with minor injuries. Rajeshwar Prasad Singh, the local Congress leader, was injured. This enraged the Congressmen who later in the evening waylaid Karyanand Sharma, the Communist rival of Sri Krishna Sinha, assaulted him so severely that he had to be sent to Patna for treatment. P.C. Joshi, after making one further attempt to hold a meeting decided that discretion was the better part of valour and gave up the rest of his tour.[91]

Rajendra Prasad, later the first President of India, expresses in his autobiography the view of the Congressman who led the election campaign in Bihar and says, 'Provoked by the Communist attacks of abuse, someone badly belaboured one of the Communist leaders in one place. I am sorry to say that the elections vitiated the atmosphere to an extent in which our principles received some setback.'[92] In the Hindi edition of his book the expression *hamara siddhant ko bhi bahut dhakka pahuncha* (our principle received serious setback) is used.[93] In fact, Rajendra Prasad had to assure Indredeep Sinha, a Communist, that he would not allow such things to continue in Bihar.

In his speech in Bihar, P.C. Joshi asked Shri Krishna Sinha to make a definite declaration that the Congress would enact the law abolishing the *zamindari* system with compensation within a year of the establishment of its ministry.[94] Bihar had one of the strongest Kisan movements in India in the 1930s, and the movement also criticized the agrarian policy of the Congress Government, 1937-9. This incident in Monghyr showed that the Congress tried to smash the recent tradition of the peasant movement in Bihar with the help of the fresh memory of the Quit India and to prove its own claim in the 1930s that the Congress was a peasant organization. Shri Krishna Sinha got 34,878 and Karyanand Sharma only 3,372 votes.

As noted earlier, in June 1946 a peasant movement over *bakasht* land for the restoration of their lands and the re-establishment of their right to the lands broke out in several districts in Bihar, and low-caste poor peasants played a significant role in this struggle. The Socialists and members of the Radical Democratic Party who had inherited the recent tradition of the Quit India movement, as well as the Communists were active in leading the *Bakasht* struggle.[95] In 1947 the State Acquisition of Zamindari Bill was introduced in the State Legislature of Bihar, and after passing through various vicissitudes of fortune this bill was finally published as the Bihar Land Reforms Act, 1950.[96] In the meantime the landlords resisted the legislation by all means—from violence to appeals to the courts.

In comparison with the studies on the Kisan movements in Bihar in the 1930s so far there have been few studies on the Kisan movement of the 1940s. To what extent the Quit India movement and the *Bakasht* struggle after the War contributed to the legislation for the *zamindari* abolition, however limited that may have been, and how the peasants understood the second Congress ministry in 1946, still awaits examination.

In Bihar there were 15 seats reserved for the scheduled castes, but there was no contest in the primary elections. The Congress won all seats, among which 7 candidates were elected uncontested. The Congress candidates who contested faced their opponents from the Scheduled Castes Federation, the Hindu Mahasabha, the Shoshit Varg, the Radical Democratic Party, and a few independents. The Congress victory was sweeping in every constituency. Jagjivan Ram who was arrested in the Quit India movement was elected unopposed in the East Central Shahabad Rural constituency. Later he was to be elected as a member of the Constituent Assembly of India and also appointed as the Minister of the Interim Government from 2 September 1946. There is no need to trace the political career of Jagjivan Ram as a Congress leader after the Independence of India. Bhola Paswan Shastri who became the Chief Minister of Bihar twice in 1969 when party defection was rampant was elected unopposed in the south-west Purnea rural constituency in 1946.

There was no serious challenge from the Scheduled Castes Federation as in Bombay, and the spirit of Quit India dominated over the scheduled castes constituencies in Bihar too.

(ii) Muslim seats

The following appeals were made by the Bihar Provincial Muslim League and a member of the Momin Parliamentary Board, Bihar:

(a) Allah-o-Akabar

Brethren in Islam. Asalamo-alaikum.

Now you yourself judge whether the bricks of votes should be used in the preparation of a fort of 'Ram Raj' or for the construction of a building for the independence of Muslim and Islam.

Take care that you should come in a body in procession on the day of election and approach the polling booth at gates and there please inform the candidates of Muslim League that the Muslim voters have come and by undergoing all the troubles they should give votes to the Muslim League. You should also know that the colour of Muslim League box would be green. The colour of our Prophet's tomb is also green. The colour of the Muslim League Box is also green. You never forget. Raise the flag of unity and perseverance.

(Original in Urdu. Official translation in English, attached with a letter from Rai Bahadur R.H. Prasad, Returning Officer, Palamau Muhammadan Rural constituency, 17 March 1946)

(b) Give one vote to Mr Lal Mohammad in the Red box.

It is a duty of Momin brothers to give their votes to their own candidates and do not come under the clutches of the enemy, otherwise the respects and honours of their community will be buried. To cast vote to other nominee will be the cause of decay of Momin brothers.[97]

(Official translation in English, attached to a letter from Khan Saheb S.K. Ahsan, District Magistrate and Returning Officer for the south Monghyr Mohammadan Rural constituency)

Rajendra Prasad writes that, in the distribution of tickets among the Congress and the Nationalist Muslims in Bihar, the Jamiat Momin (Momin Conference) got more than any other parties. The Momins won five seats in the elections, while the Jamiat Ulema got none. Rajendra Prasad recollects that, even in the constituency where it was said that all voters were the followers of the candidate who belonged to the Jamiat Ulema, he lost the contest.[98]

It was a great shock for the Congress to find that Professor Abdul Bari lost the election.[99] Abdul Bari jumped into the freedom struggle during the days of the Khilafat movement, and became a leader of the Tata Workers' Union in 1936, and also the President of the Jamshedpur District Congress Committee. With the arrival of Abdul Bari, the labour movement in Jamshedpur gained new vigour.[100] He was arrested in the Quit India movement.

Anugraha Narayan Sinha reports a rumour that, in the constituencies where the Momin candidates did not stand for the contests, the Momin voters did not cast their votes for the Congress, but for the Muslim League. He says that the Congress did not believe in this rumour, because bitterness between the two would only increase if the Congress investigated it.[101]

Two prominent Congress leaders in Bihar had to admit the bitter results of the defeat in the Muhammadan constituencies.

However, Abdul Qaiyum Ansari, leader of the Momins, was elected from Ranchi Muslim constituency. He was the only non-Congressman in the second Congress ministry. He had declined to sign the Congress pledge as he thought it would be a betrayal of the Momin community which had elected him to the Assembly. Patel had asked for an exception in his case and recommended his inclusion.[102]

In the election Abdul Qaiyum Ansari faced a Momin candidate from the Muslim League. In all about 10 Momin candidates from the League were arrayed against the 'Congress Momins' (the expression of the *Dawn*).[103]

It is also interesting to note the following report under the headline 'Novel Method of League Propaganda in Champaran' which appeared in the *Dawn*:

A NOVEL method for fighting out the elections has been adopted by the Muslim League in North Champaran Division where there is an important contest between the Congress candidate Dr Syed Mahmud and the Muslim League candidate, Mr Zubail Khan.

Hundreds of educated men have poured into the constituency in the garb of fakirs, hakims and pirs of Arabic designs who make passing remarks to the unsuspecting villages in favour of the Muslim League and go on.

This type of propaganda is having very great effect as against the regular propaganda and if things so stand, Dr Mahmud may suffer a defeat—so bewails the Bettiah correspondent of the Congress daily, 'The Searchlight'.

It may be mentioned here that a very strong contingent of the League workers including Mr Jafar Imam and the Aligarh students has gone to the above constituency which is one of the three places where the arch enemies of the Millet are pitched against the Musalmans, patted by the soft hands of Dr Prasad and financed by the 'black market' money.

But which side the wind is to blow will be apparent by the Congress daily itself.[104]

In this contest Dr Syed Mahmud won the only Muslim seat for the Congress in Bihar, defeating Zubail Khan by 1,374: 1,167.

On the other hand, Jafar Imam, whom the Communists expected as one of the leaders of the 'Progressive' group inside the League, was elected in Patna City Muhammadan Urban constituency. After the Independence of India he joined the Congress. He was a minister under two chief ministers, Binodanand Jha (1961-2) and K.B. Sahay (1963-7).

The official reports on the Quit India movement in Bihar write that the Muslims as a whole did not participate in the movement even as they did not support the British. Despite the fact that the Quit India movement had the support of the broad masses of the peasants and rural labourers in Bihar, the election results indicated that the movement failed to penetrate deep enough into the Muslim masses.

Like the students of Lahore, many students in Patna left their studies and fanned out in various parts of Bihar to intensify the election campaign for the League.[105]

In this connection, Taqui Rahim, an Urdu writer, recollects that during the years 1945-7, the Muslim League was more popular among the Muslim masses than the intellectuals.[106] He analyses that the Muslim intellectuals were divided into three groups, pro-British, pro-Congress and pro-League. As in other provinces, the Communists supported the League and its Pakistan slogan in Bihar too. Their leader was Ali Ashraf, and under their influence the members of the

Progressive Writers' Association also supported the League's demand for Pakistan.

According to the Census of India, 1941, out of Bihar's total population of 36,340,151 the population of Muslims was 4,716,314, that is, 12.9 per cent of the total population.

Though it is not so well-known as the demand for the 'Independent States' in the Muslim majority areas, the Lahore Resolution adopted by the Muslim League on 23 March 1940 provided safeguards for the minorities both in Pakistan and India:

> That adequate, effective and mandatory safeguards should be specifically provided in the constitution for minorities in these units and in the regions for the protection of their religious, cultural, economic, political, administrative and other rights and interests in consultation with them, and in other parts of India where the Musalmans are in a minority adequate, effective and mandatory safeguards shall be specifically provided in the constitution for them and other minorities for the protection of their religious, cultural, economic, political, administrative and other rights and interests in consultation with them.[107]

In this resolution the movement of the minorities to the areas where they were to become the majorities was not anticipated.

From 25 October 1946, Bihar experienced a serious communal riot in which many Muslims were killed and many others escaped to Bengal. The number of dead was estimated to be about 5,000. Though the riot started as a reaction to riots in the Muslim majority areas of rural Bengal, the political climate which the Provincial Elections created was at least partly responsible for this tragedy which hit the lives of many disenfranchised people.

(iii) Labour Seats

In the Jamshedpur Factory Labour constituency, Michael John, a Congress candidate, won the contest against his opponent, Manek Homi. Manek Homi came to the scene of the labour movement in Jamshedpur at the end of the 1920s. He founded the Jamshedpur Labour Federation in 1936, but soon the management succeeded in winning him over to their side.[108] On the other hand, Michael John was the General Secretary of the Tata Workers' Union under the leadership of Abdul Bari. It is well-known that the workers responded to the call of Quit India with a long strike. Michael John who was preparing for the strike was arrested on the night of 15 August 1942 before the strike actually started.[109] After the release of the labour leaders in 1945, they again tried to organize the workers and after the tragic death of Bari on 28 March 1947, Michael John became the President of the Tata Workers' Union.

This union, along with the Ahmedabad Textile Labour Association, became one of the founding members of the Indian National Trade Union Congress which started under the strong leadership of Sardar Vallabhbhai Patel, President of the Hindustan Mazdoor Sevak Sangh on 3-4 May 1947. As in the case of Kanpur, the 1946 elections provided the Indian National Congress a momentum for the emergence of post-Independent leaders on the labour front. As regards this front the Quit India worked favourably for the Congress and curbed the Communist influence in Jamshedpur.

(iv) Landholders' Constituencies

The Landholders' constituencies were formed under the very limited franchise system. In the case of the Patna Division, a relatively large constituency, the number of electors was 128 in Patna District, 115 in Gaya District and 50 in Shahbad District. It was only 11 in Champaran District.[110]

In four constituencies, independent candidates were elected. Out of these four, Chandeshwar Prasad Narain Sinha in Tiruhut Division and Raja Bahadur Kamakhya Narayan Singh in Chota Nagpur were elected unopposed.

C.P.N. Sinha was a zamindar of the Sheoharh Raj, and spent his political life as a legislator from 1927 to 1948. He was one of the leading zamindars, along with the Maharaja of Darbhanga, a member of the Constituent Assembly, who tried to foil the proposals to abolish the *zamindari* system.

The role of Sinha as the Ambassador of India before and after the collapse of the Rana regime in Nepal (1950-1) is also very well known. K.P. Karunakaran once wrote his view on India's foreign policy during this critical period as follows:

> In regard to Nepal the Indian Government wanted to avoid interfering in the internal affairs of the country. But at the same time, it wanted to follow a firm policy so far as protecting India's strategic interests on her borders was concerned. It was not always possible to reconcile these two attitudes and

very often the Indian Government was led to a situation where it had to take some part in the politics of its neighbour.[111]

However, in the 1960s his view became more critical of India's neighbour policy which could not understand the will of the people correctly.[112] Why Sinha was posted as the Ambassador is worth examining, because its answer may give us a key to find out the character of India's neighbour policy in the late 1940s.

Raja Bahadur Kamkhya Narayan Singh was a landholder of the Ramgarh estate in Hazaribagh District. His family ruled over the majority of the people in this backward district.[113] He founded a regional party, the Chota Nagpur Santhal Parganas Janata Party in 1949, the object of which was to 'drive out the Congress from Chota Nagpur and Santhal Parganas and cleanse Bihar politics of casteism, corruption and to restore the Zamindari rights'. K.B. Sahay who piloted the Zamindari Abolition Act and later became the Chief Minister of Bihar was his political opponent. For the purpose of obstructing the anti-*zamindari* trend in Hazaribagh, K.N. Singh took 'populist' measures like the remission in the land revenue of his estate. He showed a political somersault by merging his party with the Swatantra Party which appeared in 1959, or by joining the Congress in 1966 and leaving soon thereafter. He was a Rajput leader who was connected with land interests.

Rameshwar Prasad Singh was elected with the votes of 135 electors of Patna Division. Later he was nominated by the Congress as a member of the Constituent Assembly.

In the 1930s he was the President of the Gaya District Board, and as a zamindar of Reora he faced the well-known Bakasht Satyagraha of 1939 which most symbolically represented the Kisan movement of these years.[114]

Taranand Sinha, a zamindar of the Banaili Raj, was elected from Bhagalpur Division. The total votes polled for him was 64. While he was studying politics under the guidance of Jawaharlal Nehru, he was called back to Bihar by Shri Krishna Sinha. His opponent in the elections represented the Landholders' Association. He mentions two reasons why he won the contest. One is that he got the whole-hearted cooperation of Shri Krishna Sinha and Anugraha Narayan Sinha, both expectant of the next chief ministership. Second, the respect which his father won as the first graduate landowner in Bihar. He adds that the landlord-peasant relations were good on his estate. He joined the Quit India movement and sent some messages to Jaya Prakash

Narayan who was working underground. In his election campaign he did not prepare any posters or pamphlets. The number of voters was not many, but the constituency was divided by a river. Therefore, campaigning was not easy. But he says there was no conflict with his opponent, Pandit Ravaneshwar Mishra as both came from the same area and the same caste. They were on card-playing terms. Taranand Sinha continued to manage his *zamindari* until 1955. After India's independence he shifted his activities to university administration and business like recruitment for Tatas.[115] He belongs to that category of landholders who adjusted to the changing situation before and after the Independence. Anugraha Narayan Sinha's book records that Taranand Sinha was supported by the Congress in the elections.[116]

However, the number of electors in this constituency was only 155 in all, out of which 102 exercised their votes including 5 women voters.[117]

In the 1946 Provincial Elections, the Congress partly succeeded in chanelling the interests of the zamindars into the constitutional framework, and the experience of the Quit India was also useful here. But the route to resistance to the *zamindari* abolition by the stubborn zamindars through the courts or by violent means was not severed in the elections.

(v) The Congress and the Adivasi Mahasabha

There were keen contests between the Congress and the Adivasi Mahasabha in both the non-reserved constituencies and 7 constituencies reserved for the Backward Areas and the Tribes. Violent scenes were observed in the election campaign.

The Chota Nagpur Adivasi Mahasabha had a pan-tribal composition and demanded the complete separation of the Chota Nagpur area from Bihar under the leadership of Jaipal Singh. The Muslim League suggested a corridor passing through the tribal areas to link East and West Pakistan and sympathized with the tribal people and gave financial support to the Mahasabha.[118]

For instance, the Second Jharkhand Chota Nagpur Pakistan Conference was held on 17-18 February 1946 at Lohardaga, Ranchi District, and this conference adopted a resolution supporting the demand for the separation of Santhal Parganas and Chota Nagpur from Bihar and the formation of these areas into 'the free state of Jharkhand as the homeland of the Adivasi'.[119] Rajendra Prasad also recollects that the Mahasabha members were shouting 'Pakistan Zindabad'.[120]

The Mahasabha won 3 seats in all. Out of 7 reserved seats for the Backward Tribes, the Mahasabha won 2 seats, one in Ranchi and the other in Sinbhum. They got one more seat in the General constituency. But, its leader, Jaipal Singh was defeated.

The Congress won 5 reserved seats (3 unopposed). All the contests except one in the General constituencies were won by the Congress over the Mahasabha.

The poor results of the Mahasabha in the elections forced it to change its line after Independence. There was no longer support from the Muslim League. India had a 'secular' constitution.[121] Jaipal Singh became a member of the Constituent Assembly. Now the Jharkhand Party appeared as a 'modern' political organization, taking a constitutional line.

The elections of 1946 were undoubtedly the 'constitutional' struggle for the Congress as it was so on the side of the Muslim League. Also, the elections in Bihar showed that there was an ethnic problem which Independent India must solve here as in Assam. The Congress won the elections but the problem remained intact.

Before concluding this chapter, a word on the two leaders of the people's movement in Bihar: Jaya Prakash Narayan and Swami Sahajanand.

Jaya Prakash Narayan who tried to organize a movement during the later stage of Quit India was released from jail on 12 April 1946. He said in his first speech in Patna that ever since the Congress was declared legal, it devoted its entire energy to fighting elections and its organizational work was neglected. Elections should provide engagement only for a few of the Congress workers. Let others prepare for struggle.[122] But the main course which the Congress took had already been fixed before Narayan was released from prison.

Swami Sahajanand who did not lead the Quit India movement because of his 'People's War' policy, had come back to the Congress while elections were in progress. On 29 June 1946, he spoke as the President on the occasion of the Thirteenth Session of the Bihar Provincial Kisan Sabha held at Bermo, Hazaribagh District. He said, 'Freedom can only be snatched away by struggle. . . . Without struggle nothing will come. Our master can give us nothing.' He hoped that the national leaders would free themselves from the deceit of the Cabinet Mission. 'The Congress is big and great, and will always remain so. This is our belief.'[123] At the stage when the Bakasht Satyagraha started again in Bihar, there was ambivalence in his ideas.

Sahajanand left the Congress on 6 December 1948. At this stage his perspective of the contemporary situation became very clear. He thought that the August Revolution (of 1942) released unlimited 'People's Power (*Jan Shakti*)', but more than anything else, strengthened the Constitutional Power (*Vaidhanik Shakti*) of the Respectable People (*Babu Log*). After the elections of 1946, there appeared a sign of the decay of the Congress and as Independence came nearer, it changed its character from an organization of sacrifice (*Yog*) to that of lust for power (*Bhog*).[124]

In 1946 it was the Congress that succeeded in transforming people's power into constitutional power. However, all of the people's energy which was devoted to the Quit India movement could not be absorbed by the Congress. The Bakasht Satyagraha which was revived in 1946 was one of the earliest voices which expressed people's dissent against the constitutional process.

NOTES

1. Wavell to the King, 22 March 1946, *TOP*, Vol. 6, p. 1234.
2. Sir Henry Knight, *Food Administration in India 1939-47*, Stanford, 1954, pp. 250-8.
3. Vyas to Rao Raja Sahib, 5 March 1946, *Files on the Marwar Lok Parishad*, RSA.
4. Patel to Sachar, 20 February 1946, Das, op. cit., p. 305.
5. *Dawn*, 30 January 1946.
6. Rai, op. cit., p. 316.
7. Asoka Mehta, *The Political Mind of India*, Bombay, 1952, p. 89.
8. Ibid., p. 86.
9. *TOP*, Vol. 7, pp. 39-45.
10. *Dawn*, 8 Arpil 1946.
11. Ibid., 7 April 1946.
12. A.B. Rajput, *Muslim League—Yesterday and Today*, Lahore, 1948, p. 110.
13. *Dawn*, 1 April 1946.
14. P.C. Joshi, 'Battle for a New United Front for Freedom', *People's Age*, 12 May 1946.
15. *Fortnightly Report for the first half of February 1946*, Madras, TSA.
16. *Fortnightly Report for the first half and second half of April 1946*, Madras, TSA.
17. *Fortnightly Report for the first half of March 1946*, Madras, TSA.

18. *TOP*, Vol. 7, p. 290.
19. 'Communist Candidate sweeps Primary Election Poll', *People's Age*, 3 March 1946 and M.R. Venkatraman, 'For the Nominees of their own Flag, Untouchable Kisans' Overwhelming Verdict', ibid., 10 March 1946.
20. S. Krishnaswamy, *The Role of Madras Legislature in the Freedom Struggle 1861-1947*, New Delhi, 1989, p. 348.
21. *Dawn*, 1 April 1946.
22. I owe most of this personal information to A.B. Shinde, *The Parallel Government of Satara—A Phase of the Quit India Movement*, New Delhi, 1990. Also, I could get a useful information from Dr Gail Omvedt.
23. Source here is from Suryanath Kamath, *Quit India Movement in Karnataka*. Also, I could get more information directly from my talk with Dr Kamath.
24. S.J.M. Epstein, *The Earthy Soil—Bombay Peasants and the Indian Nationalist Movement 1919-1947*, Delhi, 1988, pp. 95-7,
25. Shinde, op. cit., pp. 172-4.
26. *TOP*, Vol. 7, p. 39.
27. *Satara District—Weekly confidential report for the week ending March 14, 1946, P5 IV 1946*, 1 April 1946 to, MSA.
28. *Dawn*, 2 April 1946.
29. W.N. Kuber, *Dr Ambedkar—A Critical Study*, New Delhi, 1973, p. 156.
30. *TOP*, Vol. 7, p. 146.
31. P.B. Rangnekar, 'Congress Leaders Plan: Police and Goondas Carry Out Terror', *People's Age*, 14 April 1946.
32. Ibid.
33. P.B. Rangnekar, 'Workers Carry Red Flag to Victory', *People's Age*, 7 April 1946.
34. *TOP*, Vol. 7. pp. 230-1.
35. Gautam Chattopadhyay, *Bengal Electoral Politics and Freedom Struggle*, New Delhi, 1984, p. 141.
36. Shila Sen, *Muslim Politics in Bengal 1937-47*, New Delhi, 1976, p. 202.
37. Amalendu De, *Islam in Modern India*, Calcutta,1988, pp. 170-2.
38. Sayyad Abudus Sultan, 'Shere-Bangalai Shreshta Janpriya Neta', in Mohammad Abdul Khaleque (ed.), *Mahapurush Fazlul Huq*, Dhaka, 1395 (Bengal calender), p. 250.
39. Abul Jafar Shamusuddin, 'Dusahasi Banglali Karmavir', ibid., p. 111.
40. Sunil Sen, *Agrarian Struggle in Bengal 1946-47*, New Delhi, 1972, p. 98.
41. 'Communist Candidate tops Poll', *People's Age*, 17 February 1946.
42. Ibid., 12 May 1946.
43. P.D. Reeves *et al.* (eds.), *A handbook to Elections in Uttar Pradesh 1920-1951*, Delhi, 1975, pp. 320-62.
44. M. Hashim, op. cit., p. 112.
45. *Dawn*, 20 March 1946.

46. *Fortnightly report for the first half of March 1946,* U.P., NAI.
47. O.P. Sangal, 'Congress leaders unleash Communal Riot', *People's Age,* 24 March 1946.
48. Paul R. Brass, *Factional Politics in an Indian State—The Congress Party in Uttar Pradesh,* Bombay, 1966, pp. 196-7.
49. *People's Age,* 12 May 1946.
50. Patel to Gilani, 24 February 1946, Das, op. cit., p. 305.
51. I.A. Talbot, 'The 1946 Punjab Elections', *Modern Asian Studies,* 14, I, 1980.
52. Ibid.
53. *Dawn,* 20 February 1946.
54. Ibid., 22 February 1946.
55. *TOP,* Vol. 6, p. 1232.
56. Ghaznavi to Patel, 4 January 1946, Das, op. cit., pp. 291-2.
57. *People's Age,* 30 December 1945.
58. Ibid., 12 May 1946.
59. Patel to Secretary, Nagpur PCC, 20 February 1946, Das, op. cit., p. 367.
60. Shukla to Patel, 20 December 1945 and Patel to Shukla, 24 December 1945, ibid., pp. 340, 342.
61. Patel to Biyani, 25 December 1945, ibid., p. 344.
62. Shukla to Patel, 20 December 1945, ibid., p. 340.
63. *Fornightly report for the Central Provinces and Berar, for the first half of April 1946,* NAI.
64. Amalendu Guha, *Planter Raj to Swaraj—Freedom Struggle and Electoral Politics in Assam 1826-1947,* New Delhi, 1977, p. 206.
65. Muhammad Shamsul Haq, *Maulana Bhashanir Rajnaitik Jivan—Tatyalochna o Mulyayan,* Dhaka, 1984, pp. 11-12.
66. Guha, op. cit., pp. 302-3.
67. Ibid., p. 303.
68. *Dawn,* 11 April 1946.
69. *People's Age,* 12 May 1946.
70. Guha, op. cit., pp. 294-5.
71. Hiren Gohain, 'Problem of Unity in Assam on the Eve of Independence', in Amit Kumar Gupta, *Myth and Reality: The Struggle for Freedom in India, 1945-47,* New Delhi, 1987, pp. 305-6.
72. D. G. Tendulkar, *Abdul Ghaffar Khan—faith is a battle,* Bombay, 1967, p. 367.
73. Talbot, op. cit., p. 20.
74. Amit Kumar Gupta, *North West Frontier Province and Freedom Struggle 1932-47,* p. 179.
75. *Dawn,* 8 April 1946.
76. Talbot, op. cit., pp. 17-18.
77. *TOP,* Vol. 7, p. 45.

78. Kishori Mohan Patra, *Orissa State Legislature and Freedom Struggle 1912-47*, New Delhi, 1979, pp. 224-6.
79. *The Orissa Report for the First Half of April 1946*, NAI.
80. Ibid.
81. *TOP*, Vol. 7, p. 43.
82. Jalal, op. cit., pp. 166-7.
83. *Dawn*, 30 January 1946.
84. Talbot, op. cit., pp. 51-2.
85. *TOP*, Vol. 7, p. 44.
86. From the pamphlets in the Palamau General constituency, *1946 Government of Bihar and Orissa, Legislative Department, Election Branch, 1945-1952*, BSA.
87. *Report on the political events in Bihar during the second half of February, 1946*, NAI.
88. 'Anti-Imperialist Awakening vilified as anti-Congress', *People's Age*, 21 April 1946.
89. 'Zamindars' men, Blackmarketeers Rallied to fight Communist Candidates', ibid., 2 December 1945.
90. Indradeep Sinha, 'Full Story of Assault on Pt. Karyanand sharma', ibid., 17 February 1946.
91. *Report of the events in Bihar during the first half of February, 1946*, NAI.
92. Rajendra Prasad, *Autobiography*, Bombay, 1957, p. 576.
93. Rajendra Prasad, *Atma Katha*, New Delhi, 1965, p. 831.
94. 'Fight the Zamindar, Mahajan, Hoarder', *People's Age*, 3 March 1946.
95. Damodaran, op, cit., pp. 322-37.
96. H.D. Malaviya, *Land Reforms in India*, New Delhi, 1955, pp. 205-6.
97. Government of Bihar and Orissa, op. cit.
98. Prasad, *Atmakatha*, p. 829.
99. Ibid.
100. Kuriakose Mamkoottam, *Trade Unionism—Myth and Reality—Unionism in the Tata Iron and Steel Company*, New Delhi, 1982, p. 24.
101. Anugraha Narayan Sinha, *Mere Sansmaran*, Patna, n.d., p. 408.
102. Hasan Nishat Ansari, *The Momin-Congress Relation— A Socio-Historical Analysis*, Patna, 1989, pp. 17-18.
103. *Dawn*, 23 February 1946.
104. Ibid., 25 February 1946.
105. Ibid., 6 February 1946.
106. I owe this part to my interview with Mr. Taqui Rahim on 8 August 1992, Patna and his letter dated 25 February 1993.
107. G. Allama (ed.), *Pakistan Movement: Historic Documents*, Lahore, 1977, p. 227.
108. Mamkoottam, op. cit., p. 24.

109. Moni Ghosh, *Our Struggle—A Short History of Trade Union Movement in TISCO Industry at Jamshedpur*, Calcutta, 1957, pp. 49-50.
110. Nandalal Sinha, *Supplement to the Report on the Elections in Bihar*, March, 1946, Patna, 1946, p. 38.
111. K.P. Karunakaran, *India in World Affairs—February 1950-December 1953, A Review of India's Foreign Relations*, Calcutta, 1958, p. 200.
112. K.P. Karunakaran, 'Non-Aligned Radicals', *Seminar*, No. 45, 1963. Also see S.D. Muni, *Foreign Policy of Nepal*, Delhi, 1973, pp. 90-1.
113. Shashishekhar Jha, *Political Elite in Bihar*, Bombay, 1972, pp. 45-55.
114. Sho Kuwajima, *Sakshatkar—Bihar ke Kisan Neta Pandit Jadunandan Sharma se Batchit*, Patna, 1996, pp. 29-34.
115. This part of information comes from my interview with Taranand Sinha, Patna, 10 February 1989.
116. A.N. Sinha, op. cit., p. 408.
117. *A letter from V.K.B. Pillai, Commissioner, Bhagalpur Division and Returning Officer for the Bhagalpur Division Landholders' Constituency* dated 27 March 1946, Government of Bihar and Orissa, op. cit.
118. K.S. Singh, *Tribal Society in India—An Anthropo-historical Perspective*, New Delhi, 1985, pp. 200-1.
119. *Dawn*, 2 March 1946.
120. Prasad, *Atmakatha*, p. 832.
121. Singh, op. cit., pp. 201-2, and Jha, op. cit., p. 110.
122. Jaya Prakash Narayan, *Towards Struggle—Selected Manifestoes, Speeches and Writings*, Bombay, 1946, p. 216.
123. *Tervan Bihar Prantiya Kisan Sammelan, Bermo (Hazaribagh), 29-30 June, 1946, Sabhapati Swami Sahajanand Saraswati ka Bhashan.*
124. Swami Sahajanand Saraswati, *Maharudra ka Mahatandva*, Patna, n.d., pp. 7, 15.

Conclusion

The Provincial Elections of 1946 in India were held in difficult conditions. India was still under the strong impact of the Quit India movement and was facing food scarcity while memory of the Bengal famine of 1943 was still fresh.

After the Second World War the British Government had to search for a peaceful transfer of power. The Provincial Elections were the first step for this purpose as they were already tested in 1937. After the elections the British Government could shift the whole responsibility for political confrontation between the Indian National Congress and the Muslim League to the Indian side.

On the other hand, all-India political forces had their own reasons to respond to the British call.

Many of the Congress leaders were in jail during the later half of the Second World War period, and those who were now free needed to divert the energy expressed in the Quit India movement into the 'right channel'. In the AICC meeting in September 1945, the Congress decided to contest the elections and to enter into negotiations with the British Government on the basis of the election results. So far, though the Congress leaders had praised the heroic spirit of the Quit India movement, simultaneously they had tried to curb the Prati Sarkar movement in Satara which was the Quit India movement in the present tense. When in November 1945 the Congress faced the upsurge of the people's movement in the form of protest against the trials of the officers of the Indian National Army, there was still some ambivalence in Congress attitudes towards the movement. But after this experience, the Congress approach to these movements was finalized. It was clearly shown in the response of the Congress towards the Royal Indian Navy Strike in February 1946.

However, Vallabhbhai Patel who was actually in charge of the Congress election office in Bombay was not satisfied with the election results. Patel who forced the striking naval ratings to surrender unconditionally was disappointed particularly with the Punjab results. Punjab was a crucial province for the elections and destiny of the subcontinent. In the Punjab the Muslim League appeared as the single largest party in the Legislative Assembly, and the elections did not prove to be the best alternative to the people's movement which Patel curbed with all his might.

In the 1937 Provincial Elections, there were heated discussions on the issue of office acceptance inside the Congress leadership though the party mainstream was ready to form the Provincial Governments. In 1946 the Congress contested the Provincial Elections on a full scale and there was no room for any doubt about office acceptance.

The Constituent Assembly of India whose members were elected on the basis of the results of the Provincial Elections framed the Constitution of India. The bureaucracy which was relentlessly criticized by the Congress in its election meetings was accommodated within this framework, and contributed to the constitutional continuity of India. The Congress ministries which appeared after the elections prepared the Zamindari Abolition bills and other similar agrarian measures though they also tried to accommodate the *zamindari* interests. On the labour front, the Congress tried to revive its influence, challenging Communist influence, and was victorious in Kanpur, Jamshedpur and other labour seats. This was a prelude to the birth of the Indian National Trade Union Congress (INTUC) in 1947 under the initiative of the Indian National Congress.

The Congress also achieved remarkable results in the scheduled caste constituencies. This victory was a step to the Congress claim after Independence that it represented the interests of the scheduled castes. But it should be discussed whether this victory really suited the spirit of the Poona Pact of 1932 which adjusted the wishes of the scheduled caste voters with those of the whole general voters. The storm of the Quit India movement seems to have absorbed the problems which the scheduled castes were facing, but this issue remained one of the main themes in the later constitution-making process.

There is no doubt that the Provincial Elections of 1946 provided constitutional continuity and the stability of Congress rule in India at least up to mid-1960s when marked social change began to appear.

After the breakdown of the Simla Conference in June-July 1945, Jinnah and the Muslim League wanted to prove through the election results that the League was the only representative organization of the Indian Muslims. This was the only and perhaps the last chance to realize the Pakistan scheme *constitutionally*. Therefore the only election issue for the League was Pakistan, and the League did not publish any election manifesto or encourage the provincial leadership to prepare election manifesto. Only the slogan of Pakistan could unite the various interests of the Indian Muslims. The 'Progressives' within the Provincial Leagues agreed to this strategy and in Bengal where there was serious conflict between the Central leadership and the emerging Bengali leadership the latter did not bring to surface their demand for an independent Bengal which had been observed since the Lahore Resolution of 1940. The conflicts were strictly limited to adjustment of nominations between the two groups.

The election results were clear. Though the Congress was predominant in the general seats, the Muslim League occupied most of the Muslim seats and in some provinces like Madras and Bombay their victory was enough to prove the theory of the 'Muslim nation'. The Convention of the League Legislators in Delhi in April 1946 became a milestone which described the Pakistan scheme as 'a sovereign independent State'.

It was in 1954 that the will of the people of East Pakistan for autonomy was clearly shown in the election results. On this occasion the Pakistan Government tried to avert political crisis with the declaration of the Emergency. This was the first grave constitutional crisis after the birth of Pakistan.

In West Pakistan, Mian Iftikhar-ud-din who had been Minister for Refugees for two months after Independence, was removed from the Muslim League in 1950. He criticized the first Constitution of Pakistan, 1956 as undemocratic and un-Islamic. He was conscious of the right of minorities and the multi-national character of the Pakistani society.

The military coup in 1958 completely buried the various trends of the political opinion that had converged for the establishment of Pakistan, and the constitutional continuity in Pakistan was finally broken. Jinnah used the *constitutional means* up to the end of July 1946 when he appealed the League workers to resort to direct action. In this respect, in the later history of Pakistan Jinnah's political idea provided the weapons for resistance and reconstruction to the anti-establishment movement.

The Communist Party of India which had propagated the theory of national self-determination since 1942 wanted to prove the correctness of its theory in the elections. Its election tactic was to support both the Congress and the League candidates in the constituencies where they did not put up their own candidates. They were miserably defeated, and in the Punjab where their theory was severely put to test they even lost the seats that they had so far maintained. After two years (in 1948) the Communists changed their policy radically at the Second Congress of the Party.

The participation of the Communists in the elections definitely contributed to the peaceful completion of the Provincial Elections. However, their participation and their conviction of the theory of 'National Unity' and self-determination delayed the development of the people's movements like the Tebhaga Struggle in Bengal. Even in Bombay where the Communists were busy with the elections when the naval strike occurred, they seemed at pains to adjust their election campaign with their support for the strike though this aspect does not appear in contemporary papers.

The elections of 1946 were held under a very limited franchise system. Most women, and people of lower classes, were deprived of their right to vote.

The Communist Party of India which discussed the meaning of the limited franchise system at the earliest stage of its election campaign did not persevere with this theme partly because of their policy of 'National Unity'. In a sense, the naval strike which was fought in the midst of the elections was the revolt of disenfranchised people. One trend of the recent historical studies in India points out the limited character of the strike in magnitude and impact. Even among the mutineers self-critical views appeared in connection with the importance of the revolt.

Even though the Provincial Elections in 1946 were fought around the issue concerning the future of the sub-continent, the franchise was limited. Only one-fourth of the people in British India who reached voting age could exercise their right, and the people of the Indian states were outside the sphere of the elections. The election results were clear and therefore became inflexible. Moreover, the Government of India Act of 1935 and the election system under the Act were basically motivated by the British desire to rule. Though the Congress and the League in particular utilized this election system fully and got their partially or fully expected results, there was a limit to their success. The movement of the disenfranchised for freedom and their daily demands complemented the limited character of the Provincial Elections, but this aspect was rejected by both the Congress and the League leadership. The response of the political leaders to the strike was noteworthy in this connection.

Despite the partial paralysis of the British administration in India by the Quit India movement during the Second World War, they had already had an experience of the Provincial Elections in 1937 and could maintain their official work during the War for the swift response to the elections which were expected immediately after the War.

Since the middle of the 1930s there remained a strong ideological trend inside the Congress under the leadership of Sardar Vallabhbhai Patel despite stiff objection from the Congress Socialists. His group wanted to transform the Congress into a Parliamentary party while not giving up completely the line of civil disobedience. The 1937 Provincial Elections and the formation of the Congress ministries were their first experiment. Though in October-November 1939 the Congress ministries resigned in protest against the British War-time policy on the freedom of India, the Congress legislators continued to occupy their positions.

Therefore, when the Congress decided to contest the Provincial Elections in September 1945, it was not just expediency for the purpose of freeing themselves from foreign rule, but was based on the long-term strategy of nation-building. Many of the Congress leaders criticized Government officials who had treated demonstrators high-handedly during the Quit India movement and even threatened to punish them after they had assumed office. But it was also true that they decided to utilize seriously 'the very apparatus that had been recently locking them in jail'.[1] We should not misread the rather standoffish statements of Jawaharlal Nehru in those days. The stable Congress rule under his leadership in the 1950s depended exactly on the electoral system which safely slid into post-Independence days from the 1930s though, of course, we have to note the significance of the 1952 General Election under universal franchise and that support of the people of all classes and strata was a decisive factor.

Though the election results in 1946 were not favourable for the Congress and it partly tried to nullify the results in the later political process as in the case of the Punjab, the Congress could still lead the people's enthusiasm against British rule into the 'right channel.' Whatever the decision of the Congress, the concession to the demand for Pakistan which was expressed in election results, and the fact that the Congress finally approved the results, at least partly, contributed to the stability of the electoral system in India. In this respect, the 1946 elections were a precursor of the political tradition established after Independence. From the late 1960s many parties in power had to step down at the Centre and provinces after the elections. Elections in India after Independence were responsive enough to absorb the enthusiasm and discontent of the people for long.

It is another theme to examine to what extent the limited franchise system of 1946, closely connected with the social structure of those days, limited the possibility of exercise of rights in various aspects of life for many years after Independence. This limited character of the elections of 1946 had its serious impact on the later history of the people of India. The new political experiment of universal electoral franchise involved a painful struggle for a new political system while inheriting the tradition of the people's struggle for their rights.

Meanwhile, as we have noted, Jinnah had been consistently a constitutionalist up to the 1946 elections, and the election results showed that the League won most of the Muslim seats. Though within limited franchise and the separate electorate system, the League could prove that most of the Muslim voters were solidly behind the demand for Pakistan. However, after 'a victory for which there is no parallel in the world', elected League legislators were now expected to achieve the goal of Pakistan by all means instead of 'working the constitution', and, whichever reasons forced the League to this decision, they finally concluded at the end of July 1946 that Muslim India had exhausted without success all efforts to find a peaceful solution to the Indian problem by compromise and constitutional means, and hence decided to resort to direct action to achieve Pakistan. This radical change of policy succeeded in the creation of Pakistan, but also led to constitutional instability in post-Independent Pakistan. Of course, the explanation for this instability cannot be complete without reference to the growth of the military leadership, caused by cold war international politics.

In Japan, the end of the Second World War relieved her people from an oppressive military regime. But in the constitution-making of post-War Japan, the role of the occupation army and, particularly, the will of the U.S., were crucial. They intervened in and led the preparation of the draft of the Constitution. The Imperial system and its idea were maintained, even as its function was forced to change. The rule of the few big business groups (*Zaibatsu*) in Japan was destroyed, but after fifty years we again find the monopolistic rule of some dominant firms and groups and their characteristic behaviour. This managing structure which achieved high rate of economic growth in Japan from the 1960s to the 1980s is under severe trial in the 1990s. Japanese education, which boasted a hundred per cent literacy, has serious problems today and has not yet been free from bureaucratic intervention. After the War Japan promised not to be a military big power again, but there are politicians and opinion leaders who assert that Japan contributed to the independence of the Asian countries with her military operations during the Second World War.

Many of these characteristics in contemporary Japan are closely connected with the nature of the constitutional and extra-constitutional continuity maintained immediately after the War. The General Election of April 1946 is to be remembered as the first constitutional step for this continuity though the elections were epoch-making in other aspects and opened the way for popular sovereignty. It was the people and the people's movement that made the post-War Constitution of Japan really people-oriented.

The problems that the people of the world faced in 1946 and the way of their solution which each area took at that critical moment are of crucial relevance to the people who live today.

NOTE

1. Henry C. Hart, 'Political Leadership in India: Dimensions and Limits', Atul Kohli (ed.), *India's Democracy—An Analysis of Changing State-Society Relations*, Princeton, 1990, p. 20. Also cf. Pradhan Harishankar Prasad, *Gandhi, Marx aur Bharat Pragati ka ek Vaikalpik Path*, Delhi, 1994, p. 39.

TABLE II: SEATS IN PROVINCIAL LEGISLATIVE ASSEMBLIES, 1946

Provinces	Total Seats	General Seats		Seats for Backward Areas and Tribes	Sikh Seats	Muham-madan Seats	Anglo-Indian Seats	Euro-pean Seats	Indian Christ-ian Seats	Seats for Com-merce, Industry, Mininig and Planting	Land Hol-ders Seats	Univer-sity Seats	Seats for Labo-urs	Seats for Women				
		Total General Seats	General Seats Reserved for Sche-duled Castes											Gene-ral	Sikh	Muham-madan	Anglo-Indian	Indian Christ-ian
1	2	3	4	5	6	7	8	9	10	11	12	13	14	15	16	17	18	19
Madras	215	146	30	1	—	28	2	3	8	6	6	1	6	6	—	1	—	1
Bombay	175	114	15	1	—	29	2	3	3	7	2	1	7	5	—	1	—	—
Bengal	250	78	30	—	—	117	3	11	2	19	5	2	8	2	—	2	1	—
United Provinces	228	140	20	—	—	64	1	2	2	3	6	1	3	4	—	2	—	—
Punjab	175	42	8	—	31	84	1	1	2	1	5	1	3	1	1	2	—	—
Bihar	152	86	15	7	—	39	1	2	1	4	4	1	3	3	—	1	—	—
CP and Berar	112	84	20	1	—	14	1	1	—	2	3	1	2	3	—	—	—	—
Assam	108	47	7	9	—	34	—	1	1	11	—	—	4	1	—	—	—	—
NWFP	50	9	—	—	3	36	—	—	—	—	2	—	—	—	—	—	—	—
Orissa	60	44	6	5	—	4	—	—	1	1	2	—	1	2	—	—	—	—
Sind	60	18	—	—	—	33	—	2	—	2	2	—	1	1	—	1	—	—

Source: *File No. 79/46, Vol. 1,* Home Department Political (I), NAI.

TABLE III: PROVISIONAL DATES OF NOMINATIONS, POLLING AND COMPLETION OF THE GENERAL ELECTION TO THE LEGISLATIVE ASSEMBLIES IN THE PROVINCES, 1945-6

Serial No.	*Province*	*Nominations*	*Polling*	*Completion of Election*
1	Assam	10 Dec. 1945	9/12 Jan. 1946	22 Jan.
2	Sind	21 Dec. 1945	18/21 Jan.1946	31 Jan.
3	NWFP	12 Dec. 1945	26–31 Jan. 1946 1–14 Feb. 1946	—
4	Punjab	12 Dec. 1945	1–15 Feb. 1946	19/23 Feb.
5	United Provinces	17 Jan. 1946 5 Feb. 1946	18–22 Feb. 4–12 Mar.	30 Mar.
		27 Feb. 1946	20–21 Mar.	
6	Bihar	18/22 Jan. 1946	22 Feb.–1 Mar.	6/8 Mar.
7	Bengal	13 Feb. 1946	16–23 Mar.	30 Mar.
8	Bombay	11 Feb. 1946	18 Mar. 20–21 Mar.	28 Mar.
9	Madras	21 Feb. 1946	18 Mar.	26 Mar.
10	CP and Berar	18/19 Feb. 1946	22 Mar.–12 Apr.	18 Apr.
11	Orissa	4 Mar. 1946	4–9 Apr.	20 Apr.

Prepared by the Bureau of Public Information, Government of India on 10 January 1946.

SOURCE: *File No. 79/46, Vol. 1,* Home Department Political (I), NAI.

TABLE IV: PROGRAMMES FOR THE WORK OF REVISION OF ELECTORAL ROLLS AND HOLDING ELECTION FOR THE BIHAR LEGISLATIVE ASSEMBLY AND BIHAR LEGISLATIVE COUNCIL

Communique
The 19 Sept. 1945

The Government of Bihar in pursuance of the policy explained in the communique dated 12 September 1945 have now drawn up the following programmes for the work of revision of electoral rolls and holding election for the Bihar Legislative Assembly and Bihar Legislative Council.

Provincial Assembly		*Provincial Council*
List of amendments and Primary elections	Preparation of fresh rolls (Labour Constituencies)	Preparation of fresh rolls
Final date for application 15 Oct. 1945	Supply of lists 15 October	Prelimininary drafts 25 October
Publication of Notices 24 Oct.–31 Oct.		
Hearing 1 Nov.–20 Nov.	Printing of lists 15 Nov.	Revised drafts 9 Nov.
Notification for primary election 6 Dec.	Draft Publication 22 Nov.–6 Dec.	Draft Publication 9 Nov.–23 Nov.
Printing of lists of amendments 11 Dec.	Notice of hearing 9 Dec.–16 Dec.	Notice of hearing 27 Nov.–4 Dec.
Publication 14 Dec.	Hearing 17 Dec.–23 Dec.	Hearing 5 Dec.–10 Dec.
Nomination for primary election 20 Dec.		
Polling 29 Dec.		
Counting of votes 2 Jan. 1946	Publication of lists 7 Jan. 1946	Final Publication 20 Jan. 1946

Contd.

TABLE IV *Contd.*

Provincial Assembly Final Election		*Provincial Council Election*	
Notification	8 Jan.1946	Notification	15 Jan.
Nomination	18–22 Jan.	Nomination	29 Jan.
Polling	22 Feb.–1 Mar.	Polling	4 Mar.
Counting of votes	6–8 Mar.	Counting of votes	9 Mar.

SOURCE: *1946 Government of Bihar—Appointment Department—Election Branch*, BSA.

TABLE V: CANDIDATES AND VOTERS IN THE ELECTIONS TO THE PROVINCIAL ASSEMBLIES IN 1946

Provinces	*Number of Seats*	*Number of seats filled without Contest*	*Number of candidates for Contested Seats*	*Total Electorates*	*Number of Scheduled Caste Voters*	*Number of Women Voters*	*Total Number of Voters in Contested Constituencies*	*Number of Electors Who Voted*	*Percentage of Column 9 on Column 8*
1	*2*	*3*	*4*	*5*	*6*	*7*	*8*	*9*	*10*
Madras	215	94	276	8,468,379	1,038,636	1,911,444	5,001,665	2,338,756	46.76
Bombay	175	29	321	4,248,757	262,326	930,368	3,685,108	1,761,542	47.80
Bengal	250	53	611	9,008,054	1,232,662	1,439,581	8,167,050	4,169,975	51.11
U.P.	228	89	350	7,237,823	687,131	1,022,199	4,305,152	1,910,307	44.37
Punjab	175	14	552	3,554,772	190,070	240,338	3,206,589	1,937,418	60.42
Bihar	152	55	214	2,844,171	68,021	387,239	1,740,308	937,807	53.89
C.P. and Berar	112	25	222	1,993,266	137,412	349,447	1,587,679	655,475	41.29
Assam	108	22	266	1,465,686	59,195	174,802	1,251,985	629,121	50.25
NWFP	50	7	130	574,634	—	n.a.	534,416	356,327	66.68
Orissa	56	37	39	680,955	18,887	99,603	224,041	82,189	36.68
Sind	60	10	178	999,342	—	65,568	880,977	453,556	51.48
Total	1,581	435	3,159	41,075,839	3,694,340	6,620,589	30,584,970	15,232,473	49.80

SOURCE: *Return showing the Results of Elections to the Central Legislative Assembly and the Provincial Legislatures in 1945-46*, New Delhi, 1948, p. 54.

TABLE VI: VOTES POLLED BY VARIOUS POLITICAL PARTIES IN ELECTIONS TO THE PROVINCIAL ASSEMBLIES IN 1946

Class of Constituency	*Total No. of Votes Polled*	*Congress*		*Muslim League*		*Hindu Mahasabha*		*Nationalist Muslims*		*Unionist*		*Communists*		*Others*	
		No. of Votes Polled	*% of Votes Polled*	*No. of Votes Polled*	*% of Votes Polled*	*No. of Votes Polled*	*% of Votes Polled*	*No. of Votes Polled*	*% of Votes Polled*	*No. of Votes Polled*	*% of Votes Polled*	*No. of Votes Polled*	*% of Votes Polled*	*No. of Votes Polled*	*% of Votes Polled*
General	13,960,536	11,294,881	80.9	—	—	257,915	1.8	—	—	136,848	1.0	516,041	3.7	1,754,851	12.6
Urban	1,474,397	1,250,664	84.8	—	—	35,701	2.4	—	—	—	—	16,154	1.1	171,878	11.7
Rural	12,486,139	10,044,217	80.4	—	—	222,214	1.8	—	—	136,848	1.1	499,887	4.0	1,582,973	12.7
Muhammadan	6,084,072	276,173*	4.6	4,547,158	74.7	—	—	391,592	6.4	277,737	4.6	7,111	0.1	584,199	9.6
Urban	674,649	15,834	2.3	531,089	78.7	—	—	33,588	5.0	—	—	—	—	94,138	14.0
Rural	5,409,423	260,341	4.8	4,016,069	74.3	—	—	358,104	6.6	277,737	5.1	7,111	0.1	490,061	9.1
Sikh	388,204	111,684	28.8	—	—	—	—	—	—	—	—	28,594	7.3	247,926[1]	63.9
Anglo-Indian	23,580	—	—	—	—	—	—	—	—	119	0.5	—	—	23,461	99.5
European	1,380			—	—	—	—	—	—	—	—	—	—	1,380	100.0
Indian Christian	181,392	61,093	33.7	—	—	—	—	—	—	2,826	1.5	—	—	117.473	64.8
Backward Areas & Tribes	35,501	17,923	50.5	—	—	—	—	—	—	—	—	—	—	17,578	49.5
Women's	193,927	132,637	68.4	8,023	4.1	11,214	5.8	4,321	2.2	—	—	10,843	5.6	26,889	13.9
General	134,403	103,157	76.8	—	—	11,214	8.3	—	—	—	—	2,041	1.5	17,991	13.4

Contd.

TABLE VI *CONTD.*

Class of Constituency	*Total No. of Votes Polled*	*Congress*		*Muslim League*		*Hindu Mahasabha*		*Nationalist Muslims*		*Unionist*		*Communists*		*Others*	
		No. of Votes Polled	*% of Votes Polled*	*No. of Votes Polled*	*% of Votes Polled*	*No. of Votes Polled*	*% of Votes Polled*	*No. of Votes Polled*	*% of Votes Polled*	*No. of Votes Polled*	*% of Votes Polled*	*No. of Votes Polled*	*% of Votes Polled*	*No. of Votes Polled*	*% of Votes Polled*
Muhammadan	15,501	—	—	8,023	51.7	—	—	4,321	27.9	—	—	—	—	3,157	20.4
Sikh	44,023	29,480	67.0	—	—	—	—	—	—	—	—	8,802	20.0	5,741	13.0
Commerce, Industry, Mining and Planting	4,116	2,999	72.9	41	1.0	13	0.3	—	—	—	—	—	—	1,063	25.8
Landholders	11,415	3,287	28.7	1,951	17.1	491	4.3	168	1.6	1,701	14.9	—	—	3,817	33.4
Labour	485,688	324,323	66.8	443	0.1	—	—	—	—	—	—	118,248	24.3	42,674	8.8
Universities	17,600	15,185	86.3	429	2.4	622	3.5	—	—	—	—	—	—	1,364	7.8
Total	21,387,411	12,240,187	57.2	4,558,045	21.3	270,255	1.3	396,181	1.8	419,231	2.0	680,837	3.2	2,822,675	13.2

SOURCE: Ibid., Table V, p. 55.

• 276,173 should be corrected as 276,175.

[1]Original footnote: This figure includes 167,289 votes polled by the Panthic Party. The percentage of the votes polled by the Panthic party on the total votes in Sikh constituencies is 43.1.

TABLE VII: NUMBER OF WOMEN VOTERS IN ELECTIONS TO BOTH RESERVED AND UNRESERCED SEATS IN THE PROVINCIAL LEGISLATIVE ASSEMBLIES

Provinces	*Number Enrolled*	*Number Enrolled in Contested Constituencies*	*Number who Voted*	*Percentage of Column 4 on Column 3*
1	*2*	*3*	*4*	*5*
Madras	1,911,444	1,134,091	393,227	34.5
Bombay	930,368	787,624	321,266	40.1
Bengal	1,439,581	1,261,268	175,451	13.9
U.P.	1,022,199	632,037	134,470	21.3
Punjab	222,360	195,197	78,087	40.0
Bihar	387,239	214,724	42,931	20.0
C.P. and Berar	349,447	148,493	68,527	46.2
Assam	174,802	151,470	39,467	26.1
NWFP	n.a.	n.a.	n.a.	n.a.
Orissa	99,603	40,928	5,262	12.9
Sind	65,568	44,695	16,950	37.9
Total	6,602,611	4,610,527	1,275,638	27.7

SOURCE: Ibid., Table V, p. 56

TABLE VIII: PROVINCIAL ASSEMBLY ELECTIONS, 1946, RESULTS AND ANALYSIS BY ECONOMIC RESEARCH DEPARTMENT, ALL INDIA CONGRESS COMMITTEE

1. MADRAS

(i) Party-wise Results

Parties	*Nominations*	*Unopposed Returns*	*Contested Wins*	*Total Wins*	*Losses*
Congress	179	71	94	165	12
SCF	13	—	—	—	13
Communist	39	—	2	2	37
RDP	11	—	—	—	11
Hindu Mahasabha	6	—	—	—	6
League	29	13	16	29	0
Majlis	9	—	—	—	9
Independent	85	10	9	19	66
Total	369	94	121	215	154

(ii) General Seats

Parties	*Nominations*	*Unopposed Returns*	*Contested Wins*	*Total Wins*	*Losses*	*% of Votes to Total Polled*
Congress	146	63	83	146	—	79
Communist	31	—	—	—	31	12.2
Independent	46	—	—	—	46	5.3
SCF	13	—	—	—	13	2.2
RDP	6	—	—	—	6	0.03
Hindu Mahasabha	5	—	—	—	5	0.01

(iii) Labour Seats

Congress	6	—	4	4	2	47.55
Communist	5	—	2	2	3	48.54
RDP	3	—	—	—	3	3.05
Independent	2	—	—	—	2	0.4

(iv) Muslim Seats

League	29	13	16	29	—	92.7
Majlis	9	—	—	—	9	2.5
Congress	4	—	—	—	4	1
Independent	3	—	—	—	3	2.8
Communist	1	—	—	—	—	0.7

2. Bombay

Parties	Nominations	Unopposed Returns	Contested Wins	Total Wins	Losses	% of Votes to Total Polled
Congress	132	11	114	125	7	80.06
League	30	7	23	30	—	5.28
SCF	14	—	—	—	14	4.54
ILP	9	—	—	—	9	1.31
Hindu Mahasabha	21	—	1	1	20	3.33
RDP	21	1	—	1	20	1.19
Communists	11	1	1	2	9	1.08
Independent	96	9	7	16	80	3.17
Total	334	29	46	175	159	

3. Bengal

(i) Party-wise Results

Parties	Nominations	Unopposed Returns	Contested Wins	Total Wins	Losses	% of Votes to Total Polled
Congress	98	15	71	86	12	42.12
League	122	11	103	114	8	36.75
Independent	254	1	7	8	246	9.11
Communists	24	—	3	3	21	2.87
Hindu Mahasabha	28	1	—	1	27	1.43
RDP	16	—	—	—	16	0.19
SCF	8	—	1	1	7	1.75
Independent Scheduled Caste	5	—	2	2	3	1.28
Kshatriya Samiti	5	—	1	1	4	0.79
Jamiat-Ulema	12	—	—	—	12	0.50
Nationalist Muslim	5	—	—	—	5	0.08
Muslim Parliamentary Board	10	—	—	—	10	0.29
KPT	44	—	4	4	40	2.36
Emrat	3	—	1	1	2	0.30
Anglo-Indian United Group	4	—	4	4	—	0.18
European	11	11	—	11	—	—
European (CI)	14	14	—	14	—	—
Total	663	53	197	250	413	100

(ii) General Seats

Parties	*Nominations*	*Unopposed Returns*	*Contested Wins*	*Total Wins*	*Losses*	*% of Votes to Total Polled*
Congress	74	9	62	71	3	75.2
Communists	11	—	1	1	10	4.1
Hindu Mahasabha	26	—	—	—	26	2.6
Independent	86	—	2	2	84	10.1
SCF	8	—	1	1	7	3.4
Independent Scheduled Caste	5	—	2	2	3	2.4
RDP	7	—	—	—	7	0.27
Kshatriya Samity	5	—	1	1	4	1.5
Total	222	9	69	78	144	100

(iii) Muslim Seats

Parties	*Nominations*	*Unopposed Returns*	*Contested Wins*	*Total Wins*	*Losses*	*% of Votes to Total Polled*
League	117	9	101	110	7	83.6
Independent	140	—	2	2	138	7.6
Jamiat-ulema	12	—	—	—	12	1.2
Nationalist Muslim	5	—	—	—	5	0.2
MPB	10	—	—	—	10	0.7
KPP	44	—	4	4	40	5.3
Emrat	3	—	1	1	2	0.7
RDP	3	—	—	—	3	0.027
Congress	6	—	—	—	6	0.5
Communists	2	—	—	—	2	0.12
Total	342	9	108	117	225	100

4. United Provinces

(i) Party-wise Results

Parties	*Nominations*	*Unopposed Returns*	*Contested Wins*	*Total Wins*	*Losses*
Congress	189	79	74	153	36
League	79	1	53	54	25
RDP	14	—	—	—	14
Hindu Mahasabha	21	—	—	—	21
Independent	88	9	5	14	74
Communists	5	—	—	—	5
Ahrar	3	—	1	1	2
Nationalist Muslim	35	—	6	6	29
Jamiat-ul-Ulema	2	—	—	—	2
Indian Federation of Labour	3	—	—	—	3
Total	439	89	139	228	211

(ii) Non-Muslim Constituencies, including special constituencies such as Labour, Commerce, Zamindars and Indian Christians

% of votes to total votes

Congress	94.8 %
RDP	2.2 %
Communists	1.5 %
Hindu Mahasabha	0.8 %
Independents	2.7 %

(iii) Muslim Constituencies including a Muslim Women's seat

% of votes to total votes

League	65.4 %
Congress	14.1 %
Nationalist Muslims	12.0 %
Independents	6.1 %
Ahrars	1.2 %
Jamiat-ul-Ulema	1.2 %

(iv) Labour Constituencies

% of votes to total votes

Congress	69.0 %
Communists	28.9 %
Indian Federation of Labour	1.5 %
Independents	0.6 %

5. Punjab

(i) Party-wise Results

Parties	*Nominations*	*Unopposed Returns*	*Contested Wins*	*Total Wins*	*Losses*
Congress	83	9	42	51	32
League	86	2	71	73	13
Unionist	101	3	17	20	81
Akali Panth	30	—	22	22	8
Communists	23	—	—	—	—
Ahrar	15	—	—	—	15
Independent	225	—	9	9	216
Total	563	14	161	175	388

(ii) General Seats—Votes Polled by Parties

Parties	*Seats Contested*	*Votes Polled*	*Percentage*
Congress	32	331,424	56.18
Unionist	22	128,705	21.82
Hindu Mahasabha	2	1,184	0.2
RDP	1	494	0.08
Communists	3	1,286	0.2
Independents	25	126,839	21.15

(iii) Muslim Seats—Votes Polled by Parties

Parties	*Seats Contested*	*Votes Polled*	*Percentage*
League	83	667,792	65.26
Unionists	69	278,463	26.81
Congress	9	4,709	0.45
Ahrars	17	41,811	4.02
Khaksars	4	3,150	0.30
Independents	54	32,442	3.12

(iv) Sikh seats—Votes Polled by Parties

Congress	26	171,954	41.14
Akalis	27	171,140	40.93
Communists	18	37,450	8.95
Unionists	1	1,216	0.29
RDP	1	1	0.00
Independents	25	36,327	8.69

(v) Labour Seats—Votes Polled by Parties

Congress	3	3,862	37.61
Communists	3	834	8.12
Independents	4	5,570	54.26

6. Bihar

(i) Party-wise Results

Parties	*Nominations*	*Unopposed Returns*	*Contested Wins*	*Total Wins*	*Losses*
Congress	109	44	54	98	11
Hindu Mahasabha	15	—	—	—	15
RDP	11	—	—	—	11
Adibasis	10	—	3	3	7
Communists	3	—	—	—	3
Independent	46	9	3	12	34
League	42	2	32	34	8
Momin (Pro-Congress)	19	—	5	5	14
Jamiat-ul-Ulema	6	—	—	—	6
Nationalist Muslim (Pro-Congress)	4	—	—	—	4
Mazdoor Union	3	—	—	—	3

(ii) Candidates set up on Congress Tickets

Constituencies	*No. of Seats*	*Candi- dates*	*Unopposed Returns*	*Contested Wins*	*Total Wins*	*Losses*
General	71	71	43	27	70	1
Scheduled Castes	15	15	8	7	15	—
Adibasis	7	7	3	2	5	2
Labour	3	3	—	3	3	—
Women	3	3	2	1	3	—
Commerce	1	1	—	1	1	—
Indian Christian	1	1	—	—	—	1
Muslim*	40	9	—	1	1	8
Landholder	4	—	—	—	—	—
Planters' Association	1	—	—	—	—	—
Mining Federation	2	—	—	—	—	—
University	1	—	—	—	—	—
European	2	—	—	—	—	—
Anglo-Indian	1	—	—	—	—	—
Total	152	110	56	42	98	12

* Original footnote; Five Nationalist Muslims from Momin community, other than our candidates, were elected. Though they are not our Party members as yet, to all intents and purposes they work as party members.

7. C.P. AND BERAR

(i) Party-wise Results

Parties	*Nomina- tions*	*Unopposed Returns*	*Contested Wins*	*Total Wins*	*Losses*	*% of Total*
Congress	96	20	72	92	4	72.44
Hindu Mahasabha	17	—	—	—	17	1.75
Independent	90	2	4	6	84	11.28
SCF	22	—	1	1	21	8.9
RDP	3	—	—	—	3	0.1
Communists	2	—	—	—	2	0.3
League	14	3	10	13	1	5.2
Khaksar	3	—	—	—	3	0.03
Total	247	25	87	112	135	100

(ii) General seats

Congress	84	17	65	82	2	78.2
Hindu Mahasabha	16	—	—	—	16	2
Independent	63	—	1	1	62	10.8
SCF	20	—	1	1	19	8.8
RDP	3	—	—	—	3	0.1
Communist	1	—	—	—	1	0.1
Total	187	17	67	84	103	100

(iii) Muslim seats

Parties	*Nomina-tions*	*Unopposed Returns*	*Contested Wins*	*Total Wins*	*Losses*	*% of Total*
League	14	3	10	13	1	82.8
Congress	2	—	—	—	2	0.1
Independent	11	—	1	1	10	17.0
Khaksar	3	—	—	—	3	0.1
Total	30	3	11	14	16	100

8. Assam

(i) General Seats

Parties	*Number of Candidates*	*Total wins*	*% of Total Votes*
Congress	47	47	79
Independents	46	—	—
Ahom Sabha	8	—	21
Communists	3	—	—
Tribal League	2	—	—
(ii) Muslim Seats			
League	34	31	66
Independents	37	0	14
Jamiat-Ulema	20	3	18
KPP	1	0	0.01
(iii) Special Seats			
Congress	11	8	61.2
Independents	16	3	35.4
Tribal League	1	0	2.2
Communists	3	0	1.2

9. North-West Frontier Province

(i) Party-wise Results

Parties	*Nominations*	*Unopposed Returns*	*Contested Wins*	*Total Wins*	*Losses*
Congress	40	7	23	30	10
Jamiat-ul-Ulema	3	—	2	2	1
Akali	3	—	1	1	2
Ahrar	9	—	—	—	9
Khaksar	13	—	—	—	13
League	38	—	17	17	21

(ii) Muslim Seats

Parties	*Nominations*	*Total Wins*	*Total Votes*	*%*
Congress	28	19	139,975	39.24
League	38	17	147,880	41.46
Jamiat-ul-Ulema	3	2	7,875	2.21
Ahrars Khaksars Independents	52	—	61,046	17.10

10. ORISSA

(i) Party-wise Results

Parties	*Nominations*	*Unopposed Returns*	*Contested Wins*	*Total Wins*	*Losses*	*% of Total*
Congress	52	34	13	47	5	80.7
Independent	18	2	2	4	14	11.1
League	4	1	3	4	0	5.2
Communist	1	—	1	1	0	2.7
RDP	1	—	—	—	1	0.3
Total	76	37	19	56	20	100

(ii) General Seats

Congress	45	31	12	43	2	87.38
Independent	13	—	2	2	11	12.35
RDP	1	—	—	—	1	0.27
Total	59	31	14	45	14	100

(iii) Muslim Seats

Congress	2	—	—	—	2	6.6
League	4	1	3	4	—	90.8
Independent	1	—	—	—	1	2.6
Total	7	1	3	4	3	100

(iv) Labour Seat

Congress	1	—	—	—	1	43
Communist	1	—	1	1	—	57
Total	2	—	1	1	1	100

11. Sind
Party-wise Results

Parties	*Nominations*	*Unopposed Returns*	*Contested Wins*	*Total Wins*	*Losses*
Congress	18	6	12	18	—
Jamiat-ul-Ulema	14	—	4	4	10
All-India Muslim League	35	1	26	27	8
Provincial Muslim League (Syed Group)	14	—	4	4	10
Indpendent (Pro-Congress)	4	—	4	4	—
European	3	3	—	3	—

Source: *AICC Papers ED-1/1946 KW II,* NMM.
No alternations were made in the names of the parties and figures in the original tables.

Abbreviations:

SCF	=	Scheduled Castes Federation
RDP	=	Radical Democratic Party
ILP	=	Independent Labour Party
KPP	=	Krishak Praja Party
European (CI)	=	European (Commerce and Industry)
MPB	=	Muslim Parliamentary Board

TABLE IX: COMMUNIST ANALYSIS OF THE ELECTION RESULTS

1. All constituencies contested by the Communists (General, Muslim, Labour, Christian and Sikh)
   Women seats are excluded as the same voters who voted in the General Constituencies voted in these women constituencies.

Province	*Total Voters Voted*	*Total Voters Voted for the CPI*	*Percentage*
Grand Total	26,50,082	5,05,284	19.0
Andhra	9,01,520	2,04,399	22.6
Bengal	6,46,232	99,338	15.3
Kerala	2,08,112	51,166	24.5
Tamilnadu	1,65 236	47,918	29.0
Punjab	1,45,292	29,572	20.3
Bombay	2,94,401	28,530	9.7
U.P.	1,18,082	20,546	17.4
Assam	71,329	12,719	17.8
Bihar	49,551	4,214	8.5
Sind	35,118	2,817	8.0
Orissa	3,924	2,234	56.9
C.P.	11,288	1,830	16.2

2. Labour seats

Province	*Total Polled*	*Congress*		*Communists*		
		Total	*%*	*Total*	*%*	*% of Congress*
Total	4,29,743	2,80,342	65.2	1,21,917	28.3	43.4
Orissa	3,924	1,690	43.0	2,234	56.9	132.1
Tamilnadu	50,567	23,583	46.6	26,108	51.06	110.7
Andhra	23,328	11,074	47.4	10,724	45.9	96.8
Bombay	55,760	32,021	57.4	16,916	30.3	52.8
U.P.	65,091	46,121	70.8	18,681	28.3	40.5
C.P.	3,347	2,454	73.3	827	24.7	33.9
Bengal	2,09,259	1,47,015	70.2	44,885	21.4	30.5
Punjab	5,305	3,859	72.7	904	17.0	23.4
Assam	13,163	12,525	95.1	638	4.8	5.0

3. Rural General Seats

Totai	17,98,799	13,80,946	76.7	3,12,499	17.3	22.7
Andhra	7,73,217	5,97,952	77.3	1,63,170	21.7	28.1
Bengal	3,81,773	2,81,227	73.6	51,209	13.4	18.2
Kerala	1,63,933	1,15,050	70.1	48,883	29.8	42.5

Contd.

TABLE IX *Contd.*

Province	*Total Polled*	*Congress*		*Communists*		
		Total	*%*	*Total*	*%*	*% of Congress*
Assam	58,166	37,085	63.0	12,081	20.7	32.5
Tamilnadu	56,092	43,587	77.7	12,061	21.5	27.6
Bombay	2,32,060	1,87,026	80.5	10.928	4.7	5.8
Bihar	49,551	45,337	91.5	4,214	8.5	9.2
U.P.	52,991	51,126	96.4	1,865	3.6	3.6
Punjab	16,920	10,517	62.1	1,176	6.9	11.1
C.P.	7,941	6,938	87.3	1,003	12.7	14.5
Sind	6,115	5,101	82.8	909	14.7	17.8

4. Muslim Seats

Province	*Total Polled*	*League*		*Congress*	
		Total	*% of Total*	*Total*	*% of Total*
Total	1,34 923	1,00,735	74.6	—	—
Bengal	55,200	46,124	83.5	1,125	2.3
Kerala	44,179	33,088	75.1	8,808	19.9
Sind	28,963	15,628	53.9	—	—
Bombay	6,581	5,895	89.5	—	—

Province	*Communist*			
	Total	*% of Total*	*% of Congress*	*% of League*
Total	8,121	8.0	—	8.0
Bengal	3,244	5.8	288.3	7.0
Kerala	2,283	5.3	25.9	7.2
Sind	1,908	6.6	—	12.2
Bombay	686	10.4	—	11.7

SOURCE: P.C. Joshi, 'Communists in the Elections—Battle for a New United National Front for Freedom', *People's Age*, 12 May 1946.

TABLE X: AMBEDKAR'S ANALYSIS OF THE ELECTIONS IN THE SCHEDULED CASTE CONSTITUENCIES IN CASE OF BOMBAY

1. Votes secured by Hindu candidates and Scheduled Caste candidates

Name of the Constituency	*Seats*	*Votes secured by Successful Hindu Candidates*			*Votes secured by Successful SC Candidates*
Bombay City (Suburban)	3	57,182	47,835	—	59,646
Bombay City (Byculla)	3	42,143	41,795	—	43,251
Kaira District	4	68,044	63,422	57,394	69,807
Surat District	4	40,232	39,985	39,610	39,849
Thana, South	3	30,581	27,587	—	11,630
Ahmednagar, South	3	25,747	20,948	—	20,908
East Khandesh, East	4	38,721	34,349	33,960	36,136
Nasik, West	4	37,218	36,794	36,555	42,604
Poona, West	3	23,758	23,454	—	24,709
Satara, North	4	44,315	42,727	41,474	43,961
Sholapur, North-East	3	19,380	16,705	—	18,264
Belgaum, North	4	55,787	50,759	49,867	27,682
Bijapur, North	3	23,083	20,838	—	16,059
Kolaba District	4	41,012	38,864	35,633	17,676
Ratnagiri, North	4	13,640	10,985	10,372	11,734

2. Relative Voting Strength of Caste Hindus and Scheduled Castes

Constituency	*Total Number of Voters in the Constituency*	*Total Number of Scheduled Caste Voters in the Constituency*	*Relative Proportion of Columns 2 and 3*
1	*2*	*3*	*4*
General Urban			
Bombay City North and Bombay Sub-urban District	167,002	34,266	1 : 4.8
Bombay City Byculla and Parel	152,991	28,520	1 : 5.3

Contd.

TABLE X *Contd.*

1	*2*	*3*	*4*
General Rural			
Kaira District	139,508	7,318	1 : 19.06
Surat District	85,670	4,765	1 : 18.8
Thana, South	67,749	4,668	1 : 14.5
Ahmednagar, South	73,162	7,382	1 : 9.9
East Khandesh, East	91,377	10,109	1 : 9.35
Nasik, West	99,274	12,698	1 : 7.7
Poona, West	73,551	13,055	1 : 5.6
Satara, North	95,459	11,152	1 :8.5
Sholapur, North-East	64,583	9,713	1 : 6.6
Belgaum, North	79,422	18,303	1 : 4.3
Bijapur, North	60,655	8,993	1 : 6.7
Kolaba District	103,828	5,001	1 : 20.7
Ratnagiri, North	32,606	3,529	1 : 9.2

3. Comparison of Primary Election and Final Election

Constituency	*Scheduled Caste Candidate who was Successful in Final Election*			*His Rank Among Candidates who Fought the General Election*
	His Name	*His Party Affiliation*	*Number of Votes Secured*	
Bombay City, North	Savlaram Gundaji Songaoker	Congress	59,646	1st among 3 (standing above 2 Hindus)
Bombay City, Byculla and Parel	N.S. Kajrolkar	Congress	43,251	1st among 3 (standing above 2 General Candidates)
East Khandesh East	Hiralal Kalyani	Congress	36,136	2nd among 4 (beating 2)

His Name	*His Position in the Primary Election treating the Constituency as a Single Member Constituency*	*Votes Obtained in the Primary Election*
Savlaram Gundaji Songaoker	2nd (failed)	2,038
N.S. Kajrolkar	2nd (failed)	2,098
Hiralal Kalyani	2nd (failed)	1,147

SOURCE: B.R. Ambedkar, *States and Minorities*, Bombay, 1947, pp. 54-79.

TABLE XI: PROVINCIAL ASSEMBLY ELECTION RESULTS, 1946

Province	*Total Seats*	*Muslim Seats*	*Congress*	*Nationalist Muslims*	*League*	*CPI*	*Others*
Madras	215	28* 29	165	—	29	2	19
Bombay	175	29* 30	125	—	30	2	18
Bengal	250	117* 119	86	—	114	3	47
United Provinces	228	64* 66	153	7	54	—	14
Punjab	175	84* 86	51	—	75	—	49
Bihar	152	39* 40	98	5	34	—	15
CP and Berar	112	14	92	—	13	—	7
Assam	108	34	58	3	31	—	16
NWFP	50	36	30	2	17	—	1
Orissa	60	4	47	—	4	1	4
Sind	60	33* 34	22	3	28	—	7

NOTE: * Women's Muslim seats excluded.
Others: 25 for Europeans and 4 for the Krishak Praja Party in Bengal, 22 for the Akalis and 20 for the Unionists in the Punjab, and 4 for G.M. Syed's Group in Sind. 5 Nationalist Muslims in Bihar are from Momins.

Compiled from the following sources:

Return showing the Results of Elections to the Central Legislative Assembly and the Provincial Legislatures in 1945-46
AICC Papers ED-1/1946 KW II, NMML
Asoka Mehta, *The Political Mind of India*
P.D. Reeves *et al.*, *A Handbook to Elections in Uttar Pradesh 1920-1951*
Harun-or-Rashid, *The Foreshadowing of Bangladesh*
Ian Talbot, *Provincial Politics and the Pakistan Movement*
Kripal C. Yadav, *Elections in Punjab 1920-1947.*

There is little difference in the statistical analysis of these sources. The only conspicuous difference is that, while Asoka Mehta mentions 4 Nationalist Muslim winners in Bengal, the AICC papers and Harun-or-Rashid mention none. This comes from the difference of interpretation on the character of the Krishak Praja Party.

APPENDIX I

The Indian Franchise Act, 1945
(9 Geo. 6, Ch. 2.)

CHAPTER 2

AN ACT TO MAKE TEMPORARY PROVISION FOR THE INCLUSION IN ELECTORAL ROLLS IN INDIA OF PERSONS RETURNED FROM WAR SERVICE, TO RELAX RESIDENCE QUALIFICATIONS FOR THOSE PERSONS AND TO EXTEND CERTAIN INDIAN FRANCHISE QUALIFICATIONS WHICH DEPEND ON SERVICE IN HIS MAJESTY'S FORCES OR ON THE AWARD OF A PENSION.

[24th October 1945]

Be it enacted by the King's most Excellent Majesty, by and with the advice and consent of the Lords Spiritual and Temporal, and Commons, in this present Parliament assembled, and by the authority of the same, as follows:

1. Inclusion in electoral rolls of persons returned from war service

(1) A person who has been engaged in war service, as defined for the purposes of this Act, may, not later than twelve months from the termination thereof or from the date of the passing of this Act, whichever last occurs, apply for his inclusion in the electoral roll for any of the constituencies mentioned in subsection (3) of this section, and the roll shall, if he is entitled to be included therein, be amended accordingly.

(2) For the purposes of this section, a person shall be treated as entitled to be included in an electoral roll if he would be so entitled if the roll were being revised at or by reference to the date of his application.

(3) Subject to the provisions of this Act

(a) the Governor-General in Council, in the case of a constituency for the election of persons to fill seats in either chamber of the Indian Legislature or for the election of persons to fill seats in the Legislative Council of the Chief Commissioner of Coorg; and

(b) the Governor of the Province, in the case of a constituency for the election of persons to fill seats in a chamber of a Provincial Legislature, may make rules regulating the manner in which and the persons by whom any question arising as to the right of a person making such an application to be included in the roll is to be decided.

2. Residence qualifications

(1) If on an application under the preceding section in respect of such an electoral roll as is therein mentioned or on the preparation or revision of such an electoral roll it appears that a person would have satisfied a residence qualification but for his absence on war service, that qualification shall be treated as satisfied in his case.

(2) In this section the expression 'residence qualification' means, in relation to the electoral roll for any constituency, any provision (however expressed) contained in any enactment, Order in Council or rules, requiring as a condition of inclusion in the electoral roll either residence or the possession of a place of residence, at or for any specified time, in the constituency or other specified area.

3. Definition of war service

(1) In this Act, the expression 'war service' means service at any time during the period which begins with the third day of September, nineteen hundred and thirty-nine, and ends with such date as may be appointed by the Governor-General in Council, either—

   (a) in any of His Majesty's naval, military or air forces; or

   (b) under the Crown in any other capacity directly relevant to the prosecution of any war in which His Majesty is at any time engaged during the said period.

(2) If any doubt arises as to whether any service of a person is or is not war service, the question shall be referred, in the case of service under the Government of any Province, to the Governor of that Province and, in the case of any other service, to the Governor-General in Council, and the decision of that Governor or, as the case may be, of the Governor-General in Council, shall be final.

4. Extension of certain franchise qualification

(1) The enactments, Orders in Council and rules mentioned in the Schedule to this Act shall have effect subject to the amendments therein specified, being amendments extending the franchise qualifications depending on service in His Majesty's regular military forces or the Auxiliary Force (India) or the Indian Territorial Force to other cases of service in His Majesty's forces or the reserves thereof, and extending the franchise qualifications depending on the award of a civil, military or political pension to cases of an award of a pension in respect of naval or air service.

(2) Any power conferred by or under any Act to amend, revoke or vary any of the provisions mentioned in the said Schedule shall include a power to amend, revoke or vary those provisions as amended in the manner specified in the said Schedule.

5. Supplementary

The functions of the Governor of a Province under this Act shall be deemed for the purposes of the Government of India Act, 1935, to be included among the functions as respects which he is, by or under that Act, required to exercise his individual judgement.

6. Printing

A copy of the Government of India Act, 1935, giving effect to—

(a) the amendments mentioned in sub-section (2) of section two of the India (Estate Duty) Act, 1945; and

(b) the amendments made by section four of, and Part I of the Schedule to, this Act.

shall be prepared and certified by the Clerk of the Parliaments and deposited with the Rolls of Parliament and His Majesty's printer shall print in accordance with the copy so certified all copies of the Government of India Act, 1935, which are printed after the said copy has been so prepared, certified and deposited.

7. Short title

This Act may be cited as the Indian Franchise Act, 1945.

SOURCE: *The Gazette of India*, Extraordinary, 26 October 1945, pp. 893-4. (Courtesy of Mr T.S. Sinha, Director of Archives, and Mr Satish Bhatnagar, Chief Electoral Officer, Government of Bihar)

APPENDIX II

Election Bill of the Palamu District Kisan Sabha

BANDE MATARAM

Red Box for the Congress, cast your vote in the Red Box of the Congress!
Gandhiji and Jawaharlal Nehru are awakening us.
  Kisan! Be awake and know the condition of our country.
There is no food, we can't get cloth.
  No oil, it's dark in our house.
Everything is under control, but
  sometimes we don't get cloth put round the dead body.
Vote for the Congress, and win our own rule;
  Then our country will be happy, Kisan!
Cast your vote in the red box of the Congress.
  Our country will be better, Kisan!
Spin all clothes with the *Charkha*,
  Weave them with the *Kargha*, Kisan!
Establish *Panchayat Raj* in seven hundred thousand villages,
  Break the shackle of slavery, Kisan!
Save our country with all physical, mental and material resources,
  Fulfill what Gandhiji has said, Kisan!
If you make mistake now, you will repent later.
  Time of voting has come, Kisan!
Jageshwar is telling us, hear, Brothers of Palamu,
  'Britishers, Quit India', we must demand it, Kisan!

Long live Revolution, Establish Kisan Raj!

Publisher
Secretary
Palamu District Kisan Sabha

The National Press, Patna

NOTE: The original of this English translation is reproduced on the next page.

बंदेमातरम्

कांग्रेस के लाल बक्स,
कांग्रेस के लाल बक्स में ही वोट दें!
गांधी जी जवाहर लाल तोहरा जगावत बाटे,
देशवा के हाल सुनि जाग हो किसनवा।
अन्न के अभाव बाटे, कपड़ा मिलत नाहीं,
तेल बिना घरवा अंधार हो किसनवा।
देशवा में सब चीज़ भइल कोंट्रोल बाटे,
मोकवा पर कफ़नो न मिले हो किसनवा।
कांग्रेस के वोट देइ आपन राज कायम कर,
तब होइ देश खुशहाल हो किसनवा।
कांग्रेस के लाल बक्स में वोट देई,
देश के कर हु उपकार हो किसनवा।
बुनि के कपास सब चरखा से सूत कात,
करघा से कपड़ा बिनाव हो किसनवा।
सात लाख गांव में पंचायत-राज कायम कर,
तोड़ि द गुलामी के जंजीर हो किसनवा।
तन मन धनवा से देश के उद्धार कर,
मानि जाहु गांधीजी के बात हो किसनवा।
अबकी जो भूल करब पीछे पछतइब तू हूँ,
चलि अइले वोटवा के बेरा हो किसनवा।
कहव जगेश्वर सुनहु पलामू - भाई,
'अंग्रेज भारत छोड़ो' यहि मांग हो किसनवा।

इन्कलाब जिंदाबाद, किसान राज कायम हो!

प्रकाशक
मंत्री
पलामू जिला किसान सभा

दि नेशनल प्रेस, पटना

Glossary

1. Organizations

Ahrars	Freedom Party
Akali Dal	Immortal Party
Bharar Sevak Samaj	Society of Volunteers for India
Grama Sevak Mantappa	Village Volunteers' Centre
Girni Kamgar Union	Red Flag Workers' Union
Jamiat-ul-Ulema	Association of Islamic Scholars
Janata Shiksha Samiti	Committee for People's Education
Khuda-i-Khidmatgar	Servants of God
Kisan Sabha	Peasant Union
Krishak Praja Party	Peasant Party
Lok Parishad	People's Conference
Mazdur Sabha	Labour Union
Momin	Believers, Muslim Weavers' Conference
Shoshit Varg	Exploited Class

2. Other Words

Akhand Hindustan	Undivided India
Bhadralog (Bhadralok)	Gentlemen
Bustee	Colony
Choukidari tax	Tax for meeting payments to watchmen
Dalal	Agent
Dhobi	Washerman
Lathial	Man armed with a club
Mandi	Market
Nyayadan Mandal	Tribunal
Patri Sarkar	Government which bastinadoes oppressors
Prati Sarkar	Parallel government
Tebhaga movement	Movement which demands the two-third of crops for tenants (*bargadars*)

Bibliography

1946 PROVINCIAL ELECTIONS

Acharya, N.C. Narasimha, *A Manual of Elections in India: Being an up-to-date and comprehensive Study of Franchise and its exercise*, Bombay, 1946.

AICC Papers—ED-1/1946 KW II—Provincial Assembly Elections—Results and Analysis, NMML.

File No. 51/2/46, Home Department Political (I), Political situation reports supplied by I & B Department, NAI.

File No. 51/3/46, Home Department Political, Weekly Political Appreciation Reports supplied to the Secretary of State for India by I & B Department, NAI

File No. 79/46, Vol. 1, Home Department Political (I), Analysis of the results of General Elections to the Central and Provincial Legislatures held in 1946-47, NAI.

Malik, Bedar, *Faislahkun Markah—1946 ke Intikhabad aur Islamia College ka Kirdar* (in Urdu), Lahore, 1987.

Mehta, Asoka, *The Political Mind of India: An Analysis of the Results of the General Elections*, Bombay, 1952.

Return showing the Results of Elections to the Central Legislative Assembly and the Provincial Legislatures in 1945-46, New Delhi, 1946.

PROVINCIAL ANALYSIS

Chattopadhyay, Gautam, *Bengal Electoral Politics and Freedom Struggle*, New Delhi, 1984.

Files of the Legislative Department, Election Branch 1945-1952, BSA.

Government of Madras, Public (Elections) Department, *G. O. No. 1943, 21st August 1943 Electoral Rolls—Provincial Legislature—Revision—1945 —Extracts of rules relating to electoral qualifications—Republished for public information, Order No. 1943, Public (Elections), dated 21st August 1945*, TSA.

Guha, Amalendu, *Planter-Raj to Swaraj—Freedom Struggle and Electoral Politics in Assam 1826-1947*, New Delhi, 1977.

Gupta, Amit Kumar, *North West Frontier Province Legislature and Freedom Struggle 1932-47*, New Delhi, 1976.

Harun-or-Rashid, *The Foreshadowing of Bangladesh—Bengal Muslim League and Muslim Politics 1936-47*, Dhaka, 1987.

Jalal, Ayesha, *The Sole Spokesman—Jinnah, the Muslim League and the Demand for Pakistan*, Cambridge, 1985.

Krishnaswamy, S., *The Role of Madras Legislature in the Freedom Struggle 1861-1947*, New Delhi, 1989.

Patra, Kishori Mohan, *Orissa State Legislature and Freedom Struggle 1912-47*, New Delhi, 1979.

Rai, Satya M., *Legislative Politics and Freedom Struggle in the Panjab*, New Delhi, 1984.

Reeves, P.D. *et al.*, *A Handbook to Elections in Uttar Pradesh 1920-1951*, Delhi, 1975.

Sinha, Rai Bahadur Nandalal, *Report on the Elections in Bihar*, Patna, 1946.

Talbot, Ian, *Provincial Politics and the Pakistan Movement, The Growth of the Muslim League in North-West and North-East India 1937-47*, Karachi, 1988.

———, 'The 1946 Punjab Elections', *Modern Asian Studies*, 14, 1 (1980).

Yadav, Kripal C., *Elections in Panjab 1920-1947*, Tokyo, 1981.

POLITICAL LEADERS

Abdul, Khaleque Muhammad (ed.), *Mahapurush Fazlul Huq* (in Bengali), Dhaka, 1395 (Bengal Calendar).

Ahmad, Jamil-ud-Din (ed.), *Speeches and Writings of Mr. Jinnah*, Vol. 2, Lahore, 1964.

Ahmad, Kamruddin, *Banglar Madyavitter Atmavikash* (in Bengali), Khand 2, Dhaka, 1382 (Bengal Calendar).

Ambedkar, B.R., *States and Minorities*, Bombay, 1947.

Azad, Maulana Abul Kalam, *India Wins Freedom*, Hyderabad, 1988.

Basu, Jyoti, *Janaganer Sange* (in Bengali), Calcutta, 1988.

De, Amalendu, *Islam in Modern India*, Calcutta, 1988.

Durga, Das (ed.), *Sardar Patel's Correspondence, 1945-50*, Vol. 2, Ahmedabad, 1971.

Gopalan, A.K., *Meri Jivani—Ek Jan-Sevak ke Sangharshon ki Kahani* (in Hindi), Lucknow, 1963.

Haq, Muhammad Shamsul, *Maulana Bhashanir Rajnaitik Jiven—Tatyalochna o Mulyayan* (in Bengali), Dhaka, 1984.

Hasim, Abul, *In retrospection*, Dhaka, 1974.

Ispahani, M.A.H., *Qaid-e-Azam Jinnah as I Knew Him*, Karachi, 1976.

Jha, Jagdish Chandra, *Bihar-Vibhuti Dr. Anugraha Narayan Sinha: Ek Jivani* (in Hindi), Patna, 1988.

Kidwai, M. Hashim, *Rafi Ahmad Kidwai*, New Delhi, 1986

Kidwai, Riaz-ur-Rahman, *Biographical Sketch of Kidwais of Avadh—with Special Reference to Barabanki families*, Aligarh, 1987.

Kuber, W.N., *Dr. Ambedkar—A Critical Study*, New Delhi, 1973.

Malik, Abdullah (ed.), *Selected Speeches and Statements of Mian Iftikhar-ud-Din*, Lahore, 1971.

Narayan, Jaya Prakash, *Towards Struggle—Selected Manifestoes, Speeches and Writings*, Bombay, 1946.

Noon, Feroz Khan, *From Memory*, Lahore, 1969.

Prasad, Rajendra, *Autobiography*, Bombay, 1957.

———, *Atmakatha* (in Hindi), New Delhi, 1965.

Prasad, Ramchandra and Ashok Kumar Sinha, *Shri Krishna Sinha* (in Hindi), New Delhi, 1988.

Rani, Shankardass, *Vallabhbhai Patel—Power and Organization in Indian Politics*, Hyderabad, 1988.

Rasul, Muhammad Abdullah, *Grame Gramantre* (in Bengali), Calcutta, 1985.

Saraswati, Swami Sahajanand, *Maharudra ka Mahatandva* (in Hindi), Patna, n.d.

Selected Works of Jawaharlal Nehru, Vol. 14, New Delhi, 1981.

Singh, Moni, *Jiban Sangram* (in Bengali), Dhaka, 1983.

Sinha, Anugraha Narayan, *Mere Sansmaran* (in Hindi), Patna, n.d.

Tendulkar, D.G., *Abdul Ghaffar Khan—Faith is a Battle*, Bombay, 1967.

PEOPLE'S MOVEMENT

Ansari, Hasan Nishat, *The Momin-Congress Relation—A Socio-Historical Analysis*, Patna, 1989.

Banerjee, Subrata, *The R.I.N Strike*, New Delhi, 1981.

Bhuyan, A.C. and Sibopada De, *Political History of Assam*, Vol. 3, *1940-47*, Gauhati, 1980.

Chakravarty, Renu, *Communists in Indian Women's Movement*, New Delhi, 1980.

Chandra, Bipan *et al.*, *India's Struggle for Independence 1857-1947*, New Delhi, 1988.

Custers, Peter, *Women in the Tebhaga Uprising: Rural Poor Women and Revolutionary Leadership (1946-47)*, Calcutta, 1987.

Das, Arvind N., *Agrarian Unrest and Socio Economic change in Bihar, 1900-1980*, New Delhi, 1983.

Dutt, B.C., *Mutiny of the Innocents*, Bombay, 1971.

Epstein, S.J.M., *The Earthy Soil—Bombay Peasants and the Indian Nationalist Movement 1919-47*, Delhi, 1988.

File No. 5/13/46, Home Department Political (I), NAI.

File No. 5/21/46, Home Department Political (I), NAI.

Ghosh, K.K., *The Indian National Army—The Second Front of the Indian Independence Movement*, Meerut, 1969.

Ghosh, Moni, *Our Struggle—A Short History of Trade Union Movement in TISCO Industry at Jamshedpur*, Calcutta, 1957.

Gupta, Amit Kumar (ed.), *Myth and Reality: The Struggle for Freedom in India, 1945-47*, New Delhi, 1987.

Home (Spl.) *File No. 503-A (3)*, MSA.

Home (Spl.) *File No. 503-I, 1945*, MSA.

Home (Spl.) *File No. 2004, 503-II, 1945-47*, MSA.

Home (Spl.) *File No. P5-I, Civil Disobedience Movement 1942, Daily reports regarding the CDM* (1.4.44-11.8.44), MSA.

Home (Spl.) *File No. P5-II, Civil Disobedience Movement 1942, Daily reports regarding the CDM* (12.8.44-30.6.45), MSA.

Home (Spl.) *File No. P5-III, Civil Disobedience Movement 1942, Daily reports regarding the CDM* (1.7.45-31.3.46), MSA.

Home (Spl.) *File No. P5-IV, Civil Disobedience Movement 1942, Daily reports regarding the CDM* (1.4.46 to), MSA.

Home Department Political (I), *File No. 5/22/1946, INA Trials Disturbances in Calcutta protesting against the Conviction of Abdul Rashid*, NAI.

Kamath, Suryanath, *Quit India Movement in Karnataka*, Bangalore, 1988.

———, *Swatantrya Sangramada Smritigalu* (in Kannada), Vols. 3, Mysore, 1974-80.

Kosambi, D.D., *Exasperating Essays—Exercises in the Dialectical Method*, Poona, 1957(?).

Mamkoottam, Kuriakose, *Trade Unionism: Myth and Reality—Unionism in the Tata Iron and Steel Company*, New Delhi, 1982.

Pandey, Gyanendra (ed.), *The Indian Nation in 1942*, Calcutta, 1988.

Ram, Moti (ed.), *Two Historic Trials in Red Fort*, Delhi, n.d.

Rasul, Mohammad Abdullah, *Krishak Sabhar Itihas* (in Bengali), Calcutta, 1969.

———, *A History of the All India Kisan Sabha*, Calcutta, 1974.

Sarkar, Jagannath *et al.* (eds.), *India's Freedom Struggle—Several Streams*, New Delhi, 1986.

Sarkar, Sumit, *Modern India 1885-1947*, Delhi, 1984.

———, 'Popular Movements and National Leadership, 1945-47', *Economic and Political Weekly*, Annual Number, April 1982.

Sen, Sukomal, *Working Class of India: History of Emergence and Movement 1830-1970*, Calcutta, 1970.

Sen, Sunil, *Agrarian Struggle in Bengal 1946-47*, New Delhi, 1972.

Shinde, A.B., *The Parallel Government of Satara—A Phase of the Quit India Movement*, New Delhi, 1990.

Singh, K.S., *Tribal Society in India: An Anthropo-historical Perspective*, New Delhi, 1985.

DOCUMENTS ON POLITICAL PARTIES AND POLITICAL MOVEMENTS

Allana, G. (ed.), *Pakistan Movement: Historic Documents*, Lahore, 1977.

Jacob, T.G. (ed.), *National Question in India: CPI Documents 1942-47*, New Delhi, 1988.

Mirza, Sarfaraz Hussain (ed.), *Muslim Students and Pakistan Movement: Selected Documents (1937-1947)*, Lahore, 1988-9.

Zaidi, A.M. and Shahada Zaidi (eds.), *The Encyclopaedia of Indian National Congress*, Vol. 12: *1939-1946—A Fight to the Finish*, New Delhi, 1981.

BRITISH POLICY

Banerjee, Anil Chandra and Dakshina Ranjan Bose, *The Cabinet Mission in India*, Calcutta, 1946.

Home Department Political (I), *File No. 101/45, Policy regarding Election Meetings etc.*, NAI.

Home Department Political (I), *Fortnightly Report from the first half of September 1945 to the second half of April 1946*, NAI, BSA and TSA.

Home Political Confidential Files 37/45, Secret Report on Political Situation in Bengal, from October to December 1945, WBSA.

Lumby, E.W.R., *The Transfer of Power in India 1945-7*, London, 1954.

Mansergh, Nicholas (ed.), *The Transfer of Power 1942-7*, Vols. 6 and 7, London, 1976 and 1977.

Menon, V.P., *The Transfer of Power in India*, Princeton, 1957.

Moon, Penderel (ed.), *Wavell: The Viceroy's Journal*, New Delhi, 1977.

Philips, C.H. and Mary Doren Wainwright (eds.), *The Partition of India—Policies and Perspectives 1935-1947*, Cambridge, Massachusetts, 1970.

Tuker, Sir Francis, *While Memory Serves*, London, 1950.

PRINCLEY STATES

Darda, R.S., *From Feudalism to Democracy—A Study in the Growth of Representative Institutions in Rajasthan 1908-1948*, New Delhi, 1971.

Files on the Jaipur Praja Mandal, the Marwar Lok Parishad and the Mewar Praja Mandal, RSA.

Gowda, K.S. Mune, *Development of Karnataka Legislature*, Mysore, 1988.

Home Department Political (I), *File No. 18/16/45, Part II, Fortnightly Report received from the Residents from July to December 1945*, NAI.

Mathur, Vishnu Dayal, *States' Peoples' Conference*, Jaipur, 1984.

OTHER SOURCES

Mitra, N.N. (ed.), *Indian Annual Register, 1945-1946.*
The Gazette of India.

RELATED STUDIES IN JAPANESE

Naito, Masao, 'Satara no "*Prati Sarkar*" Nomin Undo—Dainiji Taisen ki Indo Minzoku Undo no ichi Kosatsu' (*Prati Sarkar* Peasant Movement in Satara—Indian National Movement during the Second World War), *Azia Africa Gengo Bunka Kenkyu*, No. 9, 1974.

Nakamura, Heiji (ed.), *Indo Gendaishi no Tenbo* (Perspective of a Contemporary History of India), Tokyo, 1972.

Sato, Hiroshi, 'Tebhaga Undo no Tenkai to sono Haikei—Dinajpur ken o chushin ni' (The Background and the Development of the Tebhaga Movement with special reference to Dinajpur district), *Azia Keizai*, October 1970.

NEWSPAPERS

Amrita Bazar Patrika.
Asahi Shimbun (in Japanese).
Dawn.
People's Age.
People's War.
Statesman.

Index

Abell, George 32
abolition of the statutory landlord system 12
Act of 1919 34
Adhikari, D. 68
Adhikari, G. 155
Ahmad, Kamaruddin 146
Ahmad, Muzaffar 107, 146
Ahmedabad 172
Ahmedabad Textile Labour Association 200
Ahom Association 188, 189
Ahrars 58, 167, 184
Akali Dal 58, 59, 156, 168, 184, 185, 186
Ali Ashraf 198
Ali, Aruna Asaf 112, 147
Ali, Asaf 23, 57
All-Bengal Muslim Students' League (ABSML) 101
All-India Congress Committee (AICC) 34, 35, 51, 56, 61, 62, 72, 77, 84, 86, 103, 108, 130, 167, 173, 179, 209
All-India Posts and Telegraphs Lower Grade Union 25
All-India Railway Strike 22
All-India States People's Conference 37
All-India Trade Union Congress 25, 188
Allahabad 87, 133
Ambala Division 155
Ambedkar, B.R. 168, 177
Ambli, C.J. 175
Amery, L.S. 30
Amritsar 100, 155
Andhra Pradesh 58, 138, 171
Angadi, S.N. 174
Anglo-Arabic College 169
Ansari, Abdul Qaiyum 197
Arambagh 20
Arunachalam, D.R. 64
Assam 57, 88, 134, 138, 139, 150, 170, 203; election results in 187-9
Assam nationalism 187-8
Assam Provincial Congress Committee 187
Atre, P.K. 77
Attlee 31, 32, 83, 109, 113
Auchinleck, General 94, 95, 96, 97, 98, 99, 100
Azad, Maulana Abul Kalam 56, 57, 58, 60, 61, 91, 96, 120, 121, 141, 144, 146, 147, 148, 156, 183

Bakarganj 46
bakasht movement 41, 42, 195, 201, 204
Baksh, Maulana 58
Ballia 82
Baluchistan 134, 138, 150, 170
Banerjee, Subrata 110, 111, 113, 121
Banerji, Sibnath 148, 149
Bangladesh 12, 19
Bari, Abdul 197, 199, 200
Barisal 20
Bashyam, K.T. 156
Basu, Jyoti 67, 144, 147, 168, 180
Batliwala, S.S. 76
Bengal 12, 20, 42, 44, 45, 53, 55, 57, 59, 60, 61, 67, 84, 89, 90, 106, 107, 108, 134, 138, 139, 143, 144, 150, 168, 169, 187, 199; elections in 144-52; election results in 179-81; Kisan movement in 151-2; partition of 12, 139
Bengal Famine of 1943 11, 13, 19, 20-1, 60, 84, 166, 209
Bengal Legislative Assembly 170
Bengal Provincial Congress Committee 107

Bengal Provincial Students Federation (BPSF) 89, 101, 102, 104
Berar, elections in 186-7
Bhagalpur 159
Bhandare, R.D. 177
Bharat Sevak Samaj 174
Bhasani, Maulana 187
Bhattacharya, Ananda 102
Bhola 20
Bihar 19, 27, 40, 41, 42-3, 47, 58, 61, 67, 80, 81, 135, 138, 141, 183; election results in 192-204; Polling and Polling Stations in 157-62
Bihar Kisan Sabha 203
Bihar Land Reforms Act (1950) 195
Bihar Legislative Assembly 46, 47, 157
Bihar Legislative Council 46, 47
Bimalprotiva Devi 92
Bombay 34, 35, 45, 51, 56, 57, 67, 72, 77, 79, 84, 85, 108-24 *passim*, 178, 182, 183, 186, 193, 196, 209
Bombay Girni Kamgar Union 178
Bombay Presidency 47-8, 62, 168, 211; election results in 172-9
Bombay Provincial Assembly 118, 124, 167
Bombay Provincial Congress Committee 117
Bose, Subhas Chandra 90
Bose, Sarat Chandra 59, 90, 91, 93, 96, 102, 106, 107, 108
Bristow 113
British Cabinet Mission 13, 21, 22, 116, 146, 166, 169, 171, 176, 177, 190, 191, 203
British General Election of 1947 21
British Government 12, 29, 30, 31, 32, 35, 44, 66, 72, 82, 83, 84, 86, 112, 150, 161, 166, 209
Burma 88, 166
Burrows, Sir Frederick 179
Butler 113

Cabinet Mission Plan 12, 21, 26
Calcutta 19, 20, 23, 26, 27, 35, 59, 60, 87-108 *passim*, 132, 133, 149
Calcutta City League 102
Calcutta Corporation employees strike 97
Caroe, Sir Olaf 190
Casey, R.G. 96, 97, 100, 104, 107, 108, 109
Central Parliamentary Board of the Muslim League 49, 55, 56, 136, 142
Central Provinces 168; election results in 186-7
Chakravarty, Nikhil 23, 26, 53, 101, 102, 105, 107, 148, 149
Chandpur 20
Chandra, Romesh 137, 138, 153
Chattopadhyaya, Gautam 89, 90, 91, 100
Chavan, Y.B. 173
Chittagong 20, 150
Chopra, P.N. 79
Chota Nagpur Adivasi Mahasabha 161, 202-4
Chota Nagpur Santhal Parganas Janata Party 201
Chundrigar, I.I. 116, 121, 122, 172
Churchill, Winston 21
Colville, J. 113, 116, 118, 122, 123, 169, 176
Communist Party of India 12, 34, 35, 38, 51, 66, 75, 89, 107, 110, 111, 116, 118, 120, 133, 138, 139, 140, 141, 149, 155, 167, 168, 171, 178-88 *passim*, 211, 212.
Congress-Communist relations 34-5
Congress Labour Union 117
Congress Mandalis 76
Congress Nyayadan Committee 76
Congress Sanstha 76
Congress Socialist Party (CSP) 89
Congress Working Committee 23-5, 34, 35, 65, 74, 92-3, 97, 108, 121, 130, 190
constitution-making process, and the role of the Provincial Assemblies 12, 30
Contai 20
Coxbazar 20
Criminal Law Amendment Act 75, 76
Cripps 32, 44, 84
Cripps Offer of 1942 32
Curzon, Lord 152

Dacca 20, 45, 46, 55, 145
Dahashatwadi Dal 76
Dalvi, N.B. 174
Dalvi, V.G. 23
Damodaran, Vinita 41

Dange, S.A. 67, 118-19, 168, 178
Das, Bishwanath 190
Das Gupta, Satish 105
Daultana, Mian Mumtaz 138, 153, 154
Davis, Kingsley 47
Dehradun 88
Delhi 29, 89, 94, 117, 166, 169, 211
Deo, S.K. 80
Deo, Shankar Rao 57, 76
Deorukhar, B.J. 177
Desai, Morarji 175
Dhillon, G.S. 94, 98, 99
Diamond Harbour 20
Dias, A.L. 76
Dinajpur 151, 180
Direct Action Day 26
Diwakar, R.R. 62, 63
Doaba Canal 137
Dodmeti, A.G. 174
Dundur, K.B. 174
Dutt, B.C. 109-10, 111, 112, 114, 116, 122
Dutt, Kalpana 150
Dutta, K.S. Alla 184
Dyer, General 100

East Pakistan 49, 180, 211 *see also* Bangladesh

Fascists 21, 35
Feni 20
Forward Block 97
franchise, restricted 37-48, 60, 68, 99, 141; universal adult 36, 37, 48, 53, 130, 138, 139, 141, 214
freedom movement 11, 109, 139
Gadgil, N.V. 76
Gandhi, M.K. 24, 26, 59, 61, 62, 64, 65, 73, 74, 96, 121, 130, 161, 173, 178, 194
Ganguli, Jyotimotee 93
Gaonkar, S.P. 175
Gaya district 41, 200
Ghaznavi, Maulana Daud 185, 186
Ghosh, Prafulla 59
Ghosh, Suren 107
Gilani, B.S. 183
Giri, V.V. 149
Glancey, B.J. 153, 169
Goalanda 20
Godfrey, Admiral 113, 114
Gokhale, P.P. 173
Gohain, Hiren 188
Gopal, S. 103
Gopalan, A.K. 67, 171
Gosavi, D.K. 173
Government of India Act (1935) 10, 12, 13, 36, 39, 40-1, 42, 65, 124, 141, 212
Governors' Conference of 1945 31
Grama Sevak Mantappa 174
Grancy, Sir Bertland 31
Gujarat 57, 138
Gunther, Frances 141
Gupta, Amit Kumar 190

Haji Dost Mohammad 137
Hallett, M. 99
Hanif, Maulvi Muhammad 191
Hari tenants 49
Haroon, Abdullah 191
Harun-or-Rashid 54, 136
Hashim, Abul 53, 54, 55, 56, 105, 136, 149-50, 170
Hashmi, Hamid 154
Hayat, Shaukat 138
Hazara district 50
Hazaribagh 46
Hazaribagh district 201, 203
Hidayatullah, Sir Ghulam Hussain 49
Hindu Mahasabha 59, 168, 195
Hindustan Mazdoor Sevak Sangh 200
Homi, Manek 199
Hoshiarpur 137, 184
Hukerikar, R.S. 174
Huq, Fazlul 146, 167, 179-80
Huzare, B.R. 175

Inamdar, K.R. 173
India and Burma Committee of the Cabinet 31, 32, 44, 93 Indian Franchise Act (1945) 124
Indian Military Academy 88
Indian National Army 11, 12, 45, 60, 85, 87, 88, 89, 90, 93, 94, 95, 97, 98, 105, 106, 111, 153, 209; and the movement against the trial of the officers 21, 27, 83, 85-108, 140
INA Defence Committee 86, 89, 98

Indian National Congress 10, 11, 12, 21, 22, 26, 30, 33, 34, 36, 38, 48-66 *passim*, 74, 75, 77, 79, 84, 85, 86, 89, 93, 94, 96, 98, 99, 101, 103, 105, 107, 109, 111, 112, 115, 117, 121, 123, 124, 130, 131, 135, 139-51 *passim*, 167, 169, 170, 172, 175, 178-87 *passim*, 209, 210, 211, 212; in Bengal 59, 60, 91; in Bihar 192, 194, 197, 202-4; Central Election Board of the 12, 57, 100, 121; in Karnataka 62, 63, 156; in the North-West Frontier Province 189, 190; in Punjab 58, 153; in Sind 59; in Tamilnadu 64
Indian National Trade Union Congress (INTUC) 149, 183, 200, 210
Iqbal 113
Ispahani, M.A. Hasan 55, 156
Isur 13

Jafar Imam 135
Jaipur 156
Jalandhar 137
Jamiat-i-Ulema-i-Banga 136, 146
Jamiat Momin 197
Jamiat-ul-Ulema 142, 188, 197
Jamshedpur Factory Labour Constituency 199, 210
Jamshedpur Labour Federation 199
Janata Shiksha Samiti 174
Japan 9, 10, 14, 166, 214, 215; and the 'Asian War of Liberation' 21; beginning of parliamentary democracy in 10; General Election of 1946 in 9, 215
Japan Communist Party 10
Japanese Army 9, 86, 87, 90
Japanese Ministry of Education 10
Jatti, B.D. 174
Jha, Binodanand 198
Jharia 44
Jharkhand Party 203
Jharkhand state, demand for 202
Jhelum 137
Jingaragacha 86
Jinnah, M.A. 22, 26, 27, 30, 32, 33, 48, 49, 50, 55, 56, 65, 100, 122, 134, 143, 154, 156, 168, 169, 179, 191, 210, 211, 214
Jodhpur 166
John, Michael 199, 200
Johnson, Alec 151-2
Jorhat 57
Josh, S. Sohan Singh 67, 185
Joshi, P.C. 133, 138, 150-1, 170, 181, 183, 186, 188, 194, 195

Kabir, Humayun 144-6, 147
Kairon, Pratap Singh 58
Kajrolkar, N.S. 177
Kamaraj, K. 64, 65
Kammins 137
Kandi 20
Kanpur 182, 183, 200, 210
Kanpur Mazdur Sabha 182
Kanthi, S.R. 175
Karachi 49, 132
Karnataka 61, 62, 138, 172, 173, 174, 175
Karnataka Provincial Congress Committee 175
Karunakaran, K.P. 200
Kashmir 156
Kashmir National Conference 86
Kasur constituency 53
Kerala 138, 171
Khaliq-uz-Zaman, Chowdhry 49, 142, 143, 169
Khan, Abdul Ghaffar 189, 190
Khan, Adul Qaiyum 190
Khan, Aurangzeb 50
Khan, Bakht Jamal 50
Khan, Khizr Hayat 153
Khan, Liaquat Ali 49
Khan, M.S. 111, 121
Khan, Shah Nawaz 94, 98, 99
Khan, Sharif 149
Khan, Shaukat Hayat 153
Khan, Zubail 198
Kher, B.G. 63
Khewra Salt Miner's Union 137
Khilafat movement 197
Kidwai, Jamil-ur-Rahman 143
Kidwai, M. Hashim 37, 142
Kidwai, Rafi Ahmad 37, 58, 142, 181-2
Kidwai, Riaz-ur-Rahman 143
Kisan Sabha 45, 137, 140-1, 146, 154
Kisan Veer 173, 175
Kosambi, D.D. 77
Kripalani, J.B. 72

Krishak Praja Party (KPP) 136, 145, 146, 147, 167, 179
Krishna Menon, V. K. 37, 77, 84, 91
Kulkarni, R.A. 174
Kumaramangalam, Mohan 122
Kumaun 39
Kutre, S.B. 175

Labour Government *see* British Government
labour movement 22-7 *passim*, 67
Labour Party of England 31, 33, 84
Lahiri, Somnath 105, 107
Lahore 34, 84, 154, 155, 198
Lahore district 137, 153
Lahore Resolution 170, 199, 211
Latifi, Daneil 154
Latthe, A.B. 62, 63, 64, 174
Lewis, Hawthorne 191
London 29, 32, 100
Lucknow 34
Ludhiana 137, 184

Madani, Hussain Ahmad 188
Madaripur 20
Madras 67, 171
Madras Presidency 149, 166, 167, 168, 211; Dravidian Federation in 171; election results in 170-2; Justice Party in 171, 172
Mahajan, Sucheta 83
Mahalanobis, P.C. 20
Maharashtra 57, 61, 63, 73, 138
Maharashtra Provincial Congress Committee 73, 76, 79
Mahars 187
Mahendra, King 28
Mahmud, Dr. Syed 198
Mahmudabad, Raja of 143
Majhail, Sardar Ishar Singh 185
Malik, Abdullah 154
Mane, S.N. 174
Manikganj 20
Marwar Lok Parishad 166
Maxwell, Sir Reginald 44
Medak, S.V. 173
Meerut 141, 142, 143
Mehta, Asoka 168
Mehtab, H.K. 190
Menon, V.P. 113
Mian Iftikhar-ud-din 51, 52, 53, 56, 58, 137, 154, 170, 184, 211
Midnapur 20, 60
Mirs 49, 50
Mishra, Pandit Ravaneshwar 202
Misra, Loknath 65
Mohammed Osman 102
Momin Parliamentary Board 196
Monghyr *cum* Jamalpur Factory Labour Constituency 44, 160, 194 Monghyr district 41, 194, 195
More, S.S. 61
Mudie, R.F. 81, 169, 191
Mukherjee, Bankim 148, 149
Munshiganj 20
Muslim League 10, 11, 12, 13, 21, 22, 25, 26, 30, 33, 35, 36, 38, 48-61 *passim*, 65, 66, 75, 87, 99-111 *passim*, 115, 117, 121, 122, 124, 130-55 *passim*, 167, 168, 169, 170, 172, 179-86 *passim*, 209, 210, 211, 212; in Assam 53, 187; in Bengal 53, 55, 56, 106, 136, 167; in Bihar 135, 196, 197, 203; in Bombay 116, 167; and the Lahore Resolution 53; in the Mysore State 156; in the North-West Frontier Province 50, 189-90; in Orissa 191; in Punjab 50, 51, 136; in Sind 50, 191-2; Working Committee of the 33
Muslim League-Communist relations, beginning of the deterioration of 150
Muslim National Guards 136
Muzaffarpur 159
Mymensingh 145, 181
Mymensingh district 146, 147
Mysore Princely state 13

Nagpur 132, 186, 187
Naikaudi, Naganath 99
Nambiar, K. Ananda 171
Namboodiripad, E.M.S. 67, 171
Narayan, Jaya Prakash 72, 201-2, 203
Narayanganj 20
Nationalist Muslims 58, 59, 60, 143, 167, 179, 181, 182, 184, 186, 191, 192, 197
National Planning Commission 86
Naval Central Strike Committee (NCSC) 111, 115, 116, 121
Nawab Ismail Khan 49

Nawab of Dhaka 53
Nawab of Mamdot 48, 153
Nazimuddin, Khwaja 54, 55, 56, 104
Nehru, Jawaharlal 9, 23, 34, 37, 48, 52, 57, 58, 59, 61, 77-92 *passim*, 96, 103, 112, 121, 123, 124, 130, 132, 133. 141, 142, 143, 167, 201
Nehru Report of 1928 66
Nepal 19, 27, 200
Nesvi, T.R. 173
Netrakona 146
New Delhi *see* Delhi
Nilganj 86
Nilpharmari 20
Noakhali 20, 145
non-cooperation movement 27
Noon, Sir Feroze Khan 33, 51, 52-3, 138, 153, 170
North-West Frontier Province 12, 50, 60, 134, 150, 156, 170, 213; election results in 168, 189-90
Nurie, M.Y. 178
Nyadata Congress Committee 76
nyayadan mandals 73, 76

Omvedt, Gail 73, 75
Orissa 138; election results in 167, 168, 190-1
Orissa Legislative Assembly 190
Oudh 39

Pakistan, movement for a Muslim majority state 10, 11, 12, 13, 26, 27, 32, 33, 35, 36, 49-60 *passim*, 68, 100, 130-40 *passim*, 146, 149, 150, 155, 156, 169, 171, 172, 179-80, 182, 184, 185, 187, 190, 198, 199, 202-3, 211, 213, 214
Pandey, Gyanendra 85
Pandu Master 173
Pant, Govind Vallabh 57, 85
Parulekar, Godavari 67
Patel, M.P. 80
Patel, Maniben 99
Patel, Sardar Vallabhbhai 12, 23, 25, 51, 52, 56-66 *passim*, 77, 78, 81, 84, 85, 91, 92, 93, 108, 109, 112, 114, 116, 120. 121, 130, 149, 156, 167, 174, 176, 179, 183-93 *passim*, 200, 209, 210, 213
Patil, K.D. 173
Patil, K.F. 174
Patil, M.P. 174
Patil, Nana 173, 175
Patil, S.K. 116
Patil, V.V. 174
Patna 13, 19, 46, 158, 159, 198
Patri Sarkar see Prati Sarkar
Patwardhan, Achutrao 75, 99
Pawar, V.P. 75, 173
Pearson, Gail 47-8
peasant movements 11, 41, 50, 67, 159, 171, 195
'People's War' theory 19
Pethick-Lawrence, Lord 31, 109, 112, 146
Pirs 50, 51, 144, 145, 183, 190
Poona 73, 79
Poona Pact 178, 187, 210
Posts and Telegraphs Department strike 23, 25, 26, 27, 171
Prabhu, R.M. 175
Prakasam, T. 13
Prasad, Murli Manohar 193
Prasad, Rajendra 57, 58, 194-5, 197, 202-3
Prati Sarkar 73, 74, 75, 76, 77, 80, 176, 178, 179
Progressive Writers' Association 199
Provincial Assembly Elections of 1946, basic framework of the 29-30; Communist candidates in the 67-8; their crucial role in deciding the political destiny of the subcontinent 10, 11, 13, 21; limited character of 123-4, 143, 212, 214; respose to the 156; and the tenants and landless labour 41-2; total electorate in the 47
Provincial Congress Committee 35
Provincial Congress Parliamentary Board 63, 64, 65
Provincial Elections of 1937 10, 33, 36, 50, 209, 210, 213
Provincial Muslim League Council 54, 55
Provincial Muslim League Parliamentary Board 49, 50, 54, 55
Punjab 12, 27, 45-61 *passim*, 67, 94, 134, 137, 138, 139, 150, 166, 169, 170, 210, 213; elections in 153-6; election results

in 167, 168, 183-6; partition of 12, 139, 155
Punjab Kisan Sabha 153
Punjab Legislative Assembly 167
Punjab Provincial Congress Committee 51, 185

Quit India movement 10, 11, 13, 19, 34, 35, 36, 37, 40, 41, 60, 61, 62, 63, 66, 73-82 *passim*, 89, 91, 98, 110, 111, 112, 120, 123, 131, 142, 147, 149, 167, 173, 174, 175, 177, 181, 182, 183, 192-204 *passim*, 209, 210, 213

Radical Democratic Party 195, 196
Rahim, Taqui 198
Rai, Lala Lajpat 182
Rajagopalachari, C. 58, 64, 65
Rajan, P.T. 171
Rajasthan 138
Ram, Jagjivan 196
Rana Regime 27, 28, 200
Ranchi 46
Rashid, Abdul 100, 101, 103, 106
Rashtriya Seva Dal 76
Ratanlal Brahmin 180
Rath, Baidyanath 191
Rattray 111, 113
Rawalpindi 153
Rawalpindi Division constituency 53
Reddy, Gopal 58
Revolutionary Socialist Party (RSP) 89
Rodger 113
Roy, Rupnarayan 180
Roy, Sudhir Chandra 108
Royal Indian Navy 11, 12
Royal Indian Navy strike 21, 27, 109-24, 140, 167, 183, 209
Ruiskar 187

Sahay, K.B. 198, 201
Sahgal, P.K. 94, 98, 99
Sajjan, G.S. 175
Samaj Seva Dals 76
Sambrani 174
Sangal, O.P. 182
Sankrityayan, Rahul 19
Satara 73, 74, 75, 76, 79, 80, 98, 99, 120, 167, 172, 175, 176, 178, 209
Satara Congress Sarkar 76
Satara district 74, 75, 79, 80; Congress Committee of 79, 173
Satara Jilha Congress Sarkar 76
Satara peasant uprising of 1942-3 77, 79, 173 *see also Prati Sarkar*
Satkhira 20
Sawant, K.S. 173
Scheduled Castes Federation (SCF) 168, 177, 178, 182, 187, 195, 196
Second Jharkhand Chota Nagpur Pakistan Conference 202
Second World War 9, 12, 14, 19, 21, 27, 34, 60, 64, 85-6, 122, 123, 132, 138, 143, 145, 151, 209, 213, 214, 215
Sen, Amartya 21
Serajganj 20
Sevagram 73
Shah, Maganlal 175
Shahabad 61
Shahabad district 41, 196, 200
Shamsher, Padma 27
Sharma, Jadunandan 159
Sharma, Karyanand 67, 194, 195
Shastri, Bhola Paswan 196
Shastri, Hari Har Nath 183
Shastri, Raja Ram 182
Shastri, S.S. 175
Shinde, B.J. 172
Sholapur 80
Shoshit Varg 195
Shukla, R.S. 186, 187
Simla Conference 13, 30, 33, 72, 210
Sind 12, 49, 50, 56, 58, 59, 134, 138, 150, 170; election results in 167-8, 191-2; Muslims in 169; Syed Party in 168
Sind Legislative Assembly 49
Singh, Baldev 185, 186
Singh, Bhagat 182
Singh, Jaipal 161, 202, 203
Singh, Madan 111
Singh, Master Tara 183, 184
Singh, Moni 67, 147
Singh, Raja Bahadur Kamakhya Narayan 200, 201
Singh, Rajeshwar Prasad 194
Singh, Rameshwar Prasad 201

Singh, Sardar Iqbal 185
Singh, Sardar Siva 185
Sinha, Anugraha Narayan 80, 197, 201, 202
Sinha, C.P.N. 200, 201
Sinha, Indredeep 195
Sinha, Krishna 81, 193, 194, 195, 201
Sinha, Rai Bahadur Nandalal 46
Sinha, Taranand 201, 202
Sinhala nationalism 28
Sinhasane, G.E. 172
Sitaramayya, Pattabhi 57
Sogaonkar, S.G. 177
Sri Lanka 27, 28
Srinagar 86
Suhrawardy, H.S. 13, 54, 55, 101, 103, 104, 105, 106, 136, 144, 146, 170
Sundarayya, P. 67, 171
Swami Sahajanand Saraswati 41, 203-4
Swatantra, S. Teja Singh 185
Syed, G.M. 49, 50, 56, 59, 191

Talbot, I.A. 183
Tamilnadu 58, 138
Tamluk 20
Tangail 20
Tapache, G.D. 172
Tata Workers' Union 197, 199, 200
Tebhaga struggle 180, 212
Tenancy Bill 142
Tendulkar, D.G. 189
Tibet 27
Tipperah 20
Tottenham, R. 82
Trade Unions 44, 45, 183
Tuker, Sir Francis 85, 86, 88, 89, 102-3, 108
Twenty-Four Parganas 20

Udaipur 37
Unionist Party 33, 48, 51, 137, 138, 153, 167, 183, 184, 186
United National Front 139-40, 180
United Provinces 37, 39, 40, 58, 82, 141, 143, 161, 167
U.P. Congress Parliamentary Board 142
U.P. Nationalist Muslim Students Federation 142

Valva 99
Varanasi 78
Venkateswaralu, P. 171
Vyas, Jai Narain 166

Wardha 24, 25
Wavell, Lord 29, 30, 31, 32, 36, 44, 83, 84, 95, 96, 97, 99, 109, 113, 166, 177, 179
working class movements 11
Wylie, Francis 169

Yusuf, Sant Singh 182

Zaheer, Sajjad 50, 51
Zamindari Abolition Act 201